T0301591

Money and General Equilibrium Theory

Money and General Equilibrium Theory

From Walras to Pareto (1870–1923)

Pascal Bridel
Professor of Economics, University of Lausanne, Switzerland

Edward Elgar
Cheltenham, UK • Lyme, US

© Pascal Bridel 1997

All rights reserved. No part of this publication may be reproduced, stored in a retrieval system or transmitted in any form or by any means, electronic, mechanical or photocopying, recording, or otherwise without the prior permission of the publisher.

Published by
Edward Elgar Publishing Limited
8 Lansdown Place
Cheltenham
Glos GL50 2HU
UK

Edward Elgar Publishing, Inc.
1 Pinnacle Hill Road
Lyme
NH 03768
US

A catalogue record for this book
is available from the British Library

Library of Congress Cataloguing in Publication Data

Bridel, Pascal, 1948–
    Money and general equilibrium theory : from Walras to Pareto,
1870–1923 / Pascal Bridel.
    Includes index.
    1. Equilibrium (Economics) 2. Money. 3. Walras, Léon,
1834–1910. 4. Pareto, Vilfredo, 1848–1923. I. Title.
HB145.B735 1997
332.4—dc21   97–12052
                                                                      CIP

ISBN 1 85898 623 0

Contents

List of Figures   vi
Acknowledgments   vii
Introduction   viii

1 The First Lausanne Decade: General Equilibrium and the
   Equation of Exchange (1871–1880)   1

2 Periodical Market, Equation of Exchange and 'Forced Saving':
   Walras's Applied Theory of Money   47

3 From the *Théorie de la monnaie* to the *Etudes d'économie politique
   appliquée:* More Variations on the Same Themes (1886–1898)   79

4 The Last Monetary Model (1899–1900), or the Ultimate
   Triumph of Internal Consistency   110

5 The Fate of a Still-born Tradition: Pareto and After   150

Bibliography   176
Index   191

Figures

1.1	The demand for commodity money I	18
1.2	The demand for real money	22
1.3	The nominal demand for money	23
1.4	The demand for commodity money II	26
2.1	The loanable-funds theory of interest	65

Acknowledgments

Despite more than a century of theoretical efforts, the best developed modern Walrasian general equilibrium models cannot find room for money. This book contains a detailed analytical reconstruction of Walras's and Pareto's various attempts at coordinating money and general equilibrium theory from 1870 to 1923. The aim of this reconstruction is of course to demonstrate that, from its inception as a model of exchange between commodities, the very logic of general equilibrium theory barred money to play an essential role as a social institution allowing monetary exchanges among individuals. In particular, the purely static nature of Walras's pure economics, and the simultaneous lack of a proper technology of exchange in which money as a means of exchange has an essential role to play, exclude *ex definitione* the integration of monetary and value theory.

This book has had a very long gestation. My original interest in this question dates back to Frank Hahn's lectures and seminars in the early 1980s. A five-year stint as an Economic Advisor at the Research Department of the Swiss National Bank as well as nearly a decade of teaching monetary theory at Lausanne University convinced me of the intrinsic 'monetary' weakness of a model inaugurated in this very university one hundred and twenty years ago. From September 1995 to April 1996, a sabbatical leave allowed me to put some sort of logic to scattered materials collected throughout the best part of a decade.

I should like to thank Roberto Baranzini, Mark Blaug, Francesco Mornati, the late Don Patinkin and members of the Centre Walras-Pareto who read parts of or the whole manuscript and saved me from many a blunder. It goes without saying that the responsibility for defects in this work must remain entirely mine.

Finally, and once again, my gratitude to Claude, and to my daughters Cécile and Claire, extends far beyond the making of this book.

Lausanne

Introduction

Despite decades of excruciating theoretical effort, it is now universally accepted that there is no place for money in modern Walrasian general equilibrium models. Even in elaborate constructions featuring sequence economies with missing markets, the integration of money is – to say the least – rather contrived. To paraphrase Hahn, in such models, money plays only an inessential role. Despite tremendous intellectual efforts, neither putting money into the utility function nor the 'cash-in-advance' hypothesis have so far yielded any satisfactory results. While innocuous if properly done and interpreted, the former procedure can clearly hinder the development of monetary theory: it has by now amply been demonstrated that the transaction role of money is not well approximated by simply putting money into the utility function. For its part, the latter procedure simply assumes what should be explained: Clower's requirement that only money buys goods simply amounts to an assumption that only makes sense if one postulates what one wishes to demonstrate, that is, that money has a positive exchange value. Since it is hard to escape from the view that money is an essential feature of real-world decentralized economies, general equilibrium theorists (or, at least, those still interested in the relevance of their model to the understanding of the working of such economies) have started to worry seriously about its analytical pertinence. Since there is no monetary theory without sequences (and, of course, no sequences without expectations), the crucial issue of the static or dynamic nature of general competitive equilibrium models is central to their viability as idealized explanations of the 'Adam Smith puzzle'. Since the late 1940s, the best brains in the profession have tried to solve within the Walrasian research programme the twin questions of a static 'price determination' and of a dynamic 'price formation'.[1] It is now generally agreed that, as a result, and under very restrictive conditions, the former issue (existence) is satisfactorily solved while the latter (stability) has been proved badly wanting if not 'in some intrinsic sense ... impossible' (Hahn, 1982a, p. 747).[2]

The wish to contribute to the understanding of the origins of this unsolved riddle is in fact the present author's principal motive for writing this book. In other words, aren't the origins of this incompatibility between money and general equilibrium already present in the inner logic of Walras's original model? Isn't the intrinsic logic of his basic theory of exchange the *fons et origo* of the notion of instantaneous equilibrium defined in a 'once-and-for-all market' from which money is absent because duration does not matter? Despite weak and early attempts at 'realism' including disequilibrium trading,[3] isn't Walras's *tâtonnement* mechanism nothing more than (or not even) an idealized representation of a virtual market process conducted as it is in terms of *numéraire* – and not money? Despite Walras's repeated claims that the mathematical solution of equilibrium is the selfsame problem that is solved in practice by a perfectly free competitive market, isn't this timeless and moneyless *tâtonnement* nothing but a mathematical technique of iteration with scant relation to its intuitive content – and certainly none to an institutional setup in which money plays a role in the transaction process? Finally, doesn't Walras eventually fall victim to his relentless search for an internal coherence to his general equilibrium model that is only congruent with a purely static approach from which any claim of describing the price formation *process* is excluded?

If hypotheses such as these could be vindicated, the overall vision of more than a century of general equilibrium theorizing would be in need of some reassessment. In essence, why is it that, despite the clarity of Walras's ultimate 1900 model, the impossibility of reconciling this intrinsically static model with money had to wait three-quarters of a century to be formally established? Why is it that despite Walras's and Pareto's early claims to the contrary, generations of theorists have been endlessly trying to turn general equilibrium models into realistic decentralized or centralized descriptions of coordinating processes? Finally, why is it that despite Walras's crystal-clear distinction between pure economics relying on Weberian 'ideal types' and applied economics based on 'real types', most historians of thought still consider the 1930s as the dividing line between 'interpretative content' and 'formal developments' as the criteria against which the validity of general equilibrium models is to be gauged? With the help of a careful reconstruction of Walras's and Pareto's monetary theories, the present book's central conclusion is that, from the beginning, 'formal developments' and 'interpretative paradigm' had a much more promiscuous life than Ingrao and Israel's so-called 'two parallel lives' hypothesis would wish to have it. In short, this volume should lead the reader to the conclusion that the mathematical analogy as the dominant validity criterion was born together with the earliest of all general equilibrium models. In other words, for the sake of saving the internal coherence of his mathematical model, Walras progressively severed the relationship between scientific abstraction and empirical evidence throughout the various editions of the *Eléments*. And money was an obvious victim of this procedure.

The argument commences (Chapter 1) with a re-examination of the logic of Walras's theory of exchange and of the role played in it by *numéraire* and by money. The problems linked to the definition of *numéraire*, to the serious consequences of a lack of any formal analysis of money as a medium of exchange (in particular the idea that money plays no role in the bargaining/*tâtonnement* process) and the relation between money and marginal utility are first discussed in turn. Walras's simple model of exchange is shown to be unable to demonstrate the superiority of monetary exchanges: from the very beginning, the exchange-facilitating properties attributed to money are simply assumed. The five monetary lessons written for the first 1874 instalment are then examined in detail: Walras's inability to extend to commodity money his marginal utility argument, his Fisherine-type quantity equation and the lack of any dynamic analysis reveal a perfectly comparative static approach to money. Finally, the role of *numéraire* and money in the all-important – and often neglected – time structure of the *Eléments* is given further attention. It is shown again that, from the very first phase of its inception, Walras's general equilibrium model is in no shape to offer a formal account of the transaction role of money.

In Chapter 2, the earlier connections between Walras's pure and applied monetary theories are explored in great detail. Despite a total lack of a proper stability analysis in the realm of his pure theory of money, Walras suggests in his more applied writings important insights about a tentative dynamic analysis on the money and commodity markets. If Walras is thus certainly not guilty of neglecting the consequences of a monetary shock on both markets, he fails to coordinate these analytical instruments (for example, substitution effect and forced saving) with his pure theory of money and his general equilibrium framework. Most marginalist economists suffered to some extent from this inability to reconcile in a satisfactory way their chapters on the theory of value with their chapters on the theory of money. In other words, Walras does offer a rather sophisticated adjustment process following a monetary shock, but this transmission mechanism (though clearly endowed with *real* effects) is not in the least articulated with his pure theory of money. Most of his efforts imply an extensive use of his quantity equation within a sequence of 'periodical markets'. His methodical application of the quantity theory to the understanding of trade cycles and his brilliant forced saving period analysis are two particularly good cases at hand.

Chapter 3 explains why, between 1886 and 1898, no breakthrough took place in Walras's pure theory of money, even if, during these twelve years, his monetary thought underwent a slow but steady reorganization. The Fisherian *circulation à desservir* is first replaced in 1886 by a cash-balance-like *encaisse désirée*. This move from an aggregate demand for money to individual demands for desired cash balances is, however, left unexplained: linked with the postulate of monetary exchange, the size of these desired balances is simply *assumed.* The structure of the *Eléments* is then completely reworked from the 1889 second edition onwards. For the sake of the overall logic of the general equilibrium model, the money section is shifted after exchange, production and capital formation. For the first time, as an add-on notion, money is considered as part of circulating capital. Finally, interesting additions are brought to the analysis of the working of the money market, in particular the definition of the rate of interest as a measure of the opportunity cost of holding money and an intuitive description of the real-balance effect. However, the line between pure and applied monetary theory is not yet clearly drawn and, apart from a few scattered elements, the gap between price and monetary theories is still wide open. All in all, the lengthy process of theoretical *tâtonnement* spreading from the *Théorie de la monnaie* to the second and third editions of the *Eléments*, led to extremely modest analytical improvements: the monetary scaffolding is still very wobbly but also not properly linked to the underlying 'real' model.

Chapter 4 is entirely devoted to a careful assessment of Walras's ultimate 1898–1900 claim to have eventually found room for money in the agent's utility function; that is, to have integrated money and value theories. The insistence with which he claims that his general equilibrium is a purely *static* theory of relative prices underlines the whole discussion of Walras's argument. This hypothesis is of pivotal importance when examining the conceptual framework and the working of the *équations de la circulation*, their connection with the simultaneous appearance of the *tâtonnement sur bons* in the capital market and the all-important reassessment of the time structure of the *Eléments*. Walras went as far as possible within the limits of his purely static framework to take account of the positive value of money while resisting all temptations to dynamize his system: the mechanisms of the money equation and Walras's utility analysis and his definition of an 'existence' theorem for a monetary equilibrium reveal a complete lack of reference to historical time. Once again, they demonstrate the instantaneous character of the *tâtonnement* 'mechanism'. Since the market system simultaneously reaches equilibrium *in principle* on all markets (including the money market), the trial-and-error 'monetary' tâtonnement 'process' to solve general equilibrium equations is at long last formally acknowledged by Walras as being a mere convenience of analytical exposition – not an attempt to describe how it actually happens on real markets. All in all, despite the introduction of money (or at least what he considers as money), Walras is able to keep unchanged the purely static nature and conclusions of his model. This eventual and formal unification of his comprehensive system is, of course, bound to be realized at the expense of its realism. Hence, the chapter closes on some considerations of a more methodological nature: the treacherous question of the antagonism between formal development and interpretative contents is reexamined in connection with the evolution of Walras's monetary theory between 1870 and 1901. Trapped from his first edition by the logic of an equilibrium model congruent only with a purely static approach, and despite heroic analytical efforts, Walras (and his monetary theory) eventually fell victim to his relentless search for an internal coherence from which any claim of describing a price formation process is finally excluded. And money as a medium of exchange, but not as a *numéraire*, was the prime victim of this first (but not last) victory of the internal over the external coherence of general equilibrium analysis, the epitome of all *rational* economic models.

Finally, Chapter 5 discusses the fate of Walras's monetary theory at the hands of his epigones. In a nutshell, between 1900 and the early 1930s, a complete nemesis fell on Walras's brilliant monetary intuition. To explain the sharp discontinuity with Walras's *encaisse désirée*, this chapter first examines in some detail the status of money within Pareto's own general equilibrium model, in order to contrast Pareto's narrow monetary theory with Walras's. The difficulty in appraising the apparent weakness of Pareto's contribution has more to do with methodological issues linked to the status of pure theory than with monetary theory proper. Very clearly, for Pareto, monetary theory does not belong to the 'first approximation' of pure theory from which it is accordingly excluded *ex definitione*. The second section of this chapter attempts to explain the fate of Walras's monetary theory at the hands of his immediate non-Lausanne epigones. The pre-1914 contributions of Schumpeter (the theorist, not the historian of thought) and Schlesinger display hardly any progress on Walras's attempt at finding a solution to the integration of money into general equilibrium theory. The (modest) efforts invested in monetary theory by Boninsegni (Pareto's successor in the Lausanne chair) and a handful of Italian disciples during the same period also confirm this sharp discontinuity. Worse, some of these contributions even mark a step backwards on the results reached around 1900: in particular, the infamous 'circularity argument' looms large over many of them.

Monetary theory as a subset of the general theory of choice resumed its course only in the 1930s with the works of Hicks and Samuelson, and another fifty years were necessary to demonstrate formally that there is no room for money in general equilibrium models of the Walrasian type. All this finally leads to the conclusion that, more than one hundred and twenty-five years after Walras's early version of general equilibrium, it is about time to call for some radical rethinking on a static construction which, from its inception as a model of exchange between *commodities*, barred money from playing its essential role as a social institution allowing monetary exchanges among *individuals*.

NOTES

1.   In a letter to Gide, Walras already explicitly linked his main intellectual effort to Smith and to 'les économistes [qui] l'ont produite il y a quelque cent ans'. However, Walras hastens to add that 'toute mon ambition a été de donner à cette thèse une valeur qu'elle n'a jamais eue en la *démontrant* scientifiquement' (Walras, 1965, II, p. 254; italics added).

2.   At this stage, suffice it to mention a few quotations from some of the most brilliant modern theorists who have been trying to unravel that particular riddle:
   *   'Money ... does not square at all easily with the theory of multilateral exchange such as has been accepted by economists since Walras' (Hicks, 1966, p. 3).
   *   'The analytical ... content of the most general of modern statements of value and monetary theory [that is, Patinkin's] is logically indistinguishable from that of the most traditional theory of a barter economy' (Clower (ed.), 1969, p. 16).
   *   'Of course, our model is in no shape to give a satisfactory formal account of the role of money' (Arrow and Hahn, 1971, p. 338).
   *   'The most serious challenge that the existence of money poses to the theorist is this: the best developed model of the economy [the Arrow–Debreu version of a Walrasian equilibrium] cannot find room for it' (Hahn, 1982b, p. 1).
   *   'Money has always been an awkward puzzle for neoclassical general equilibrium t heory ... How can fiat money command any value in terms of the goods and services that enter utility and production functions? The question is not answerable in the standard general equilibrium framework ... Money [has] no place in an Arrow–Debreu world' (Tobin, 1985, pp. 108 and 123).
   *   'It is not clear if what we know as Walrasian general equilibrium is compatible with a model in which money as a medium of exchange plays an essential role' (Ostroy, 1987, p. 515).

3.   Allowing, of course, endowment and path-dependency effects.

1. The First Lausanne Decade: General Equilibrium and the Equation of Exchange (1871–1880)

Economists frequently go too far when they assume that economic laws they have deduced on barter assumptions may be applied without qualification to actual conditions, in which money actually affects practically all exchanges and investments or transfers of capital. (Wicksell, 1901–06, II, p. 6)

Indeed, in [Walras's] theories of exchange, production and general equilibrium, money as a medium of exchange made no appearance; the omniscient, superhuman auctioneer obviated any need for it. (Tsiang, 1989, p. 9)

Considering how little formal theory was available when Walras applied in 1870 to the newly established chair at Lausanne, the three and a half years that were to lead to the *Eléments*' first instalment (1874) are crucial in the development of his general equilibrium model. Within these forty-two months, besides the heavy teaching load of a full-time professor, Walras thought out and wrote down single-handed 'the basis of practically all the best work of our time' (Schumpeter, 1954, p. 1026). In particular, and besides actually *discovering* independently the notion of marginal utility[1] and integrating it into his pure theory of exchange, Walras also clearly worked out during that same fruitful period[2] Part III *Of Numéraire and Money*. This fact is of the utmost importance in understanding the part Walras wanted money to play in his general equilibrium model: the chapters on money were in fact thought out and written well *before* the 'Theory of Production' and the 'Theory of Capital Formation', which only appeared in the *Eléments*' second instalment (1877).

Thus, beside this 1874 end product, various earlier drafts and some only recently published material should help clarify Walras's very first foray into the pure theory of money (1869, 1872). Section 1 examines the problems linked to the definition of *numéraire*, the serious consequences of a lack of any formal analysis of money as a medium of exchange (in particular the idea that money plays no role in the bargaining/*tâtonnement* process) and the relation between money and marginal utility. Walras's simple model of exchange is shown to be unable to demonstrate the superiority of monetary exchanges: from the very beginning, the exchange-facilitating properties attributed to money are simply assumed. Section 2 explores in detail the five monetary lessons written for the first instalment: Walras's inability to extend to commodity money his marginal utility argument, his Fisherine-type quantity equation and the lack of any dynamic analysis reveal a perfectly comparative static approach to money. Section 3 investigates the role of *numéraire* and money in the all-important – and often neglected – time structure of the *Eléments*. It is shown that, from the very first phase of its inception, Walras's general equilibrium model is in no shape to offer a formal account of the transaction role of money.

1   *NUMERAIRE*, MONEY, UTILITY AND THE THEORY OF EXCHANGE

As innocent as a confusion between money which serves as a unit of account (that is, *numéraire*) and money which serves as a medium of exchange may seem at first, it is necessary to examine very carefully this distinction in order to understand the thorny theoretical issues raised by the fact that, for Walras, these two functions 'have to be played by the same commodity' (*Oeuvres économiques complètes,* henceforth *OEC*, VIII, p. 540). Repeated failures to understand this distinction have given rise to frequent confusion (not least by Walras himself) about whether a general equilibrium system is based, or not, upon barter assumptions and what such an assumption means. In particular, this lack of a careful separation between these two functions – if rather innocent for existence theorems – would lead to significant misunderstanding of stability/*tâtonnement* theorems.[3] Moreover, and in view of Walras's lifelong deliberate attempts to include money in the utility function, some preliminary remarks on the non-zero marginal utility of (or positive price for) money are already offered at this stage; notably in connection with the part *not* played by marginal utility in his first equation of exchange. The three parts of this section should thus prepare the ground for Walras's early pure theory of money in which the same commodity displays both functions and, at the same time can also be traded *per se*.

1.1 Money as a *Numéraire*

In the first edition of the *Eléments*, Walras devotes the whole of Lesson 25 to the definition of the concept of *numéraire*. At this stage, not a word has been uttered about money: the entire discussion of the notion of *numéraire* thus makes its first appearance in Part II, which is entirely assigned to the theory of *exchange*.[4] This *numéraire* is a commodity, which, in all and every respects, is like any other commodity except that it also serves as a standard in terms of which all the others are expressed:

The situation of a market in a state of general equilibrium can be completely defined by relating the values of all commodities to the value of any particular of them. That particular commodity is called *numéraire* [or *standard commodity*]; and a unit quantity of this commodity is called a *standard* [*étalon*]. (1874, p. 144; *OEC,* VIII, p. 222; 1954, p.185)[5]

Starting with this definition, and following Marget (1935, pp. 170–75) and Jaffé (in Walras, 1954, p. 515), it is essential to realize that the concept of *numéraire* is always considered by Walras as a *concrete* commodity and not as some abstract 'ideal money' or 'unit-of-account' (Patinkin, 1965, p. 15).[6]

That said, it would be a clever linguist who could assert with total conviction that Walras's idiosyncratic use of the term *numéraire* is to be understood in the sense in which it was (and still is) in ordinary French speech. If, for Walras, *numéraire* is not to be used in the sense of an abstract unit of account,[7] it should be used neither in the ordinary sense of hard cash nor of *specie*.

In all later editions of the *Eléments*, the concept of *numéraire* is also introduced in the lesson in which Walras discusses for the first time the 'problem of exchange of several commodities for one another; the theorem of general equilibrium' (1954, p. 161). Clearly, and in all editions, the idea of a concrete standard commodity in terms of which the relative values of all other commodities can be expressed is closely related to Walras's central contribution to economic theory expressed in terms of his general equilibrium theorem, that is, in terms of Walras's Law.[8]

This argument is made even more forcefully by Walras himself. Barely two months after the publication of the first instalment of the *Eléments*, in a letter answering Jevons's very first comments[9] on his book, Walras is very clear about (i) the origins of his concept of *numéraire*, (ii) Cournot's and his distinction between absolute and relative values and (iii) how his theory of money stands in relation to his general equilibrium theorem:

Rest assured that I am deeply moved by what you told me [about my book] and particularly about my chapters on money ...; but I must draw your attention to the fact that *the foundations of that* [monetary] *theory are those of the theory of exchange*: that is, the principle of proportionality of values to *raretés* [that is, marginal utilities] (Lessons 20 and 23), the distinction between *numéraire* and money (Lesson 25), and, above all, the discussion of absolute and relative changes in value (Lesson 28). ... I have been frequently asked to lecture or to write articles on that complex and delicate question [of money]. I have always answered that it was not possible, that the place of the theory of money in the political economy I teach is akin to Newton's binomial in algebra, that is, that [monetary theory] is the topic of the 25th Lesson of my course of lectures, the understanding of which relies necessarily on the twenty-four previous lessons ... (1965, I, p. 431; italics added)

In modern parlance, the aggregate excess demand function of an economy with n commodities is formally expressed as

$$f : S \Rightarrow \Re^n,$$

where

$$S = \Re^n_+ - [0].$$

The interpretation is that $f(p)$ is the vector of aggregate excess demands (positive) or excess supplies (negative) expressed as the price system p. A basic property of f is that it is homogeneous of degree zero, that is, that $f(tp) = f(p)$ for all positive t.

It is this very property which justifies the use of a *numéraire*. If, of course, the scalar t is set appropriately, the commodity n can be chosen as the *numéraire* so that $p_n = 1$ The price system q can then be replaced by the *numéraire* price system p with $p_n = 1$ by multiplying q by $t = 1/q_n$ Nothing 'real' changes since, by definition, if $f(tp) = f(p)$ then $f(p) = f(tq) = f(q)$. q has, however, to be positive. And Walras was to add, right from his very first edition: 'To shift from one *numéraire* to another, it is only necessary to divide the prices expressed in terms of the old *numéraire* by the price of the new *numéraire* in terms of the old' (1954, p. 186).[10]

The introduction of this concept of *numéraire*, that is of money as a unit of account only, marks such an important turning point in both price and monetary theories that it is worth inquiring somewhat further into its origins and antecedents.

For once, no similarity – genuine or spurious – with anything found in his father's writings is invoked by Walras out of filial piety. In *De la Nature de la Richesse*, Auguste Walras also draws a distinction between the unit-of-account (*numéraire*) and the medium-of-exchange functions of money ('real' money). However, and perfectly in line with a very long French tradition in monetary matters, *numéraire* is only, for the father, an abstract unit of account which may or may not coincide with 'real money' (that is, cash in hand) (*OEC*, I, p. 212). Even if '[les physiocrates] n'ont pas mis assez de soin à distinguer la *monnaie* du *numéraire*' (p. 211), nowhere does Auguste define *numéraire* as a *physical* commodity. He then devotes a further two pages (pp. 212–13) to 'two essentially different things, *real money* and *money of account*' (*numéraire*). Though a unit of account, *numéraire* is thus no longer cash in hand but not necessarily a physical good.

In return and, as it has been discovered by Boven (1912, pp. 58–60) and carefully documented by Jaffé (in Walras, 1954, p. 499 and 1983, p. 76), Walras must have borrowed this concept consciously or not, from Isnard, this most ubiquitous of intellectual ghosts in the *Eléments*.[11] Having built his entire theory of exchange on a logic identical to Isnard's idea that the value in exchange is a term in a ratio which is inversely proportional to the ratio of the quantities exchanged (1781, pp. 16–18), in his treatment of money and *numéraire*, Walras seems also to have drawn more than passing inspiration from Isnard.

On the one hand, and to the best of the present author's knowledge, nowhere else in the entire pre-1870 literature does one find such a clear-cut definition of *numéraire* in the Walrasian sense:[12]

> If one has several commodities, M, M', M'', M''', M'''', etc., whose values are known, and which are in the proportions a to b to c to d to e, etc., all of these items can be evaluated in terms of one of their number. Thus we have $M:M'::a:b$, $M:M''::a:c$, $M:M'''::a:d$, etc. The values of M', M'', M''', M'''' will thus be bM/a, cM/a, dM/a, eM/a, etc.
>
> From this it follows, first, that the measure of one of the commodities can serve as a common measure for all of the others and that one can always relate the value of all the other goods to this item.
>
> Second, if this good is very valuable it also follows that it can serve as a convenient medium of exchange for all of the others. Goods which thus serve as common measures and media of exchange are called monies. (1781, I, pp. 21–2; as from Baumol and Goldfeld, 1968, pp. 256–7; for the word *numéraire*, see also 1781, I, p. xiv)

On the other hand, Walras's own wording is so close to Isnard's that it is difficult to consider such similarities as the result of a mere coincidence.[13]

Finally, Isnard anticipates, in a strikingly similar fashion, the connection Walras himself draws between the two essential functions of money when the commodity serving as *numéraire* is identical with the commodity serving as money in the sense of medium of exchange:[14]

> Nous avons vu dans la première section comment on pourrait ... rechercher quelles valeurs [les marchandises] ont entre-elles sans l'intermède des monnaies ... Un tel calcul serait très compliqué dans le système d'un grand nombre de marchandises. Nous avons vu dans la seconde comment l'usage d'une mesure commune ou de la monnaie était propre à simplifier ces calculs. (1781, I, pp. 18, 26–7)

In Walras's case, two main consequences were to follow this move from money being a *numéraire* only to money being also a medium of exchange. On the one hand, such a move brings out strongly the need to discuss in detail the barter assumption sometimes attributed to Walras's general equilibrium model; on the other, and in view of his subsequent attempts to include money in the utility function, Walras's first undertaking to analyse the exchange-facilitating properties of money and the idea that money (though neutral) increases the efficiency of the economic system also calls for careful reading.

1.2 Money as a Medium of Exchange: an Optional Add-on Component of the Theory of Exchange

Walras's argument is constructed around a move from a 'direct exchange' – unit of account – *numéraire* economy to an 'indirect exchange'– means of exchange – money economy. In his Geneva Lectures (1872), as well as in practically identical terms in the first edition of the *Eléments*, Walras provides a wealth of theoretically fascinating comments around the same theoretical core: money is different from other goods in degree rather than in kind; monetary phenomena are an optional add-on rather than an integral component of the mechanism of exchange:

> il y a un avantage incontestable à ce que la richesse soit évaluée en la marchandise qui doit l'acheter, autrement dit, à ce que la même marchandise qui doit être choisie pour monnaie soit désignée comme numéraire ...
>
> L'intervention de la monnaie substitue [ainsi] deux échanges à un seul, et, en cela, elle complique les choses. Il est vrai qu'elle substitue deux échanges très faciles et très rapides à un seul échange qui serait très difficile et très long, sinon tout à fait impossible [15]; c'est en quoi elle est un élément de simplification. *En somme, elle constitue une simplification pratique et une complication théorique*; c'est pourquoi, quand nous aurons bien défini son rôle, *nous en ferons très souvent abstraction dans l'étude scientifique des phénomènes de la vie économique.* Il est [cependant] certain que l'intervention de la monnaie décompose l'échange unique de marchandise contre marchandise en deux échanges, dont l'un est l'échange de marchandise contre monnaie et s'appelle *vente*, et dont l'autre est l'échange de monnaie contre marchandise et s'appelle *achat*. (1874, pp. 174–5, first italics added; same passage in *OEC*, VIII, p. 544; for a similar text in the 1872 lectures, see *OEC*, XI, p. 455)

In this 1874 first instalment, Walras leaves no stone unturned about this distinction between 'the intervention of money and the intervention of *numéraire*' (1874, p. 150; *OEC*, VIII, p. 228). Indirect exchange occurs when a commodity is sold for money and then money is used to buy another commodity; direct exchange happens when a non-monetary commodity is exchanged for another non-monetary commodity. Indirect pricing is valuing a commodity in terms of a medium of exchange; direct pricing is valuing a commodity in terms of another commodity. The presence or absence of the *numéraire* affects the way the pricing is done but not the manner of exchange, that is, whether exchange is direct or indirect: this is determined by the presence or absence of money.

In other words, and at the risk of being unduly repetitive, if there is no *numéraire* and no money, barter takes place with direct prices; if there is a *numéraire* and no money, then there is direct exchange and prices are calculated indirectly. Finally, if there is money, it implies the existence of a *numéraire* and exchange and pricing are indirect. In a nutshell, Walras 'simply' anticipates the so-called Clower (or cash-in-advance) constraint that practically 'goods do not buy goods'[16] thus the need for a medium of exchange: 'nous ne pouvons échanger directement les marchandises contre des marchandises' (1874, p. 172; *OEC*, VIII, p. 541).

'On the assumption of the intervention of money' (1874, p. 149; *OEC*, VIII, p. 227), Walras reasserts that the role of medium of exchange is clearly assigned to money, not to *numéraire*. In other words, Walras *assumes* that money plays no essential role in the *tâtonnement*/bargaining process. Hence, already, at this stage, this assumption gives rise to the uncomfortable feeling that the *tâtonnement* cannot be a historical time process of price formation involving money but an iterative timeless mechanism conducted in terms of *numéraire*.

Thus, from the very beginning of his analysis of the role played by money in his general equilibrium model, Walras 'simply' put his finger on the crucial distinction between 'micro-money' and 'macro-money', between choice-theoretic money and money as a social institution, between an inward-looking approach and an outward-looking approach to monetary theory. The former can easily be reconciled with the idea (central to general equilibrium analysis) that exchange is a relation between commodities. The latter, which tries to provide a transaction role for money, implies a completely different starting point: exchange is a relation among individuals; and this relation is clearly, for Walras a mere '*complication théorique*'. Unfortunately, more than a century after the *Eléments*, economists have not yet managed to solve satisfactorily this 'little theoretical complication' fraught as it is with frightful – and maybe insuperable – difficulties. Clearly, the *fons et origo* of that central issue is already present in Walras's earliest writings. For grossly underestimating this theoretical difficulty, one may even wonder if Walras himself is not responsible for introducing such a mortal weakness into his model.

The best illustration of the inability of Walras's general equilibrium model to incorporate *monetary* exchanges is offered unintentionally by Walras himself in his Theorem of Equivalent Distributions:[17]

> *Given several commodities in a market in a state of general equilibrium, the current prices of these commodities will remain unchanged no matter in what way the ownership of the respective quantities of these commodities is redistributed among the parties to the exchange, provided however, that the value of the sum of the quantities possessed by each of these parties remains the same.* (1874, p. 142; *OEC*, VIII, p. 221 as in 1954, p. 185; italics in original)

Under Walras's assumptions, equilibrium prices are thus invariant to changes in the initial distribution of commodities between consumers. Building on this innocent-looking and straightforward demonstration, it is possible[18] to take one crucial step in the understanding of the pure logic of Walras's exchange model. With p standing for prices, x_i for agent i's final allocation of commodities and (w_i), for the same agent's initial allocation of commodities, if $[p,(x_i)]$ is an equilibrium final allocation for agents having certain (independently given) preferences and initial distributions of commodities (w_i), then $[p,(x_i)]$ is also an equilibrium final allocation for agents having the same (independently given) preferences and any other initial distributions (w'_i) under Walras's assumptions that $\Sigma w'_i = \Sigma w_i$ and $p w'_i = p w_i$, for all i. Now, if i's final allocation of commodities is identical with i's initial endowment it simply means that, at prices p, the individual does not want to trade. Thus, the no-trade distribution $(w'_i = x_i)$ is in the same equivalence class with an initial allocation of commodities in which the pattern of net trades between agents and commodities is somewhat more realistic.

For the sake of clarity, this argument can be restated with the money-in-the-utility-function approach initiated paradoxically by Walras himself in 1899–1900.[19] To determine the utility of their cash balances, agents must first have a clear idea of the volume of transactions that these balances will have to perform; and this can be known only after the agents have determined the outcome of the process to utility maximization itself. Thus, in the case mentioned above in which the composition of an agent's initial endowment is the same as his or her optimum one, he or she will not plan to carry out any transactions, and, hence, the holding of money balances will not generate any utility, that is, for this agent the marginal utility of money is zero. In other words, the transaction role of money, or alternatively the idea that money has a special role as means of payment, is not well approximated by simply putting money into the utility function.

Hence, Walras's class of equivalent distributions is much too crude to provide a role for the exchange-facilitating properties generally attributed to money. For Walras, trade or no trade, it is all the same to his highly centralized model of exchange. In other words, and even if intuitively and with the help of history Walras illustrates the real-world inferiority of barter exchange, his exchange model is unable *to demonstrate* the superiority of monetary exchanges; it is simply assumed.[20] The lesson drawn from the absence of any formal role for money in the single-period version of the pure exchange economy characterized by Walras's Theorem of Equivalent Distributions is devastating for the entire general equilibrium model. Even before any argument is raised in favour of monetary exchanges, Walras's model logically rules out *ab initio* any essential role for money in the exchange technology. As Ostroy sums it up:

> When subjected to the scrutiny of the inward-looking approach to money and general equilibrium, this goal of integration [of money] does not appear to be very satisfying. By introducing money after he had completed his theory of exchange, Walras clearly made monetary phenomena an optional add-on rather than an integral component of the mechanism of exchange. Further it was an add-on that would have to be valued for its own sake rather than as a component enhancing the performance of the rest of the system. (1992, p. 784; see also Howitt, 1973, p. 495 for a similar argument)

This central issue linked to the transaction role of money will reappear with added force in Walras's 1900 attempt to include money into utility functions: it is dealt with in great detail in Chapter 4, Section 2, below.

Walras's arguments in favour of monetary exchanges are thus strictly circumstantial. Instead of postulating, like Isnard, the need for such a medium of exchange, Walras attributes it to something he regards as more fundamental than Smith's traditional division of labour.[21] His main idea is to link directly the need for a medium of exchange to his theory of social wealth (the *Eléments'* very subtitle) by way of his father's concepts of utility and value linked to 'possession' for one and to 'consommation' for the other (*OEC,* XI, pp. 453–5; 1874, pp. 172–3). The whole of Walras's analysis is in fact nothing other than a straightforward reproduction, sometimes *word for word*, of parts of Chapters 2 and 3 of Auguste Walras's *Théorie de la richesse sociale* (1849, pp. 23–52 and in particular pp. 37–45): the source of inspiration is, here, very clear. It is utility which makes a thing an object of consumption for an individual according to his or her current preferences; but it is the limitation in quantity of goods endowed with utility that gives it a value in the market[22] and makes it an object of possession whether an individual possessor cares to consume the good or not. Should an object be 'durable', 'divisible', 'generally cognizable' and 'more stable in value' than most others (*OEC,* XI, p. 455; 1874, pp. 173–4),[23] it can serve not only as a medium of exchange, but also as something that can be held for eventual exchange against the less durable, less divisible and less generally cognizable objects of consumption. For the first time in economic theory appears the idea that:

> Celui qui échange de la monnaie contre de la marchandise considère l'utilité de cette marchandise qui répond à son besoin particulier; celui qui échange de la marchandise contre de la monnaie considère la valeur de cette monnaie qui représente la richesse sous sa forme la plus générale. (1874, p. 175; *OEC,* VIII, p. 545)

At this stage, Walras does not carry his analysis (actually his father's!) any further. Apart from specifying that one should not confuse his argument with the old Mercantilist 'chrysohedonic illusion', nothing more is said about this vague concept of utility; in particular, no connection whatsoever is drawn with a still undiscovered *marginal* utility.

Nevertheless, for Walras, money is clearly much more than a straightforward *numéraire*. Does it mean that, in his first edition, Walras managed to escape from the logic of a barter economy in which money is neutral after all? Certainly not. Clearly, even before any technical discussion of this model and of the exact part money is playing in its logic, the reader is faced with the fundamental and formidable question economists have been trying unsuccessfully to solve for more than a century: *is there room for money in a general equilibrium framework of the Walrasian type?*[24]

The preceding discussion shows with great clarity Walras's deep understanding of the respective logic of both a barter and a monetized economy. However, it also contains no less clearly the seeds of the fundamental confusion between what Hahn (1973b, p. 160) has called a *sequence economy* and an *inessential economy*. Walras is unambiguous about it and anticipates by a century Hahn's recent statement according to which 'there is nothing we can say about the equilibrium of an economy with money which we cannot also say about the equilibrium of a non-monetary economy [that is] the money of this construction is only a contingent store of value and has no other role' (1973b, p. 160). In other words, no monetary variable needs enter into the determination of that economy's equilibrium – a property quite different from the concept of neutrality of money which asserts that the set of equilibria of an economy is independent of the *quantity* of money.

Thus, though well aware of the crucial distinction between a barter and a monetary economy, Walras also laid the foundations for the idea that difficulties linked with money can be kept out of the theoretical picture without altering in the least 'a scientific study' of 'real world' economies: 'on peut toujours, si l'on veut, faire abstraction de l'intervention de la monnaie, et considérer les marchandises comme échangées les unes contre les autres' (1872, Lesson 6; *OEC*, XI, p. 455).

The inconsistency is obvious and runs throughout the whole of Walras's monetary theory. Money for him is plainly more than a veil. Hence, he cannot view his model as that of a barter economy. But how could a positive value for money be reconciled with his theory of exchange and more generally with his general equilibrium model without destroying its essential characteristics? The successive upheavals undergone by his monetary theory 'from 1876 to 1899' (1954, p. 38) are precisely the best proof that he understood the difficulty of his undertaking and perceived the need for a device to bridge that gap. The fact that he ultimately failed in an enterprise that nobody has yet succeeded in bringing to fruition more than a century later is no good reason to accuse him of considering his general equilibrium as a barter model.[25]

1.3 Money and Marginal Utility Theory I

Considering Walras's lifelong attempt to explain the positive value of money by the application of the same analytical apparatus that he used to explain the value of other goods, one last remark is necessary in connection with the early developments of the concept of marginal utility.

In two classic articles on Walras's role in the 'marginal revolution', Jaffé (1972, 1976) has convincingly shown how Walras has succeeded far better than either Menger or Jevons in forging a clearly defined theoretical link between marginal utility and prices. Leading his readers through Walras's convoluted argument, Jaffé concludes effectively, though rather surprisingly, that Walras proceeded from general equilibrium *to* marginal utility and not from marginal utility to general equilibrium: 'Instead of climbing up from marginal utility to the level of his general equilibrium analysis, Walras actually climbed down from that level to marginal utility' (1972, p. 313).[26]

Although obsessed with his priority over Jevons and Menger in discovering what he called (out of filial piety) *rareté*, Walras was nevertheless perfectly aware of the order of precedence between marginal utility and general equilibrium. And this fact is of great importance for the development of his *monetary* theory.

Relying again on scholarly evidence collected and presented by Jaffé, it is possible to date with great accuracy Walras's first successful derivation of demand curves from considerations of utility and quantity. According to Jaffé, the decisive turning point was only reached by Walras some time in the second half of 1872 (1965, I, pp. 309–11; Jaffé, 1972, pp. 300–305). Only at that time, and with the decisive help of one of his mathematical colleagues, did Walras succeed in integrating *rareté* (that is, marginal utility) into his model. Put in other words, despite frantic groping with strange concepts such as *virtual* and *effective* utility inherited from Dupuit (1844), until that date Walras was still confusing demand curves with utility curves.[27] Eventually dispelled by a re-definition of *rareté* in terms of a differential coefficient, this confusion formally made room for Walras's definitive version of the marginal utility theory in his 1873 maiden paper on economic theory.

Be that as it may, everything written by Walras before that crucial second half of 1872 is definitely not 'powered' by the engine of marginal utility – although the conceptual general equilibrium framework is unmistakably already present. And that includes, of course, his all-important chapters on monetary theory.

However, and while a comparison between Walras's early Geneva Lectures (1872) and the first instalment of the *Eléments* shows very clearly the fundamental changes brought about by marginal utility to his price theory, *the chapters on the 'price of money' do not display any such substantial alterations.* In other words, the 1872 advent of marginal utility, while forcing drastic revisions on Walras's theory of value, left his monetary theory practically unchanged. In view of the subsequent upheavals this monetary theory underwent from the late 1870s onwards, this curious (and early) dichotomy between money and prices needs to be carefully documented and discussed.

2   *OF THE VALUE OF MONEY* AND THE *EQUATION OF EXCHANGE*: WALRAS'S PURE THEORY OF MONEY (1871–1874)

The material gathered up and analysed so far allows now a much more organized and fruitful discussion of Walras's first venture into pure monetary theory. Two steps are in order. Section 2.1 examines briefly how and why Walras chose precious metals as commodities serving both as *money* and as *numéraire*; furthermore, it is shown that, between 1871 and 1874, marginal utility did invade 'the law of establishment' of their prices *as commodities*. However, both the 'equation of exchange' and the geometric analysis of the 'value of money' suggest in Section 2.2 that Walras utterly failed to apply the same argument to gold and silver demanded not as commodities but as money. Finally, Section 2.2 also examines how Walras extends his 'equation of exchange' to include money substitutes (that is, fiduciary or paper money).

2.1 Money and Marginal Utility II

Section III of the *Eléments'* first edition is entitled *Of Numéraire and Money*. In addition to Lesson 24, which is devoted to exchange rates, it is made up of five other lessons appearing in the following order:

*   Lesson 29: *Conditions du numéraire et de la monnaie*;
*   Lesson 30: *Problème de la valeur de la monnaie*;
*   Lesson 31: *Qualités des métaux précieux*;
*   Lesson 32: *Système rationnel de numéraire et de monnaie*;
*   Lesson 33: *De la monnaie fiduciaire*.

Although under slightly different titles, the outline of these five lessons matches *exactly* that of Walras's 1872 Geneva Lectures. Of course, the lecture notes are not as elaborate and polished as the 1874 printed version, but the ordering of the argument and all the key (italicized) words are unmistakably present. The only, but crucial, difference appears in Lesson 31 'Of the Quality of Precious Metals'; while nothing original is said in the 1872 version about *why* precious metals are chosen as money *par excellence*, in 1874, the entire discussion is recast in terms of the relative stability of their *marginal* utility. Surprisingly, this glimmer does not shed any light either on the previous (or following) lessons from Section III or on their logical ordering.

Evidently, since Lesson 31 discusses the value of money in terms of the interaction between a demand curve for metal used as money and a demand curve of metal remaining in ordinary commodity use, one could clearly expect this lengthy demonstration in terms of the marginal utility of precious metals not only to *precede* the *equation of exchange* but also to prepare the ground for a straightforward extension of these results to the purely monetary demand. Such a move will have to wait until the fourth edition in 1900, with Walras's inclusion of money in the utility function by way of an analysis in terms of indirect utility via his *encaisses désirées* and the *service d'approvisionnement*. Reflecting a quarter of a century later on this first version of his theory of money, Walras comments in the introduction to his fourth edition that he 'continued on the second and third editions, as in the first, to write the equation of offer and demand for money apart from the other equations *and as empirically given*' (1954, p. 38; italics added).

One recurrent theme throughout Lessons 29, 30 and 31 as well as in the Geneva Lectures is that 'only a commodity can be money' (1874, p. 177; *OEC*, VIII, p. 438). And the whole of Lesson 31 is devoted, and with more than passing help from his father's *Richesse sociale*,[28] to a justification of this restrictive choice perfectly in line with both a very long tradition in monetary theory and above all to Walras's concept of *numéraire* as one of the *n* commodities.

Il n'y a qu'une marchandise ... qui puisse être adoptée comme intermédiaire d'échange; en d'autres termes, la monnaie doit être une des espèces de la richesse sociale. On essayerait vainement d'employer comme monnaie une chose qui n'aurait pas par elle-même de valeur d'échange. (1874, p. 178; *OEC*, VIII, p. 448)

Money is different from other goods, but in degree rather than in kind. Gold and silver are commodities and, as such, are endowed with two standard qualities: they are useful and their quantity is limited. Their marginal utility, therefore their prices, are thus positive. But, what makes these two commodities particularly suited to playing the various money functions? Once again very traditional qualities, the list of which remains unchanged between 1872 and 1874: 'universal utility', 'uniformity of qualities', 'indestructibility', 'divisibility', and 'transportability' (*OEC*, VI, p. 200; 1872, Lesson 6 as in *OEC*, XI, pp. 452–5; 1874, pp.184–5, *OEC*, VIII, pp. 549–51). All these characteristics make precious metals the best possible standards of value (*étalon*) not because their value is fixed once and for all but because 'their variability [in utility, quantity and thus in value] are smaller and more regular' (*OEC*, XI, p. 455). After discussing and rejecting various alternatives (notably corn), Walras's 1872 argument stops at that point. All this is fairly standard and does not break in any way from his father's idiosyncratic reading of the then dominant classical wisdom.[29]

But in 1874, in the second half of Lesson 31 (paras 181–4), Walras departs radically from this standard wisdom. Referring his readers to his marginal utility theory of prices (and particularly to paras. 135 and 164), Walras for the first time breaks new ground in monetary theory. Not that he goes very far or very deep. He simply uses his marginal utility discoveries to explain the reason why precious metals are not *fixed* standards of value:

> Il faudrait, pour que les raretés [that is, marginal utilities] des métaux précieux fussent constantes, que ni leur quantité, ni leur utilité ne changeassent, ou que cette quantité et cette utilité changeassent de telle sorte que les raretés [that is, marginal utilities] ne changeassent pas. (1874, p. 186; *OEC*, VIII, pp. 551–2)

Among other reasons explaining the instability of the marginal utilities of precious metals used as money (as opposed to commodity), Walras goes as far as to mention shifts in the demand for money: 'Si l'on considère l'emploi de ces métaux comme monnaie, les exigences de la circulation augmentent également en même temps que les quantités de marchandises qui circulent et leurs coefficients de circulation' (1874, p. 186; *OCE*, VIII, pp. 551–2).

Clearly, a positive growth rate of the economy increases the demand for money and raises simultaneously the marginal utility of a given stock of metallic currency and thus its price. Besides this straightforward reason for the variability of the *rareté* of money, Walras mentions the part played by an increased production of precious metals, changes in the volume of fiduciary money, a geographical segmentation of the money market and, last but not least, exchange-rate fluctuations (1874, pp. 186–7; *OEC*, VIII, pp. 552–3).

On a more sophisticated level, Walras goes one theoretical step further when, in a passing remark on the necessary conditions for the marginal utility of money (or of any one of the $n-1$ commodities) to be constant, marginal utilities of all the other commodities have to be constant as well (1874, p. 185; *OEC*, VIII, p. 551).

Be that as it may, these various marginalist themes, and the pivotal idea that the value of money has to be determined in the same way as other commodities, are completely separated from Walras's discussion 'Of the Value of Money'. On the one hand, in 1874, this piece of analysis is included in Lesson 30 while these important remarks concerning 'money in general equilibrium' appear in an uncoordinated manner, as an afterthought, in Lesson 31 only; on the other, both the equation of exchange and the geometrical determination of the value of money are left absolutely unchanged between 1872 and 1874. Clearly, Walras did not re-work his 1872 monetary theory considering his breakthrough in marginal utility and price theory

2.2 The 'Equation of Exchange' and the Value of Money

In his classic 1931 article, Marget demonstrates quite convincingly that, in the first edition of the *Eléments*, Walras worked out an *equation of exchange* 'which was in all respects equivalent to equations of the so-called "Fisherian" type' (1931, p. 573). Basically correct, and in view of the new Walras material now available, Marget's argument is, however, in need of a comprehensive overhaul that will bring it one step further.

Reflecting in later editions on his equation of exchange, Walras wrote in the *Preface* to his fourth edition: 'In the first edition, this solution [to the problem of the value of money] was founded on a consideration of the "circulation to be cleared" ["circulation à desservir"[30]], which I had borrowed from the economists' (1954, p. 38).

To clear first the question of the origins of the 'demand for money' used in 1872 and 1874, it is of some importance to attempt to trace the antecedents to this pre-Fisherian $MV = PT$ type of equation.[31] Walras's reference to 'les économistes' (a term still used at the time in France for Quesnay and the Physiocrats) is, to say the least, not very helpful. Although, in the absence of any reference, it is, of course, impossible to say with any degree of certainty which authors influenced Walras, and to what extent (if any) one can connect his equation with previous attempts, two possible lines of inquiry are possible: the all-important family tradition on the one hand, and the writings of other contemporary French economists on the other.

Surprisingly, the first line leads nowhere. In the various chapters Auguste Walras devotes to money, none offers a detailed discussion of the quantity theory itself; and even less an algebraic version of Léon's equation of exchange.

The second line is hardly more conclusive. Surprisingly for a man obsessed with priorities but very scrupulous in his recognition of the work of his predecessors and contemporaries, with the exception of Hume, not a single reference to monetary theorists appears in the first edition of the *Eléments*.[32] Of course, and given the relative intellectual isolation in which Walras worked out his theory (at least until 1874), it is fairly easy to get an idea of what he *might* have read by the early 1870s: his working library (part of which belonged to his father) was his only source of information and has fortunately been preserved at Lausanne.[33] However, apart from most of the standard pre-1870 discussions on the quantity theory,[34] the very few formulations similar to Walras's 'equation of exchange' available then[35] appeared in volumes not to be found on Walras's shelves. The only possible implication is obviously that Walras developed his *equation of exchange* (including its label) totally independently. The level of sophistication reached is thus all the more remarkable.

Walras's fundamental equation appears in identical form in the Geneva Lectures and in the first edition of the *Eléments*.

$$\alpha'' Q_a' V_a = \alpha' Q_a' V_a + \beta Q_b v_b + \gamma Q_c v_c + \delta Q_d v_d + ... \qquad (1.1)$$

in which:

Q_a' = part of the stock of money-metal A remaining in ordinary commodity uses;

Q_a'' = part of the stock of money-metal A used as money (M in the Fisherian notation);

$$Q_a = Q_a' + Q_a'' \quad [36]$$

$Q_b, Q_c, Q_d, ...$ = quantities of commodities $B, C, D, ...$ bought and sold on the markets;

α' = 'coefficient of circulation' [that is, 'velocity'] of the money-metal in its commodity uses;

α'' = 'coefficient of circulation' [that is, 'velocity'] of the money stock;

$\beta, \gamma, \delta, ...$ = 'coefficients of circulation' of commodities $B, C, D ...$

These various *coefficients of circulation* (the value of which can be anything between zero and, theoretically, infinity)[37] are simply an extension to the ($n - 1$) commodities of what is (in traditional quantity equations), and for no good reasons, applied to money only:

> J'appelle *coefficient de circulation* le nombre par lequel il faut multiplier la quantité existante d'une marchandise pour avoir la quantité totale de cette marchandise entrée en échange, c'est-à-dire vendue et achetée, pendant une certaine période de temps ... (1874, p. 179; *OEC*, VIII, p. 460; see also 1872 in *OEC*, XI, p. 457)

Finally,

$$V_a, v_b, v_c, v_d, ... = \text{'values' of commodities } A, B, C, D, ...$$

Since commodity A has been chosen as the medium of exchange, it is clear that, in equilibrium, the price of the portion Q_a' used as commodity is identical to the price of Q_a'' used as money: '[o]therwise, one would either turn money into good or good into money' (1874, p. 179; *OEC*, VIII, pp. 464–5). Furthermore, Walras also draws (for the first time) the now obvious conclusion that 'la valeur de la quantité totale de monnaie entrée en échange est égale à la valeur des quantités totales de toutes les autres marchandises entrées en échange' (1874, p. 180; *OEC*, VIII, p. 466).

Using the *numéraire* technique, Walras reduces these *values* into *prices*. Since, for example, the price of A in terms of B would be obtained by dividing V_a by v_b [that is, $P_a = V_a / v_b$], it is of course easy to derive, as in equation (1.1), the prices of n - 1 commodities in terms of commodity money by dividing through by V_a:

$$\alpha'' Q_a'' = \alpha' Q_a' + \beta Q_b p_b + \gamma Q_c p_c + \delta Q_d p_d + ...^{38}$$ (1.2)

And Walras concludes that 'we have here a genuine equation of exchange' (1874, p. 180; *OEC*, VIII, p. 468). Substituting M for Q_a'', V for α'', T for $Q_a' + Q_b + Q_c + ...$, v (the *average* velocity of circulation of goods) for $\alpha', \beta, \gamma, \delta$ and P for $p_b, p_c, p_d, ...$, one gets a notation very close to Fisher's own equation of exchange: $MV = PTv$.

Walras's last and seminal step in his attempt to present a mathematical and a geometrical formulation of the forces determining the value (price) of money takes account, of course, of both the monetary and the industrial demands for money-metal.

Once again, the algebraic as well as the geometric demonstrations are identical in both sources. Considering Figure 1.1, and reverting to Walras's original notation of prices of money and goods not in terms of money but in terms of commodity B, it is possible to further substantially the understanding of his quantity theory.

Walras considers first commodity A and its *courbe de prix* (1874, p. 178; *OEC*, VIII, p. 452).[39] Furthermore, he begins his argument with an 'existing' fixed quantity Q_a of A at a *given* price p_a. Then, if and when commodity A is chosen as the medium of exchange, a portion Q_a' of Q_a only remains in ordinary commodity use while portion Q_a'' is used as money. Other things being equal, this reduction from Q_a to Q_a' of commodity A available for ordinary uses raises the price from p_a to P_a. Walras concludes: 'C'est ici que se pose clairement le problème de la valeur de la monnaie, qui consiste, étant connus Q_a et p_a, ainsi que la courbe $A_q A_p$ ou son équation $Q = F(p)$, à déterminer Q_a', Q_a'' et P_a' (1874, p. 179; *OEC*, VIII, p. 458).

Using the original version of his equation of exchange (1.1), Walras rearranges its terms and divides it by α'' and v_b:

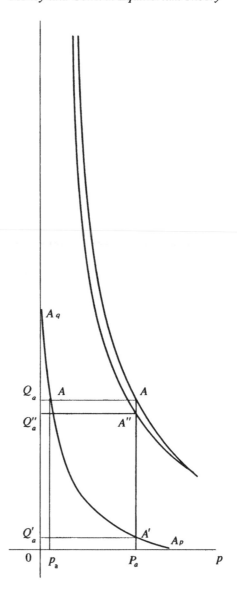

Source: Walras, *Eléments,* Figure 9, Plate II, *OEC*, viii, p. 454.

Figure 1.1 The demand for commodity money I

$$\left(Q_a'' - \frac{\alpha'}{\alpha''}Q_a'\right)P_a = \frac{\beta}{\alpha''}Q_b + \frac{\gamma}{\alpha''}Q_cP_c + \frac{\delta}{\alpha''}Q_dP_d + \cdots .$$

Assuming, then, the right-hand side of this equation to be constant[40] and naming it H, Walras is eventually able to formulate the equation of the demand for monetized metal, that is, his price curve for money:

$$Q_a'' = \frac{H}{P_a} + \frac{\alpha'}{\alpha''}F(P_a). \tag{1.3}$$

Walras comments:

> This ... equation, ... that of the price-curve for commodity A considered as money (a curve going through point A"), *tends* to be a rectangular hyperbola ... for the reason that α' ... is very small compared to α'' and that $(\alpha'/\alpha'')F(P_a)$ is very small compared to H/P_a; it means that the price or the value of money *tends* to vary inversely with its quantity. (1874, pp. 180–81; italics added; *OEC*, VIII, p. 472)[41]

This first appearance of such important notions – still at the heart of most discussions in the field of monetary theory – needs very careful assessing. Using modern standards of judgement, a detailed critical study of the hypotheses underlying these algebraic and geometrical stepping-stones to neoclassical monetary theory should help clear the ground for a better understanding of the part played by money in Walras's grand theoretical design.

If, for a given quantity of Q_a, the metal has only non-monetary uses, its equilibrium value p_a is determined at A by the intersection of A_qA_p and Q_aS.[42] If, however, and as is shown on Walras's diagram, metal also has monetary uses, its equilibrium value is determined by the intersection of the north-easternmost curve which represents the composite demand for both types of uses.

The demand curve for metal in its non-monetary uses only displays – as any demand curve for a normal good – a *different* elasticity at each point; if metal has monetary uses as well, the demand for non-monetary uses will simply move down[43] the demand curve from A to A' in response to the change of price p_a to P_a. The composite demand curve for both types of uses – whatever the slope and the nature of the demand curve for metal in monetary uses – will also display a different elasticity at each point. Furthermore, this composite demand curve will necessarily be steeper than A_qA_p and intersect Walras's price curve for money when – following a rise in prices – the demand for metal in non-monetary uses falls to zero. The intersection of that composite demand curve with the (unchanged and exogenously given) supply curve for metal in both uses determines the new equilibrium P_a.

This demand curve for metal in non-monetary uses is clearly a demand curve in the usual Walrasian or Marshallian sense of the term. By definition, such a curve illustrates the outcome of individual experiments: to what extent is the quantity of a commodity demanded by an agent, or a collection of agents, affected by changes in the price (and the price only) of that commodity. Walras's functional relationship $Q'_a = F(p_a)$ excludes by definition any other determining variable but P; in particular, no mention is made of a change in the quantity supplied. As a matter of fact, the whole point of the marginalist approach is precisely to organize the forces which determine an equilibrium price into two categories – supply and demand – which, ideally, are mutually exclusive. In particular, the shape of the demand curve for a commodity cannot depend on the supply of that same commodity. And that seems to be precisely the implicit hypothesis behind Walras's price curve (demand curve) for money. Clearly, this calls for a very careful assessment of the argument behind the shape of 'this price curve ... that tends to be a rectangular hyperbola'. In that respect, two main questions need to be answered. On the one hand, why is it that, for Walras, this price curve only *tends* to be a rectangular hyperbola?[44] On the other, that explained, does it bring back Walras's argument to the standard, and well-documented, Marshallian confusion between a demand curve and a market-equilibrium curve?

The first problem is easy to solve. The fact that this price curve for money is not an exact rectangular hyperbola but only tends to be such a particular curve is clearly linked to the ratio $(\alpha'/\alpha'')F(P_a)$ on the right-hand side of equation (1.3). Considering rather realistically that α' is 'very small' compared to α'',[45] the relative size of this ratio is also 'very small' compared to H/P_a. In fact, even if α' and α'' are direct functions of P_a, it seems reasonable to assume that they would both vary in roughly the same proportion, leaving the value of their ratio fairly stable, if not constant. In more familiar terms, and using the suitably amended Fisher equation $MV = PTv$, Walras's argument would consider both velocities (for money and goods) and, hence, their ratio v/V as constant, or, at least stable enough to be safely neglected in the course of the discussion of the demand for money. All in all, and despite a brave attempt at refining the standard quantity theory argument with the introduction of v, the second term of equation (1.3) is for Walras only a token sign of reservation to the traditional quantitativist proposition. The reader is finally left with an analysis conducted in terms of a perfect rectangular hyperbola as the price curve for metal in its monetary uses. For Walras, such a curve is simply the geometrical equivalent of the straightforward 'theorem of the [long run] proportionality of prices to the quantity of money' (1954, p. 366).[46]

The second issue at hand is precisely for Walras to justify the argument hidden behind the shape of that particular curve. Although somewhat intuitively better than other marginalists at hiding his hyperbola behind a smoke-screen of reservations, Walras does not really crack that much tougher theoretical nut. On the basis of this rectangular hyperbola hypothesis, Walras is usually and rightly lumped with economists of the Cambridge School even if he never argued explicitly that the demand for money has uniform unitary elasticity.[47] Patinkin's systematic critique addressed at the neoclassical economists (in particular at Marshall; 1965, pp. 603–10) can be extended, with some minor alterations, to Walras.

In standard monetary theory, this rectangular hyperbola is directly connected to the absence of money illusion – one of the pillars of any version of the quantity theory. By definition, the amount of money demanded by an agent is equal to his or her initial money holdings plus the current amount of his or her excess demand for money. Since any individual adjusts his or her money balances so as to maintain a desired relationship between them and his or her planned expenditures on commodities, it follows that the agent is guided by the *real* value of these balances *only*, that is, by what Walras, as an heir to a very long tradition, calls the money balances 'expressed in terms of commodity B' (1954, p. 335). It then follows that an individual confronted with a proportionate change in money prices *and* initial money holdings will always change the amount of money demanded in the same proportion so as to keep the *real* value of his or her nominal demand for money constant. Alternatively, such a result is equivalent to the assertion that the demand function for *real* money depends on *relative* prices and *real* wealth only.

At this stage, the discussion can also be restricted to equiproportionate changes in prices by keeping at bay the substitution effect. Hence, all commodities can be viewed as a single composite good with price p, 'the absolute price level'.[48] In other words, p can also be defined as the price of the good *real* money holdings. A demand curve for real balances as a function of p is simply the geometrical expression of the absence of money illusion: the verticality of that demand curve (Figure 1.2) illustrates the fact that the demand curve for *real* money holdings is perfectly inelastic (or of uniform zero elasticity) with respect to an equiproportionate increase in all money prices (that is, the price of the single composite good) *and* in all initial money holdings.

These straightforward considerations can now be easily connected with Walras's rectangular hyperbola. The reciprocal of the price level $1/p$ can be defined as the real (or relative) price of the nth good *nominal* money holdings.[49] The curve which describes this demand for these nominal holdings as a function of their relative price $1/p$ is precisely Walras's hyperbola: the *nominal* demand for money is the product of the price level by the *real* demand (Figure 1.3). The fact that it is a rectangular hyperbola, that is, that it displays a uniform unitary elasticity, is the logical counterpart of the zero elasticity of the demand curve for real balances. To illustrate the argument with the traditional case: since a doubling of initial money holdings and all prices leaves the demand for *real* balances unchanged, it must also induce a doubling of the demand for nominal balances.

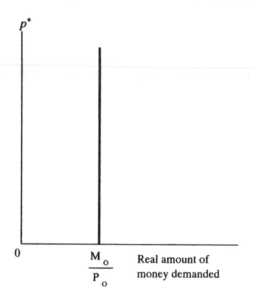

Source: Patinkin (1965, p. 28).

Figure 1.2 The demand for real money

Put in another way, and to use Walras's own terminology, at any point on that rectangular hyperbola curve, the real value of the amount of nominal balances demanded is constant and equal to H/P; that is, the area of any subtended rectangle is constant and equal to the product of the quantity of money by its price:[50]

> our solution to the problem of the value of money shows very well how and why the quantity of money in circulation is unimportant. *The product of this quantity by its value is constant*; and the value increasing proportionately to the diminution of the quantity, it is of no importance that this quantity be large or small. (1874, p. 191; italics added; *OEC*, VIII, p. 557)

One could hardly wish for a clearer statement of the neutrality of money in terms of Walras's price curve for money !

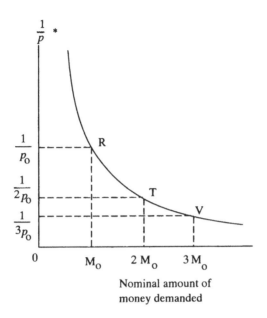

Source Patinkin (1965, p. 28)

Figure 1.3 The nominal demand for money

All this of course changes if the increase in money prices is not accompanied by an equiproportionate increase in nominal money holdings. With characteristic sharpness, and anxious to relate his discovery to the quantity theory tradition, Walras refers the reader to the 'great deal of truth' that can be found in Hume's essay 'Of Money' (1752). While basically in agreement with Hume's demonstration, Walras adds, however, one extra and crucial condition for the standard results of that theory to be verified:

Hume should have supposed not an addition or a subtraction of an identical amount of money to or from all purses, but a multiplication or a division of the amount contained in every purse *by the same figure*. (1874, p. 181; italics added; *OEC*, VIII, pp. 474 and 476)

In modern parlance, Walras had in fact grasped perfectly one of the main conditions for the long-run neutrality of money to be strictly verified: the absence of distributional effects linked with a change in the money supply;[51] that is, all agents' money holdings *have to* be altered *proportionately* to the initial money holdings. Such a change does not affect relative prices (the so-called composite commodity with price p), and hence does not generate any substitution effect. This brilliant piece of analysis shows once again Walras's fastidious analytical procedure: an equiproportionate change in all prices being clearly the type of price change that has always been the primary concern in monetary theory, one has, however, to eliminate from the outset the possibility of having an increase in money prices not accompanied by an equiproportionate increase in nominal money holdings.[52]

This remarkable piece of analysis makes all the more surprising the gaping hole Walras subsequently left in his discussion of the total effect of a change in money prices *accompanied or not* by an equiproportionate increase in money holdings. Whatever the case may be (that is, independently or not of the substitution effect), changes in prices do however, *always* cause an opposite change in the *real* value of initial money holdings, and hence, generate an all-important *wealth effect*.

Without fear of being unduly repetitive, it seems useful to recapitulate here the repercussions introduced in Walras's monetary theory by the absence of that wealth effect. Walras's price curve for money (that is, demand function) depends on relative prices and real wealth ('the command over commodities'). To make the issue simpler, the latter is here measured as the sum of the initial money holdings. In the case traditionally dealt with in monetary theory and adopted by Walras as 'the usual case', a doubling of the money supply distributed to each and every agent equiproportionately to their initial money holdings generates a *wealth effect* that *ultimately* – through an adjustment process – should lead to a doubling in all money prices. To adopt the modern terminology introduced by Patinkin (1965, p. 20), this wealth effect (at the exclusion of any substitution effect) is henceforth called the *real-balance effect:*[53] an injection into an economy in equilibrium of an additional quantity of money distributed among agents equiproportionately to their initial money holdings makes – at these equilibrium prices – these new real balances higher than in the original equilibrium position (relative prices and non-monetary wealth remaining the same). At these original prices, as a consequence of the excess supply of money, a situation of excess demand on each and every market replaces the original state of general equilibrium. Such pressures on the demand side of commodity markets initiate in turn a series of successive approximations which push upwards each and every original money price until they have all increased equiproportionately to the original increase in money supply.[54] If, of course, the system is stable, relative prices and real balances corresponding to this new general equilibrium position are the same as in the original equilibrium.[55]

As will become evident with the 1900 fourth edition, the absence of such a stability analysis is one of the central weaknesses of Walras's monetary theory. In particular, and as will be shown presently, Walras's early confusion between a demand curve for money based on individuals' experiments and a market *equilibrium* curve is the mirror image of that lack of stability analysis; that is, it is the result of a lack of understanding of the pivotal role played by the real-balance effect in the commodity market in the course of the adjustment process. For, as made equally plain in Chapter 4 below, without this effect, there would be *no* market forces to stabilize the absolute level of money prices, that is, *following* a change in the money supply, the price level would remain *indeterminate*. The time structure used in the *Eléments* and the strictly static characteristics of Walras's general equilibrium model will be shown to explain this apparent weakness. Or, put in other words, the structure of Walras's model did not call for such an analysis.

Reverting to Walras's own rectangular hyperbola price curve for money, and with the benefit of what has just been recalled, it is now possible to understand exactly where his argument went awry.

Using Figure 1.4, a diagram introduced by Walras in the second edition of the *Eléments* only (1954, p. 335),[56] but already used for a slightly different purpose in an 1880 article, it is possible to concentrate the discussion on the demand for metal in its monetary uses only, that is, on his rectangular hyperbola. Assuming once again a classic equiproportionate change in all money and prices *and* in initial money holdings, it appears clearly from this diagram that points H, h' and h'' (and all other possible equilibrium points between supply and demand for money) are generated by changing the quantity Q_a'' of monetised A, that is, by shifting S. It is obvious that, *by construction*, this curve is *not* a demand curve: it is the locus of intersection points between all the demand curves and their respective supply curves. As already mentioned above, the slope of a demand curve cannot logically depend on the supply for the same commodity. Similarly, any of these demand curves has to display a slope steeper than one. Hence, Walras's price curve is not a demand curve but a market equilibrium curve for money.

The whole point is obviously for any stability analysis to explain how the system moves from one equilibrium point (say H) to another (say h'') following an increase of monetized A from α to α''. Patinkin's lucid remark apropos that confusion in the neoclassical monetary theory applies particularly well to Walras:

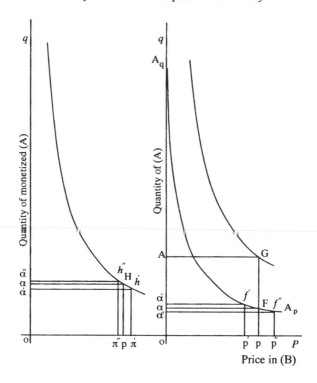

Source: Walras (1954, p. 335)

Figure 1.4 The demand for commodity money II

To be more precise, [behind that hyperbola] there is a conceptual market-experiment in which we take an economy in equilibrium, introduce into it a disturbance in the form of an equiproportionate change in initial money holdings, and then let this disturbance work out itself in all its manifestations until the economy return again to an equilibrium position ... By continuing to change the quantity of money ... [w]e generate additional points ... these points must trace out a rectangular hyperbola ... (1965, p. 49)

Two questions – which are in fact the two sides of the same coin – are clearly begging for an answer. Where is – if any – Walras's demand curve? Where is – if any – Walras's stability analysis?

Before suggesting what are going to be straightforward answers, and in order to be fair to Walras, two preliminary remarks are called for. On the one hand, not in his first 1874 edition or in any other edition[57] or in any other writing or article does Walras ever call his rectangular hyperbola a demand curve for money: this locus is always referred to as the price curve for money. This may seem a trivial distinction but why should Walras, who was so obsessed with symmetry, make an exception for money, were it not to display at least some degree of theoretical uneasiness. More about that issue will be said later when tackling Walras's 1880 writings on money.

On the other hand, while the famous *tâtonnement* process through which an economy reaches a theoretical equilibrium solution of its market excess-demand equations is unmistakably already there in the 1874 theory of exchange (see, for example, 1874, p. 127; *OEC*, VIII, p. 188), nowhere does Walras offer in his first instalment a similar mechanism on the money market. In that respect, he does not even try to coordinate formally his theory of exchange (Section II) with his theory of money (Section III). The question of the part played, or rather not played, by money in the *tâtonnement* process in a production economy is dealt with by Walras only in the 1877 second instalment of the *Eléments*: this tricky topic linked to the static nature of Walras's equilibrium equations and to the time structure used by Walras in the *Eléments* will accordingly be examined in detail in Section 3.

So far as the state of Walras's monetary theory during the 1870s is concerned, the answers to two of the questions raised above are simple: this analysis displays neither a demand curve for money nor a stability analysis. The diagrammatic as well as the algebraic versions of the equation of exchange are market-equilibrium conditions only. To put things even more bluntly, Walras does not suggest the slightest hint of a possible mechanism (either in the money or in the commodity market) that – following a monetary shock -- would bring the economic system back to equilibrium. But was he preoccupied with such a theoretical question? Probably not if one considers the concluding, and approving, remark about Hume's comparative static approach to the quantity theory: 'the end-result of such an event [that is, a change in the money supply] would be a rise or drop in prices proportionate to the increase or decrease of the quantity of money' (1874, p. 181; *OEC*, VIII, p. 476).[58]

Reverting now to Walras's main argument, and adding the equation for the price curve for Q_a'

$$Q_a' = F(P_a)$$

to the equation for the price curve for Q_a''

$$Q_a'' = \frac{H}{P_a} + \frac{\alpha'}{\alpha''} F(P_a),$$

Walras eventually derives the price curve for commodity A considered both in its commodity and monetary uses:

$$Q_a = \frac{H}{P_a} + \frac{(a'' + a')}{a''} F(P_a).$$ (1.4)

And, with optimism, he concludes his Lesson 30 with the following words: 'We have thus solved the problem of the value of money' (1874, p. 182; *OEC*, VIII, p. 480).[59]

However, after a lengthy discussion of the 'rational system of *numéraire* and money' and an equally drawn out and at time questionable primer on book credit[60] (Lessons 32 and 33), Walras amplifies his equation (1.2) only including so far 'metallic currency' only (or 'real' money) to take care of the 'fiduciary circulation' (or paper money):

$$a''Q_a'' + F = a'Q_a' + \beta Q_b p_b + \gamma Q_c p_c + \delta Q_d p_d + \dots$$ (1.5)

where F is made up in obscure proportions of book credits, bills of exchange, cheques and, last but not least, of a term equal to the difference between banknotes in circulation and 'cash in till multiplied by a coefficient of circulation' (1874, p. 201; *OEC*, VIII, p. 522).[61]

Be that as it may, and even if the definition of that extra variable is highly dubious, it allows Walras to recognize explicitly that 'the use of fiduciary money has a certain influence on prices' (1874, p. 201; *OEC*, VIII, p. 524). A fuller development of the influence of banknotes on money and commodity markets was only to appear in 1880 with his forced saving argument (see below Chapter 2, Section 2). Armed with this sophisticated *equation of exchange*, Walras concludes rather overoptimistically that he is now ready to discuss short-run fluctuations and crises: '[This] *equation of exchange* allows an analysis of the crisis phenomenon: 1. Monetary crisis – 2. Industrial crisis – 3. Commercial and financial crises' (1872 as in *OEC*, XI, p. 463).

Clearly, whatever the causes of crises may be, and in anticipation of a good number of interwar cycle theories, this equation of exchange is for Walras the best indicator of short-run tensions in the economic system; that is, more than any other single standard, a change in the price level resulting from a variation in one or another of the components of this equation expresses the degree of disequilibrium present in the economy. This is the topic of Chapter 2, Section 1. However, the gap between that intuitive and very plausible argument and an attempt at a rigorous stability analysis in terms of a *tâtonnement* process in the money market is left wide open.

3 *NUMERAIRE* AND MONEY IN THE THEORIES OF EXCHANGE, PRODUCTION AND CAPITAL: THE TIME STRUCTURE OF THE *ELEMENTS* (1874–77)

Between 1874 and 1877, the main thrust of Walras's research was aimed at producing the second instalment of the *Eléments*. The three central contributions around which this second part was built dealt with the theory of production (1876), the theory of capital formation (1877) and the pseudo-dynamic of the 'Continuous Market' (1877). Money plays no role whatsoever in this second instalment.

Walras should have attempted to integrate money when moving from a pure exchange economy to production and capital formation. The logical crowning of such an extension would be to offer a fully dynamic and integrated monetary model. It is in fact exactly the logic followed by Walras in his thirteen-component structural model developed in Parts IV, V and VI of the second instalment. Money is clearly provided with three niches of its own and added to this model by means of Equations 11, 12 and 13. Cash holdings of consumers (Equation 11) and cash holdings of producers (Equation 12) are part of the circulating capital while money savings (Equation 13) is part of the income category (money is thus considered both as a stock and as a flow). However, having already introduced his monetary analysis in Section III of the 1874 first instalment, and short of completely rewriting it, Walras was no longer able (could not or had no wish) to make it congruent with his overall model. The slots provided for money in this thirteen-equation model are either left empty or, more properly, are exogenously filled.[62] The almost *pro memoria* reference to money in the 1877 instalment, the crucial new orderings of chapters from the 1889 edition onwards[63] coupled with the 'important changes' (1954, p. 38) that his monetary theory underwent right up to 1899 are clear indications that in the first edition, Walras's monetary theory is extremely loosely – if at all – connected with exchange, production and capital models. In fact, in a desperate attempt to beat time (and Jevons!) in order to 'prendre date pour [sa] découverte' (1965, I, p. 320), Walras published his first instalment without having thought through his model to its logical end. In particular, the time dimension introduced by the theories of production and capital formation was not and could not be reconciled with a pre-existing monetary theory itself not properly connected with the theory of exchange. In fact, it is only in the penultimate Part V of the first edition, that, in 1877, and almost as an afterthought, Walras tries to handle the analytical time structure of the *Eléments*. By providing a solid framework for discussion, this neglected threefold distinction should greatly help to clear up the confusion surrounding the use of money and *numéraire* and the static or dynamic nature of the Walrasian *tâtonnement* mechanism.

In Lesson 50 on 'The Continuous Market', and for the first time,[64] Walras outlines three time dimensions into which he will struggle to constrain sequentially his general equilibrium:

- the 'once-and-for-all market' (1877, p. 307; *OEC*, VIII, p. 576);
- the 'periodical market' (1877, p. 307; *OEC*, VIII, p. 576);
- the 'continuous market' (1877, p. 310; *OEC*, VIII, p. 579).

That this distinction appears in this order and at the extreme end of Walras's theoretical chapters immediately leaves the reader with the uneasy but very clear suspicion that Walras's general equilibrium might well be regarded as working like a huge 'once-and-for-all' static model in which equilibrium is 'instantaneous'. At this point, it is also evident that, with such a typology, Walras was trying to build a bridge between theoretical rigour and some sort of 'realism'. If pure theory has to be of any use for applied and social economics, some indications should be offered on the links between them in the concluding part of the *Eléments*. Finally, this triple distinction is already unmistakably present in the *first* edition of the *Eléments*: a fact important to keep in mind when assessing various interpretations of the part money might or might not be playing in the *tâtonnement* mechanism in subsequent editions.[65]

In the next three sections, the role of *numéraire* and money in these successive time dimensions is accordingly examined in a general equilibrium model which, for the first time includes exchange, production and capital.

3.1 The 'Once-and-for-All Market'

The 'once-and-for-all market' is beyond doubt the clearest expression of a durationless, equilibrium, stock version of Walras's price formation (or *tâtonnement*) mechanism. At one point in historical time, exchange, production and capital markets are all and simultaneously open once and for all; trading comes to a halt; *tâtonnement* takes place and the vector of equilibrium prices is *instantaneously* reached.

Even if, in 1877, Walras had not yet properly got under his skin all the subtleties of the no-trade-out-of-equilibrium hypothesis (in particular in the theory of production), this version of the *tâtonnement* cannot deal with a genuine dynamic path along which markets move towards equilibrium. It is a purely virtual mechanism – not an attempt to understand the behaviour of actual markets. In 1896, Walras gives retrospectively the fullest account of this procedure, the logic of which dominates the first three editions:

J'ai reconnu, dans mes *Eléments d'économie politique pure*, notamment en énumérant les *éléments* et en décrivant le *mécanisme de la production* (18è leçon), et en définissant le *marché permanent* (27è leçon), que toutes les espèces de la richesse sociale, sauf les terres, étaient soumises à un continuel mouvement de disparition par suite de la consommation et de réapparition par suite de la production, qu'elles étaient ainsi 'comme autant de tiges qui, sans cesse coupées à l'un de leurs bouts, repousseraient sans cesse par l'autre bout'.[66] Entre toutes ces espèces, les services immatériels de capitaux sont tout spécialement à l'état de courant continu; ils sont consommés au fur et à mesure qu'ils sont produits. Mais j'ai expliqué en posant les *équations de la production* (20è leçon) qu'au moyen de ces deux unités: 1° l'unité, naturelle ou artificielle, de quantité du capital, et 2° l'unité de temps, on pouvait évaluer les quantités de ces services et, par conséquent, les supposer offerts et demandés, vendus et achetés, **par stocks** sur le marché. J'ai expliqué enfin, après avoir posé et avant de résoudre les *équations de la production* (20è leçon) et celles *de la capitalisation et du crédit* (24è leçon), que, pour faire la théorie de la détermination des prix courants des services et des produits, **je supposais le mouvement économique de la production et de la consommation arrêté pour un instant, afin de considérer une quantité déterminée de richesse sociale et un marché hypothétique sur lequel les tâtonnements pussent se faire jusqu'à l'établissement de l'équilibre.** En opérant ainsi, j'ai fait comme les mathématiciens qui, pour constituer rationnellement toute la mécanique, élaborent *la statique* avant la dynamique. S'il y a des savants qui aient trouvé le moyen de procéder à l'inverse en économique, on doit souhaiter qu'ils se décident, sans trop tarder, à nous faire part de cette remarquable découverte. (1896, p. 336; see also *OEC*, X, pp. 306–7; original italics, bold emphasis added)[67]

Before investigating the consequences of this first approach on the use of *numéraire* and money, two comments on its application to exchange, production and capital markets are in order.

First, this technique allows the stock method borrowed from the theory of exchange to be applied to production and capital.[68] Accordingly, and for the sake of the argument, the production and capital processes can be considered as instantaneous exchanges between *stocks* of commodities. If this procedure allows Walras to determine the prices of productive services of *given* quantities of land and personal capital, he is compelled to admit that the 'quantities' (stocks) of capital proper are *unknown*. Using Walras's own words taken from the summary of Lesson 46:

Terres, capitaux naturels inconsommables; leurs quantités sont données. Personnes, capitaux naturels consommables; leurs quantités sont aussi données. *Capitaux proprement dits*, capitaux artificiels consommables; *leurs quantités sont inconnues*. (1877, p. 278; *OEC*, VIII, p. 344; emphasis added)

In other words, on the once-and-for-all markets, so far as stocks of land and personal capital are concerned, 'there is no action of price on quantity or reaction of quantity on price' (1877, p. 278; *OEC,* VIII, p. 352). However, such a two-way relationship exists on the market for capital proper (the stock of which is accordingly an unknown):

> Les capitaux proprement dits sont des capitaux artificiels; ce sont des produits; leur prix est soumis à la loi des frais de production. Si le prix de vente est supérieur au prix de revient, la quantité produite augmentera et le prix de vente baissera; si le prix de vente est inférieur au prix de revient, la quantité produite diminuera et le prix de vente s'élèvera. A l'état d'équilibre, le prix de vente et le prix de revient sont égaux. (1877, p. 279; *OEC*, VIII, p. 353)

On this once-and-for-all market, the selling price of a capital good proper k is the direct result of the relation $P_k = \pi_k/i$, that is, the quotient of its net income by the general rate of net income. Capital goods proper are thus the only capital goods the net income of which (resulting from the quantity produced) are in a position to alter their selling prices. In modern parlance, while markets for land and personal capital goods undergo price adjustments only, both quantity and price adjustments take place on the market for capital goods proper. This variability of the quantity of capital appears therefore to be in contradiction with the stock hypothesis of the once-and-for-all market.

However, to avoid, in the first edition, this problem of 'false transaction/production' Walras calls to the rescue the so-called 'foreign market' fiction: he assumes that producers/entrepreneurs can import the productive services they need from abroad where their elasticities of supply are presumed to be infinite at a given set of prices to produce commodities sold on the home market. Once equilibrium in production is reached, entrepreneurs pay back these imported services not in the same quantities but in quantities having the same value in total; the 'supposition du marché étranger' can then be eliminated (1877, pp. 252–7; *OEC,* VIII, pp. 312, 314 and 320–22).[69]

Second, on this once-and-for-all market, the vector of equilibrium prices resulting from this purely theoretical and timeless *tâtonnement* mechanism is *ex definitio* identical with the solution reached 'in principle' by solving the general equilibrium equations. The so-called selfsameness view[70] is thus assumed between 'existence' and 'process': the relative prices which emerge from the process of free competition on the once-and-for-all markets are identically the same as the roots of the system of equilibrium equations. As in the theorem of equivalent distribution, the exclusion of trading at 'false prices' from this hypothetical competitive market mechanisms implies that preferences and asset holdings are assumed to be constant prior to trading at equilibrium prices.[71] How, then, could the auctioneer reach at the end of this pseudo-dynamic *tâtonnement* mechanism a set of equilibrium prices different from the solution of a system of $(n - 1)$ equations? Bertrand's famous (1883) allegation, according to which Walras's *tâtonnement* (in exchange) is path dependent, is here groundless. Given Walras's hypothesis about the working of his once-and-for-all market, the vector of equilibrium prices is not contingent upon the order in which the transactions are taking place, since none takes place before equilibrium prices are reached. Once again, and to use Solow's terms, Walras's *tâtonnement* is a 'swindle' (1956b, p. 88). It teaches us nothing whatsoever about an adjustment process on real markets: reality is constrained in such a manner into the fiction of a 'hypothetical regime of perfect competition' (Walras, 1954, p. 40), that the trial-and-error *tâtonnement* led by a handy auctioneer is bound to offer the same vector of equilibrium prices as that reached by solving the equation system.[72] In the end, even if Walras likes to keep the illusion of a *tâtonnement* 'process' actually taking place on such a hypothetical market, the realism of this mechanism is no more than a delusion, or even a mirage.

Nevertheless, Walras is largely responsible for the origin of Bertrand's perplexity. In 1874, and despite the assumption of no 'false trading' indispensable for the validity of the theorem of equivalent distribution, it appears from all the evidence available that Walras was probably unaware of the analytical consequences of disequilibrium transactions, endowments and path-dependency effects. As shown above, it is only in 1877 that the first clear-cut discussion of the theoretical once-and-for-all market appeared in Lesson 50. Bertrand's critique being addressed at Walras's original 1874 theory of exchange,[73] the mathematician could not be aware of either Walras's threefold time dimension or his crucial once-and-for-all market hypothesis.

The coordination between these two pieces of analysis had to await a footnote in Walras's 1885 article on Gossen. This answer to Bertrand is clearly coined in terms of the once-and-for-all market:

Bertrand m'objecte que le problème de l'échange n'est pas déterminé par la raison qu'en cas d'excédent de la demande sur l'offre ou de l'offre sur la demande, selon qu'on satisfera en premier lieu tels ou tels des acheteurs et des vendeurs, il faudra faire ensuite plus ou moins de hausse ou de baisse pour satisfaire les autres. Je réponds à cela que, *sur le marché théorique,* en cas d'excédent de la demande sur l'offre ou de l'offre sur la demande, on ne satisfait personne, mais que *l'échange demeure suspendu*[74] jusqu'à ce que la hausse ou la baisse ait amené l'égalité de l'offre et de la demande; après quoi on satisfait alors tout le monde. *Le prix courant théorique est essentiellement un prix unique résultant, à un moment donné, d'un échange général.* Dans ces conditions, le problème de l'échange est parfaitement déterminé. (1885 in *OEC,* IX, p. 312, note 1; see also 1965, II, p. 630; italics added)

Well before the 1900 *tâtonnements sur bons*, to consolidate the internal coherence of his model, Walras is compelled to outline with greater clarity the no-trade-out-of-equilibrium condition (only implicit in the *Eléments*) and its connection with a durationless *tâtonnement* mechanism (not process). Caught once again (and certainly not for the last time) between theoretical rigour and greater realism, Walras gave up without hesitation the latter for the sake of the former. All in all, to keep calling *tâtonnement* a theory discarding disequilibrium trade by means of the once-and-for-all market hypothesis amounts to end up with a theory called *tâtonnements* but without any groping.

Hence, from his very first edition, Walras is faced with the difficult problem of reconciling a durationless equilibrating mechanism taking place in 'logical time' with an intuitive process of price formation taking place in successive historical time instants. Walras's constant oscillations between reality and abstraction, between process and mechanism, between a market process and a mathematical iterative mechanism, are at the core of the contradictory interpretations given to *tâtonnement* and, of course, to the part money plays or does not play in it. Walras's repeated claims that the mathematical solution of equilibrium is the *selfsame* problem[75] that is solved in practice in the market by the mechanism of free competition is the best illustration of this difficulty, which implies that *tâtonnement* is an idealized representation of the market process or that it mimics market forces. Such an interpretation is often[76] considered as an early acceptance of the *tâtonnement* terminology dropped by Walras in the 1900 fourth edition in favour of the theoretically sounder (but empirically weaker) *tâtonnement sur bons*. Of course, the present author does not wish to deny the possibility of such a reading of Walras's evolution. However, he firmly insists on the equally important presence in the very first edition of the *tâtonnement* hypothesis considered as a timeless mathematical technique of iteration used by Walras on his fictitious once-and-for-all market to find a solution to the general equilibrium system of simultaneous equations. As a matter of fact, one of the main goals of this book is to demonstrate that, from Walras's earliest 1874 venture into pure theory, these two interpretations of *tâtonnement* are clearly both present. Prisoner from the start of the necessities of the mathematical rigour of general equilibrium analysis, Walras unsuccessfully grappled during thirty-five years to reconcile the instantaneous analytical mechanism of the once-and-for-all theoretical market conducted in terms of *numéraire* with the trial-and-error process of market forces in which money has a central part to play in a trading process taking place in historical time. In other words, and from his very first attempt at formalizing Adam Smith's intuition, Walras devised a model which would allow him to explain only the definition – not the formation – of equilibrium prices.

To illustrate further the contrast between these two versions of *tâtonnement*, it seems useful to examine briefly the solution to this tension suggested by Donzelli (1989, pp. 269–81) with the introduction of an apposite contrast between 'historical' (or 'real') and 'logical' time:

> The set of 'real'[77] time instants is the time set over which the economy under theoretical investigation is supposed to evolve; the set of 'logical' time instants is instead the time set over which the equilibrating process is assumed to take place. The simultaneous presence within the analytical model of these two distinct notions of time allows to solve the apparent paradox of the Walrasian theory of *tâtonnements* ... .
>
> [B]y virtue of that distinction [between 'real' and 'logical' time], the process of adjustment towards equilibrium, though being interpreted as an enduring process with respect to 'logical' time, can nevertheless be viewed as a durationless phenomena with respect to the 'real' time set through which the evolution of the economy is supposed to take place. But, being durationless with respect to 'real' time, the adjustment process cannot give rise to any observable disequilibrium phenomenon; as a consequence, it has the character of a purely virtual process that is structurally unable to affect the data constellation characterising the economy at the instant (of 'real' time) to which the analysis is meant to refer. By the same token, the equilibrium state associated with that data constellation, though it can be conceived as a rest point of an adjustment process unfolding itself in 'logical' time, can at the same time be supposed to be instantaneously reached by the economy at the relevant instant of 'real' time. (1989, pp. 276–9)

Using Donzelli's distinction, Walras's once-and-for-all market technique[78] is thus based on a notion of *instantaneous equilibrium* completely different from the dominant stationary equilibrium approach.[79] While the latter goes back to the classical notion of gravitation (adjustment is seen as an enduring process in which disequilibrium trading is considered as a normal phenomenon even if the data of the economy are not allowed to change), the former notion of instantaneous equilibrium puts at the heart of Walras's theory the disturbing idea that duration is irrelevant to general equilibrium models and, hence, not a basic feature of the economic system it purports to analyse.

The part played by *numéraire* and money in Walras's complete 1877 model of the once-and-for-all market is now easy to appreciate. As in the theory of exchange, the durationless *tâtonnement* mechanisms in production and capital formation are conducted in terms of *numéraire* only. Since there is no trading or production out of equilibrium, the *tâtonnement* goes on in term of *numéraire* as long as, in 'logical' time, the vector of equilibrium prices has not been reached. By definition, in such a model, the role of money is non-existent. In fact, in Walras's 1877 model, money is *inessential*: the *tâtonnement* mechanism is not in the least hampered if money is absent; or, again, to quote Howitt, 'money plays no role in the bargaining process' (1973, p. 495). In line with the logic of the once-and-for-all market, the *tâtonnement* mechanism is a device expressly introduced to abstract from time, transaction and information costs – the very rationale of money as a means of exchange.[80]

In Walras's own words, in the pure exchange model: 'the use of money in trading has peculiarities of its own, the study of which must be postponed until later, and not interwoven at the outset with the general phenomenon of value in exchange' (1874, p. 52; *OEC*, VIII, pp. 73–4). Similarly, in the production model: 'We can now see how this procedure [the 'foreign market' fiction] makes it possible to abstract, if not from *numéraire*, at least from money' (1877, p. 252; *OEC*, VIII, p. 312).

3.2 The 'Periodical' Market

Walras defines the 'periodical market' by contrasting it with the timeless once-and-for-all market:

> Granting all this and supposing that all the accessory facts that we have hitherto neglected are taken into account, let us drop the assumption of a 'once-and-for-all' market and imagine, instead, *a determinate period of, let us say a day, or better a year,* in order to allow for seasonal variations. (1877, p. 307; *OEC*, VIII, p. 576; italics added)

These 'accessory facts' are 'simply' those eliminated at the beginning of the theory of production when – for the sake of the once-and-for-all market – Walras introduced the hypothesis of exchanges between 'stocks' of commodities and services. In fact, this switch to a determinate period in historical time involves the reintroduction of *circulating* (or *working*) *capital*[81] and thus of *money*:

> not only the entrepreneurs' working capital in the form of raw materials, new capital goods,[82] new income goods and cash on hand, but also the consumers' working capital in the form of accumulations of income goods, cash and money savings. (1877, p. 244; *OEC*, VIII, p. 298)

However, this move to a periodical market within a determinate period of historical time by way of the reintroduction of circulating capital and money forces Walras to give up the entirety of his timeless general equilibrium model. In short, as soon as historical time is brought into his theoretical picture, Walras has – in his own words – to 'discontinue using abstract symbols and replace them by concrete numbers ... to make our general system of economic phenomena readily understood' (1877, p. 307; *OEC*, VIII, p. 576). Still in other words, a modest attempt at injecting a greater dose of realism into general equilibrium by way of circulating capital, money and time renders its rigorous use highly questionable. Walras reverts in fact to the traditional gravitation theory implying short-run disequilibrium transactions oscillating through historical time round a long-run equilibrium centre of gravity.

Stock of productive factors (social wealth)

Land	Persons	Capital Goods
80	50	60
of which	of which	of which 40 fixed
32 consumers' services;	14 consumers'services;	capital of which
48 productive services	36 productive services	12 consumers' services
		28 productive services
		20 circulating capital
		of which 4 consumers
		(2 consumers' goods
		+ 2 cash and savings)
		16 entrepreneurs (4 new
		capital goods + 4 stocks
		raw material + 6 income
		goods + 2 money)

Income

Rent	Gross wage	Gross Income
2	5^{83}	3^{84}

To take into account all the elements of 'social wealth',[85] Walras drops his entire general equilibrium analysis and switches to a rather primitive macro-model very similar to Quesnay's *Tableau économique*. Assuming an equilibrium rate of net income of 2.5 per cent, at the end of this periodical market (typically a year), Walras outlines in the following table the economy of an 'imaginary country'. For the first time, *all* thirteen categories of

Walras's elements of production can now be taken into account; quite a few assumptions have, however, to be made explicit. First, the ratio between an annual turnover estimated at 100 thousand million and the amount of working capital implies an average period of production of one-fifth of a year. Second, out of the 10 thousand million income, 8 are consumed and 2 are capitalized; the latter being in turn divided between 1.5 thousand million for depreciation and insurance premiums on existing capital goods proper, there remain 500 million for the production of new capital goods proper. Yet – and in contrast to the once-and-for-all market – the '500 millions [earmarked] for the production of new capital goods proper' (1877, p. 310; *OEC*, VIII, p. 579) will be put to productive use during the *following* period only. Walras takes his model no further than the brink of a dynamic analysis: within his periodical market, the constancy of the stock of capital is clearly preserved.

This periodical market is in fact a way to homogenize the various economic flows linked to a certain length of time; to turn them into stocks to analyse how they are distributed between economic agents at the end of the period. This technique allows for a periodization of the temporal continuum into slices of time. But this annual market period does not reflect any dynamic process through time: in particular, it does not explain in any way the dynamic the economic system is going through to reach the equilibrium situation described by Walras's 'concrete numbers'.[86] In particular, and even if Walras 'revert[s] to the thirteen categories of elements of production' (1877, p. 308; *OEC*, VIII, p. 578), nothing is said about the way the money stock is distributed between consumers and entrepreneurs and, even worse, why agents hold money at all. In general, this technique can be seen as a sheer preliminary manipulation in an attempt to use a sequence of successive periods in an exercise in comparative static.

At this point, it is not really surprising to realize that the equation of exchange linked to the idea of *circulation à desservir* is the only other piece of theoretical work in the first edition of the *Eléments* in which appears the notion of period. As shown in Section 2, above Walras's equation of exchange[87] contains coefficients of circulation $\left(\alpha'', \alpha', \beta, \gamma, \delta \ldots\right)$ for every good including, of course, money:

> J'appelle *coefficient de circulation* le nombre par lequel il faut multiplier la quantité existante d'une marchandise pour avoir la quantité totale de cette marchandise entrée en échange, c'est-à-dire vendue et achetée, **pendant une certaine période de temps déterminée, un an, un mois, un jour.** ... Ce coefficient est naturellement d'autant plus élevé que la marchandise entre plus fréquemment en échange. Il pourrait être inférieur à l'unité; il pourrait être nul. (1874, p. 179; *OEC*, VIII, pp. 460-62; original italics, bold emphasis added)

As far as money is concerned, the coefficient α'' is none other than the velocity of circulation of the part of the stock of money-metal used as money. Since, by assumption, Walras's monetary theory excludes barter (and hence postulates monetary exchanges), in equilibrium, the *equation of exchange* is confirmed even if – as abundantly shown earlier – not a word is said about the dynamic process leading to such a monetary equilibrium.

Accordingly, the congruence between the 'periodical market' (1877, Part V) and the Equation of exchange (1874, Part III) is perfect: the time period used in both models is strictly formal; equilibrium positions only are considered; preliminary *tâtonnements* conducted in terms of *numéraire* (not money) are accordingly completed; the vector of equilibrium prices (and hence general equilibrium) is determined by real variables only; though forced by assumption (*circulation à desservir*) into the periodical market, money is inessential, money is neutral.

In the realm of applied monetary theory and with the use of a sequence of such periodical markets, Walras will suggest his only attempt at a monetary disequilibrium analysis in terms of 'forced saving'. Paradoxically, and Chapter 2, Section 1, below should confirm such a suspicion, whenever Walras endeavours to inject a dose of realism into his model, he has to 'discontinue using abstract symbols and replace them by concrete numbers' (1877, p. 307; *OEC*, VIII, p. 576). In other words, whenever Walras wants money to play an essential part in his analysis, he has to give up his general equilibrium model and revert to a more rustic quantity-theory macro-type of approach.

3.3 The 'Continuous Market'

The 'continuous market' is the third and last time dimension to be found in all four editions of the *Eléments:* it reflects the ultimate move away from a purely static general equilibrium towards a 'real-world' dynamic: 'Finally, in order to come still more closely to reality, we must drop the hypothesis of an annual market period and adopt in its place the hypothesis of a continuous market. *Thus, we pass from the static to the dynamic state*' (1877, p. 310; *OEC*, VIII, p. 579; italics added).

Annual production and consumption are no longer constant magnitudes and 'change from instant to instant along with the basic data of the problem'. 'Every hour, nay every minute', the flows of circulating capital are disappearing and reappearing leading to similar movements ('but much more slowly') in the stocks of personal capital, capital goods proper *and money*.[88] This grand stock-flow dynamic was – and still is – light years away from Walras's strictly static general equilibrium, like a promised land at which

Walras could only briefly glimpse in the concluding theoretical chapter of the *Eléments*:

> Such is the continuous market, which is perpetually tending towards equilibrium without ever actually attaining it because the market has no other way of approaching equilibrium except by *tâtonnements*, and, before the goal is reached, it has to start groping afresh, all the basic data of the problem, e.g. the initial quantities possessed, the utilities of goods and services, the technical coefficients, the excess of income over consumption, the working capital requirements, etc., having changed in the meantime. (1877, p. 310; *OEC*, VIII, p. 580)

The contrast between the dynamic of the continuous market and the purely static once-and-for-all market on which the whole general equilibrium edifice rests is an essential part of the 1874–77 edition. Contrary to whatever Morishima may argue (1977, pp. 4–5), the continuous market is not meant to be considered an integral part of Walras's general equilibrium edifice. This *coda*, as Jaffé aptly named it, 'was meant rather to serve as a link between Walras's pure statical theory and his applied and "social" theories, which are intrinsically dynamics'[89] (1980, p. 367). As early as this first edition, and even if he lends an air of empirical relevance to his equilibrium equations throughout his two instalments, Walras attributes this durationless hypothesis to his general equilibrium model. In particular, the theory of *tâtonnement* conducted in term of *numéraire* is a theory of the mechanics, not of the history in real time, of the emergence of a vector of equilibrium prices in a hypothetical competitive economy. Accordingly, and from the very first phase of its inception, general equilibrium analysis cannot offer a formal account of the role of money as a medium of exchange.

NOTES

1. For a step-by-step discussion of Walras's great difficulties in first understanding and then integrating the concept of marginal utility into his price theory, see Jaffé (1983, pp. 300–305).

2. So fruitful indeed that – in the Spring of 1873 – victim of what seems to have been his first nervous breakdown, Walras had to stop all activities for two months (1965, I, p. 320). This 'névrose cérébrospinale' (1965, I, p. 503) was to regularly pester him throughout his entire life, hamper more than once his research and eventually drive him into early retirement in 1892. About the crucial importance of this 1871–74 period in the making of general equilibrium analysis, it is worth quoting Walras himself. In the *Preface* to the fourth edition of the *Eléments* (1900), reflecting (with characteristic optimism) about thirty years of research, he writes: 'this volume, despite the aforementioned changes, is, as I have already said, simply the definitive edition of the book that I first published in 1874–77' (1954, p. 39).

3. As shown later, the premises of the classical dichotomy can be traced, at least in part, to this confusion.

4. Within this Section II, the *numéraire* is, however, introduced at a fairly late stage in the argument. The mechanism of arbitrage between two, three and *n* commodities is first conducted without the benefit of a unit of account, that is, prices in the first edition are not expressed in *numéraire*. See Jaffé (1954, p. 573, n. (h) and pp. 575–6, n (i)) for the peculiarity of this *tâtonnement* without *numéraire*.

5. This text will incidentally remain *unchanged* throughout the five successive editions. The same terrain is already covered in a much shorter fashion in Lessons 4 and 6 of the 1872 Geneva Lectures but under the same title: 'Choice of an Instrument of Measurement and a Medium of Exchange' (*OEC*, XI, p. 439).

6. Many prestigious theorists have been guilty of attributing such a confusion to Walras or, at least of some sloppiness of expression on this matter. See, for example, Pareto and his statement about 'ideal money ... which does not exist materially' (1896, p. 167; 1909, p. 450); Cassel and his 'scale-of-reckoning' concept of money (1924, p. 51); Hayek and his *numéraire* 'which serves merely as a unit of account, ... and consequently there will be no additional demand for it to hold it as money' (1941, p. 31) and Hicks (1966, p. 8). But see Wicksell (1919, pp. 224–5) for an apposite and healthy warning against that confusion.

7. A detailed discussion of this concept would obviously take us too far afield. Besides Walker's classic doctrinal treatment of 'ideal money' (1877, pp. 290–301), Guggenheim's discussion (1978) of the pre-Classical French use of abstract units of account ('ghost moneys' and other macute) provides a good introduction to understanding the tradition from which Walras sharply departed.

8. This term expressing the interdependence among the excess demand equations of a general equilibrium system was introduced by Lange (1942, p. 50). Footnote 2 on that same page offers the first demonstration that Walras's law also holds in the absence of a uniform medium of exchange, that is, 'in a moneyless system ... [in which] one of the commodities [is] taken arbitrary as *numéraire*'.

9. 'I have begun to read your work, especially the part on Money which happens to be of much interest to me because I am engaged upon a book having the same subject' (1965, I, p. 426).

10. The difficult problem of the price of the chosen *numéraire* being zero or the even trickier question of the relevance of the choice of one *numéraire* to considerations of stability are of course not mentioned by Walras.

11. Jaffé goes as far as to assert that he has gathered 'evidence enough to indicate that Isnard was not merely "a precursor of Léon Walras" [Schumpeter, 1954, p. 307, n. 14] but actually a direct progenitor of the Walrasian general equilibrium model' (1983, p. 56). See also Klotz, (1994, pp. 42–3).

12. Even Cournot, with his 'fictitious and invariable modulus' (1838, p. 26) cannot be invoked as a possible forerunner.

13. Such a 'coincidence' is all the more difficult to admit when one realizes that ninety-three years separate Isnard's *Traité* (1781) from Walras's *Eléments* (1874), that Walras actually had in his own library his father's copy of Isnard's exceedingly rare book and that it is on Walras's intervention that this title found its way into Jevons's List of Mathematico-Economics Books, Memoirs and Other Published Writings (Jevons, 1879, p. 301). For Walras's one and only reference to Isnard, see Walras's letter to Jevons (1965, I, pp. 568–9) in which Walras notices that 'the ratios of value between commodities exchanged are expressed altogether correctly in algebraic language and which should, I think, be placed at the head of the list'.

14. That is, and to use Walras's terminology, *numéraire* is simultaneously *real money*.

15. That is, none other than Jevons's later double coincidence argument (1875, p. 34). See also Walras's earlier discussion in *Le Travail* (1867 as in *OEC*, VI, pp.199–200).

16. Clower (1967, p. 86).

17. The text of this Lesson 24 (1874, Part II, The Pure Theory of Exchange) appears immediately before the introduction of the idea of *numéraire* (Lesson 25); it remained unchanged throughout all editions. Given the crucial part paid by the 'no-trade-out-of-equilibrium' hypothesis in Walras's *tâtonnement*, it is worth observing here that this theorem of equivalent distributions is only valid with trading at equilibrium prices. See below pp. 30–6 the crucial problem raised for a proper understanding of the *tâtonnement* mechanism by Walras's early recognition of this hypothesis.

18. With the help of Ostroy and Starr (1990, pp. 6–7) and Ostroy (1992, p. 784).

19. See below, Chapter 4, Section 1.

20. A century later, in the midst of the 'cash-in-advance' versus 'money-in-the-utility-function' debate, Patinkin made (explicitly this time) the same admission: 'Most discussions of monetary theory ... simply assume (as I too do in this book [that is, *Money, Interest and Prices*]) that money exists and serves as a unique medium of exchange in the economy' (1989, p. xxix).

21. '[E]very prudent man in every period of society, after the first establishment of the division of labour, must naturally have endeavoured ... to have at all times by him ... a certain quantity of some one commodity or other, such as he imagined few people would be likely to refuse in exchange for the produce of their industry ... [M]oney has become in all civilized nations the universal instrument of commerce, by the intervention of which goods of all kinds are bought and sold, or exchanged for one another' (Smith, 1776, pp. 37–8 and 44).

22. In fact none other than Auguste Walras's ubiquitous idea of *rareté* applied to money (for example, 1849, pp. 23–4; 1831, p. 290).

23. These very characteristics are those already listed and discussed in exactly the same words by Auguste Walras (1849, pp. 24–5 and 51–2).

24. See the sample of references to leading theorists given above on page viii, note 2.

25. The wish to go back to the origins of this still unsolved question is in fact the present author's principal motive for writing this book. In 1933, Hicks made for the first time the (now) perfectly sound argument that 'in [Walras's] world in which there is perfect foresight there is no use for money at all' (1933, p. 447). In other words, money can have no positive value, therefore it is a mistake to attempt to introduce demand for money functions into general equilibrium equations: Walras's model is one of barter. If strictly theoretically true, it took the profession nearly six decades to come to terms with such a severe limitation to Walras's model. In his answer to Hicks's argument, flying to Walras's rescue, Marget concludes rightly on Walras's *intentions* in the field on monetary theory: 'Though he did not pretend, by his incorporation of money into his general theory of equilibrium, to go beyond the limits of static theory, Walras ... made it clear that he hoped he had cast that theory into such a form that future workers in the field of what he himself called 'dynamics' *could take hold of the problem at the point at which he left off*' (1935, p. 186; italics added). In short, by setting thus the agenda for further research, Walras could hardly be accused of thinking in barter terms even if this very agenda was to lead Hicks to demonstrate the barter nature of Walras's model.

26. Jaffé is in fact refuting (with an important array of documentary evidence) one of Schumpeter's arguments (thus these movements up and down a ladder): '[The] analysis of Walras's schema discloses the fact that marginal utility was the ladder by which Walras climbed to the level of his general-equilibrium system' (1954, p. 918). However, Schumpeter (to Jaffé's obvious delight) was among the first to recognize that the general equilibrium structure 'was the achievement of Walras': 'So soon as we realize that it is the general equilibrium system which is the really important thing, we discover that, in itself, the principle of marginal utility is not so important after all as Jevons, the Austrians, and Walras himself believed' (1954, p. 918). See also Walras's own Autobiography *in Correspondence* (1965, I, pp. 5–6).

27. Even worse, Walras was in fact not identifying the agent's utility curve with the same agent's demand curve but an individual's utility curve with a market demand curve. Such a confusion obviously implied interpersonal comparisons of utility and the assumption of

a constant marginal utility of money (or whatever that was given in exchange for the commodity demanded).

28. Notably, and even if not referred explicitly to Chapters 2 and 3.

29. Just as Laidler did for Marshall (1991, pp. 7–47); it would probably not be too difficult to connect this line of argument with the position taken by leading French monetary economists of the time, notably Coquelin, Cernuschi, Chevalier, Wolkoff and above all, Victor Bonnet (1859, 1865, 1866, 1870). Say and Ricardo are, however, the two authors whose works were used by Auguste Walras to build the chapters his son used so freely in his own discussion (see 1849, pp. 26–30). Mill, however, is curiously completely absent from Léon's references.

30. This is Jaffé's translation. Marget suggests 'the circulation [presumably of goods] to be disposed of' (1931, p. 575, n. 14). In his obituary notice of Walras, Schumpeter suggests *notwendige Zirkulation* (that is, necessary circulation) (1910, p. 401).

31. Irving Fisher's equation appeared only eleven years later on page 26 of the first edition of *The Purchasing Power of Money* (1911). In a well-known footnote 2 on page 25, Fisher puts Simon Newcomb (1885, p. 546) at the head of a rather short list of precursors including Edgeworth (1887), Hadley (1896, pp. 196–7) and Kemmerer (1907). However, Fisher hastens to add that 'while thus only recently given mathematical expression, the quantity theory has long been understood as a relationship among several factors: amount of money, rapidity of circulation and amount of trade' (1911, pp. 25–6). He then refers the reader to the classic Book III, Chapter 11 of Mill's *Principles* (1848), never quoted by Walras.

32. Later on, Bagehot will be added but, as shown below on p. 97, in a wholly different context.

33. It is now housed in the library of the Walras–Pareto Centre.

34. Copernic, Bodin, Locke, Montesquieu, Hume, Smith, Say, Ricardo, J. Mill, Tooke, Senior and, of course, J.S. Mill.

35. Roscher (1854), Bowen (1856) and Levasseur (1858).

36. This equality appears in (1872) only.

37. The higher the coefficient the more often the corresponding commodity is exchanged.

38. This exact formulation appears on page 200 only. In his Lesson 30, Walras argues not in terms of 'money' (that is, commodity A) but in terms of commodity B.

39. And not its demand curve. See above, Section 1, for an explanation of Walras's confusion between utility and demand curves.

40. In other words, and as mentioned earlier, in the first edition, the demand for money is exogenously given.

41. This curve which is 'sensiblement hyperbolique' and the idea of a price that varies 'sensiblement en raison inverse de sa quantité' appear already in the Geneva Lectures. In this 1872 version, Walras goes formally one step further than in 1874 and defines this hyperbola as $M = q'_a p'_a$ (*OEC*, XI, p. 457).

42. This exogenously given supply curve does not appear explicitly on Walras's original diagram.

43. And not up; remember Walras's reversal of axes.

44. In opposition to the opinion expressed by Marshall and his pupils for whom this curve *always* displays a uniform unitary elasticity; see Marshall (1923, p. 283) for his *Constant Outlay Curve*; Pigou (1917, p. 196); Patinkin (1965, pp. 605–9) and Bridel (1987, pp. 28–35).

45. 'Obviously, the more often a good is exchanged the higher its coefficient of circulation' (1874, p. 179; *OEC*, VIII, pp. 462–3).

46. To be fair one must acknowledge the fact that whenever Walras refers to that curve he always mentions *pro memoria* that it approximates, sometimes 'closely' (1954, p. 334), sometimes only 'partially' an equilateral hyperbola 'if we neglect a negligible term' (1880, p. 557).

47. See Marget (1942, II, p. 648). According to Patinkin, Wicksell should be considered as an exception (1965, p. 583).

48. Consider an economy with n goods, the n'th good being fiat money. The money prices of the $(n-1)$ goods are $p_1/p_n, ..., p_{n-1}/p_n$. The relative prices of the $(n-1)$ goods in terms of the first one are $1, p_2/p_1, ..., p_{n-1}/p_1, p_n/p_1 \cdot p_n/p_1$ is the relative price of money in terms of good 1, that is, the number of units of good 1 that have to be given up to obtain a unit of fiat money, that is, Walras's 'price of money in terms of B'.

49. When the price level goes up the real (or relative) price of the good nominal money holdings goes down and vice versa. Figures 1.2 and 1.3 are borrowed from Patinkin (1965, p. 28).

50. Or, alternatively, that $Q''_a P_a = H$. The various numerical examples set up by Walras in connection with his forced saving argument (below Chapter 3, Section 2) will dispel any remaining doubts about the constancy of this ratio.

51. This argument is obviously nothing but a recantation of the then already century-old Cantillon effect (Cantillon, 1755, pp. 98–9). Walras returned only once, briefly, to this issue in the 1900 fourth edition of the *Eléments* (*OEC*, VIII, p. 469; 1954, p. 328). See below Chapter 5, Section 2.

52. In view of Walras's detailed discussion of the forced saving process (see below Chapter 2, Section 2) – a mechanism entirely based on a distribution/substitution effect – a preliminary assessment of that effect is obviously called for. With a doubling of the money supply *not* distributed equiproportionally to the initial money balances, at the end of the adjustment process, the economy would not be restored to equilibrium by a doubling of all prices. On the money market, the real value of the increased money holdings of each agent are not going to be identical to those ruling in the original equilibrium. Consequently, the various excess demands for goods will not be the same either, that is, the system of relative prices is no longer homogeneous of degree zero in money prices: the new equilibrium involves higher relative prices for the goods favoured by agents whose money holdings have more than doubled and lower relative prices for the goods preferred by individuals whose holdings have less than doubled. However, it should be equally self-evident that, at the end of this adjustment mechanism and despite the distributive effect, a doubling of the money supply will nevertheless have induced a doubling of the price level as a whole.

53. Taking Patinkin's terminology one step further, one could dub 'non-monetary-wealth effect' the impact of the price change on the real value of the individual's non-monetary wealth.

54. As far as the end result is concerned, the assumption about the way these price rises are taking place is irrelevant: the new equilibrium set of prices corresponding, for example, to a doubled quantity of money, is one in which each and every price is doubled.

55. In other words, excess demands for each commodity and for real money holdings are also the same in both positions, that is, equal to zero.

56. In order to clarify his demonstration, Walras is simply splitting his original 1872–74 figure into two separate diagrams. The reader's attention can thus be focused on the demand curve for money that is drawn for the first time in a quantity-price space of its own.

57. For editions 2–5 see *OEC*, VIII, p. 481 and for Jaffé's translation, 1954, p. 334.

58. It should be noted that the preceding analysis has, of course, implicitly assumed a unitary elasticity of expectations with respect to future prices; that is, there can be no substitution between present and future commodities.

59. In an article on bimetallism, Walras works out the number of equations necessary to solve a system in which 2, 3, 4, ..., n metals can be simultaneously used as currencies. He rightly concludes that 'in the case of a unique standard [only] is the problem fully determined' (1876, p. 4). See also a letter to Cernuschi (1965, I, p. 511).

60. Apparently marred by a stock-flow confusion.

61. With Marget, it is possible to consider this coefficient as a premonition by Walras of the use of a term corresponding to Fisher's V' (1931, p. 579, n. 26).

62 See Chapter 4, Section 1 for a discussion of Walras's only attempt at subsuming money under the logic of his general equilibrium model.

63. The theories of production and capital formation appear before the monetary chapters.
64. No trace of this argument can be found in any previous article or publication. It is hard to resist the impression that this trilogy was added more or less as an afterthought in order to attempt a reconciliation between the real world and pure theory. See Billoret (1988) for a brief discussion of this issue.
65. It is shown in Chapter 4 below that the radical change brought to monetary theory in the 1900 edition is closely related to (or even the result of?) the substantial alterations brought to this time framework.
66. 1877, p. 310; *OEC*, VIII, p. 579.
67. The version of this text comes from the 1896 original; for the alterations brought after the fourth edition see *OEC*, X, pp. 306–7.
68. In that respect, Walras uses exactly the same technique as Marshall with his temporary equilibrium (1890, I, pp. 331–6).
69. This stratagem was replaced in the second (and third) edition by the fiction that borrowing and lending productive services from landowners, capitalists and workers on the home market (under the additional proviso that 'false quantities' are irrelevant because 'pour chaque reprise du tâtonnement, nos entrepreneurs trouveront, dans le pays, des propriétaires fonciers, travailleurs et capitalistes possédant les mêmes quantités de services et ayant les mêmes besoins des services et des produits' (1889, p. 235; *OEC*, VIII, p. 308); finally, the fiction of *bons* was introduced into the fourth edition. Although Walras had moved from one fiction to another, the aim was exactly the same in all five editions: to find a way of keeping the necessary parameters and asset holdings constant, that is, to exclude historical time from the analysis by collapsing the future into a durationless present.
70. See *OEC*, VIII, p. 307 and 1954, pp. 241–42 for the origin of this terminology.
71. More rigorously, these constant parameters are (1) the total resources; (2) the technology (or production functions); (3) the utility functions; and (4) the initial distribution of wealth (endowments).
72. 'The reason why we need [this] assumption is that otherwise the empirical assumption is not consistent with the mathematical assumption' (Negishi, 1989, p. 263).
73. In his famous joint review of Cournot and Walras, Bertrand was dealing with Walras's *Théorie mathématique de la richesse sociale* (1883), a collection of essays nowhere mentioning the time structure of Walras's model.
74. From the second edition onwards, and without any further comment, Walras introduced the sentence 'Theoretically, trading should come to a halt' in the *tâtonnement* in exchange (*OEC*, VIII, p. 72; 1954, p. 85). On this difficult problem of interpretation linked to the 'no-trade out-of-equilibrium' hypothesis, see Jaffé (1967, pp. 224–7; 1981, pp. 245–7); Newman (1965, pp. 101–3); Walker (1972, pp. 347–8; 1983, pp. 9–11; 1990, pp. 963–9).
75. See, among numerous instances, the example of the *tâtonnement* in the theory of exchange (1877, p. 69; *OEC*, VIII, p. 93).
76. See, for example, Jaffé (1967, pp. 224–7), Walker (1983, pp. 9–11).
77. What is called above, 'historical' time.
78. And even more clearly the fourth edition 'preliminary *tâtonnement* process' discussed at length below in Chapter 4, Section 1.
79. Hayek, Hicks and the Swedes in the 1930s were only developing the stationary equilibrium conception shared by, for example, Marshall and Cassel but emphatically rejected by Pareto (below Chapter 5, Section 1).
80. Note once again that this is not synonymous with *neutrality of money*. If money is neutral, equilibrium quantities and price ratios in the system are independent of the volume of money, but not of the use of money as such.
81. In terms of Walras's thirteen-component model (1877, pp. 221–4; *OEC*, VIII, pp. 275–7), equations 7 to 13 (income goods) are added to equations 1 to 6 (capital goods proper). See also 1877, p. 306; *OEC*, VIII, p. 572.
82. Not yet productive of income, new capital goods are part of the working capital.

83. 1.25 thousand million in net income and 3.75 thousand million in depreciation and insurance charges.
84. 1.5 thousand million in net income and 1.5 thousand million in depreciation and insurance charges.
85. *The Theory of Social Wealth* is after all the *Eléments'* subtitle.
86. This analysis of the periodical market remained practically unchanged throughout the four editions. The only exception (added in the fourth edition) is the explicit acknowledgement of an assumption implicit in the first three editions: the 'basic data of the economic problem [have to remain] fixed [that is] we assume not only that the preliminary phase of groping has been completed with equilibrium established *in principle*, but also that the phase of static equilibrium has actually commenced, so that equilibrium is established *in fact*'(OEC, VIII, p. 577).
87. $\alpha'' Q_a V_a = \alpha' Q_a' V_a + \beta Q_b v_b + \gamma Q_c v_c + \delta Q_d v_d + \ldots$
88. Only the stock of landed capital escapes by nature this process of renewal.
89. More on this connection in terms of the Weberian ideal/real types below, pp. 141–45.

2. Periodical Market, Equation of Exchange and 'Forced Saving': Walras's Applied Theory of Money

[Walras] proposait des réformes monétaires qui auraient été inutiles si le théoricien avait eu raison. (Denizet, 1977, p. 565)

It is no accident that among the series of articles on applied monetary theory and banking written by Walras, all that was to be eventually reprinted appeared either in his *Etudes d'économie politique appliquée* (1898) or in his posthumous *Mélanges d'économie politique et sociale* (1987). Clearly, and Walras is not a particular case among the leading marginalist economists, his contributions on money and banking, as opposed to his pure theory of money, are to be found in applied economics articles mostly connected with trade or business cycles issues. It is thus no surprise to find under this heading much analytical work that would, today, be considered as part of monetary theory.

This is, of course, the consequence of the well-known gravitation theory which draws a distinction between short-run disequilibrium and long-run equilibrium forces; between market and natural (or equilibrium) prices and between permanent forces at work in decentralized economies on which can be grafted (almost as an afterthought) temporary forces; short-run factors that make an actual economy fluctuate in historical time around an 'equilibrium', 'normal', full-employment centre of gravity. Subscribing to that analytical method, Walras uses as an illustration the then already century-old metaphor of the theoretical equilibrium level of a surface of water as opposed to the actual level of the same but constantly moving mass of water (1874–77, p. 311; *OEC*, VIII, p. 580). The link between a theoretical equilibrium and a real-world permanent state of disequilibrium is precisely to be drawn by way of a stability analysis; and money should, of course, play a crucial role in such a dynamic process.

The lack of such a proper stability analysis in the realm of Walras's pure theory (for example, in terms of a real-balance effect) is discussed later, in Chapter 4. However, there are important pieces of tentative dynamic analyses on the money and commodity markets in Walras's *applied* economics writings. If Walras is thus certainly not guilty of neglecting the consequences of a monetary shock on the money as well as on the commodity markets, he does *not* properly coordinate these analytical instruments (for example, substitution effect and forced saving) with his pure theory of money and his general equilibrium framework. Most marginalist economists suffered to some extent from this inability to reconcile in a satisfactory way their volume on the theory of value 'with their volume II, or more often [with] a separate treatise, [on] the theory of money and [nominal] prices' (Keynes, 1936, p. 292). In other words, Walras does offer a rather sophisticated adjustment process following a monetary shock but this transmission mechanism (though clearly endowed with *real* effects) is not in the least articulated with his pure theory of money. Most of his efforts imply an extensive use of his quantity equation within a sequence of 'periodical markets'. His methodical application of the quantity theory to the understanding of trade cycles (Section 1) and his 'forced saving' period analysis (Section 2) are particularly good cases at hand.

1   CRISES, CYCLES AND THE TRANSMISSION MECHANISM, OR HOW TO USE THE EQUATION OF EXCHANGE

In the closing paragraph of Lesson 33, Walras concludes that a thorough discussion of the influence of money on prices has to be postponed until the reader gets a proper understanding of 'credit combinations', that is, 'bills of exchange and banknotes' (1874, p. 201; *OEC*, VIII, p. 524). Accordingly, and in line with his distinction between pure and applied economics, such a problem falls well outside the scope of the *Eléments*. Even if his promise to come back 'later' to this crucial question will not develop until his 1880 '*Théorie mathématique du billet de banque*', it is nevertheless possible to get a first inkling of the general outline of Walras's overall argument by putting together various hints scattered in unpublished or long-forgotten articles written for obscure journals on somewhat surprising occasions.[1]

Though certainly not thought through to its logical end, the pregnant hints to be found in his Geneva Lectures (1872), in 'Des billets de banque en Suisse' (1871) and in 'Loi fédérale sur l'émission et le remboursement des billets de banque' (1875) improve considerably Walras's previous attempts at understanding the part played by money and credit during the cycle. In particular, the use of his equation of exchange as an instrument of analysis of short-run fluctuations and a first attempt at discussing the consequences of variations of money supply (banknotes) and bankcredit on fixed and circulating capital offer a clear anticipation of his later monetary and forced saving analysis.[2]

1.1 Trade Cycles and the Equation of Exchange

Immediately after the first full-length discussion of the algebraic and geometric version of his equation of exchange, Walras offers one of his clearest and most definitive statements about the long-run, comparative static or equilibrium conditions of the validity of his formulation of the quantity theory:

> [In this equation], we assumed $\alpha, \beta, \gamma, \delta$ (coefficients of circulation) to be fixed; *and it is only under this hypothesis that we get the rectangular hyperbola $Q''_a = H/P_a$.*[3] *Should $\alpha, \beta, \gamma, \delta$ vary, both the hyperbola and the demand for money-metal Q''_a would vary* [that is, the curve would no longer be a strict rectangular hyperbola]. (*OEC*, XI, p. 462; italics added)

The exercise is subsequently repeated for each component of the equation of exchange to explain different types of crises. But every time, even if not as explicitly as for the coefficients of circulation, the context makes abundantly clear that whenever there is an external shock on one of these variables, the demand curve for money-metal temporarily departs from its long-run uniform unitary elasticity. Thus, Walras introduces intuitively in his analysis the other argument that explains why the demand curve for money 'only tends to be a rectangular hyperbola' (1874, p. 180; *OEC*, VIII, p. 472). As shown presently, Walras is, of course, far from offering either a complete 'direct' or a full-blown 'indirect' transmission mechanism between money and prices, but at least he does leave room for some sort of adjustment process. If a niche is clearly provided for such a piece of analysis, it is eventually left empty. Clearly, there is little or nothing to object to a typical comparative static reasoning such as the quantity theory, providing one is aware of its limitation; and Walras clearly realized this. Even if his argument lacks an articulate coordination between long-run neutrality and short-run disequilibria (off-rectangular hyperbola positions), Walras's typology of crises is certainly the earliest and most detailed to be found in the writings of the founding fathers of marginalism. In particular, it anticipates parts of the protracted interwar debates on business, trade and credit cycles.

Walras's own definition of cycles is worth reproducing in full: 'Les phénomènes économiques qu'on appelle du nom de *crises* ... sont comme des maladies ou des indispositions aiguës qu'une société peut avoir' (1871, p. 321). Perfectly in line with the century-old Classical tradition, and of course with other marginalist contributions to cycle theory (notably those by Jevons, Marshall, and Menger), a crisis is considered as a short-run, temporary oscillation around a long-run 'natural' equilibrium determined by 'real' variables only.[4]

Reorganising his three fold distinction under two headings only, Walras differentiates commercial/financial/industrial crises from monetary crisis. The former types occur only when 'speculative excesses on goods or public papers take place; the latter when metallic currency is temporarily in short supply'(1871, p. 321).

Monetary crisis[5]

This most obvious of crises follows a variation of the supply of money-metal. Typically, Walras refers to a contraction of the stock of metallic currency.[6] Unless there is compensation through an increased supply of banknotes, commodity prices would contract[7] and the ensuing deflationary process would saddle producers with heavy losses. However, and fully in line with Walras's dictum that only metallic money is genuine money, such a substitution would put only a temporary brake on deflation. If the supply of currency (gold and/or silver) is not brought back to its former level (through, for example, imports), a return to the original price level could be only temporary. A discussion of the reason why banknotes can only temporarily and partially replace gold is deferred until Section 1.2 below, where Walras's complicated banknote theory is considered in detail.

Commercial, financial and industrial crises[8]

Under this extremely broad heading, Walras puts together all the possible disruptions brought to the economic system by changes in the volume of credit. In other words, barring shocks on the supply of money, the system is considered as stable as long as fiduciary circulation F is not out of step with real variables. Clearly, in more general terms, Walras provides his reader with the very first elements of his own version of the indirect mechanism from which Wicksell will draw later much more than passing inspiration to build his cumulative process on which was subsequently erected all the interwar monetary equilibrium literature down to today's 'money and general equilibrium' contributions.

Using again equation (1.5) and introducing changes in the volume of F, it is easily shown that in fact industrial crises on the one hand and commercial and financial crises on the other are simply variations on a basic credit-cycle theory. Put in another way, Walras examines here the various consequences of short-term credit fluctuations according to the channels through which these changes of bank credit are injected or withdrawn from the economy. Leaving for Section 2, below, a thorough analysis of the exact working of this indirect mechanism,[9] suffice it here to summarize the four cases mentioned by Walras.

- An increase of the coefficients of circulation β, γ, δ and so on of commodities $B, C, D, \ldots$ (right-hand side) following a growth in F (left-hand side). Typically, there is for Walras an increase in the velocity of circulation of capital and consumption goods process. Despite the implicit full-employment starting-point, the price level is left unchanged, that is, in Hawtreyan fashion the increased demand for goods resulting from cheap money is met in the short run by a depletion of stocks (what Walras calls an industrial crisis).

- A speculative increase in commodity and/or bond prices $(p_b, p_c, p_d \ldots)$ following an increase in F: cheap credit leads speculators to be bullish on 'certain goods' leading to an excess demand for them and in turn to a rise in their prices (self-fulfilling prediction); it is what Walras calls a commercial crisis.

- A drop in prices $(p_b, p_c, p_d \ldots)$ following 'a sharp contraction of F'[10] is paradoxically going to increase the demand for goods now cheaper in terms of money (v_a is kept constant) and fosters a rise in the level of production (another type of industrial crisis with, this time, growing output). This case (which disappears from Walras's later argument) is highly questionable: it implies a very large proportion of payments to be made in cash.

- A similar argument, but this time the production of goods is constant, the excess demand being met through imports.

In general, Walras's argument is extremely primitive: it amounts to nothing more than a mechanical application of his equation of exchange. It has, however, not only the merit of existing but also to be the first ever marginalist attempt at building some sort of transmission mechanism. Keeping in mind again that during these years (1871–77) Walras also built alone the whole general equilibrium structure, one can hardly complain of the relative weakness of his trade-cycle theory.

1.2 Banknotes and the Equation of Exchange

At the junction between pure and applied monetary theories, the 'theory of banknote' was destined to play a crucial role in Walras's (failed) attempt at integrating cyclical phenomena into his equilibrium framework. Furthermore, and as it often happens in monetary theory, the dominant institutional framework plays (often implicitly) a rather large part in shaping the more rigorous thinking of the theorist. Walras's involvement in some heated debate on the nature of credit and banking, bimetallism and other protracted contemporary discussions could not but influence his attempts at formalizing his theory of money. The fundamental question of the exact nature of what Walras was trying to achieve with his general equilibrium model (a theoretical benchmark or an attempt at describing a genuine economy) is, of course, particularly relevant here.

In 1860, Walras had already devoted some twenty pages to an interesting, though non-technical, discussion of credit and banking in connection with capital in 'a prosperous [that is, growing] society' (1860, p. 160). In particular, in his extremely witty and devastating critique of Proudhon's 'free credit' (or zero-interest) doctrine, Walras had already brought forward his 'theory of banknote' as part of his more general credit theory (1860, pp. 96– 100). In view of the part played later by this 'theory' in Walras's forced saving adjustment process, it is necessary to examine the additions brought between 1871 and 1875 to the basic ideas that banknotes are:

1. nothing but bills of exchange payable to the bearer on sight (short-term credit);
2. that a change in their quantity might alter the velocity of circulation, though not the quantity, of circulating capital; and finally
3. that there is nevertheless a connection between short-term credit, savings and the velocity but not the quantity of circulating capital.

Even before the first formalization of his equation of exchange, within six months of his arrival at Lausanne, Walras had again taken up his 'théorie du billet de banque'. The liquidity crisis the Franco-Prussian war had brought to Switzerland and the ensuing heated debate on the necessity of creating a Central Bank reawakened Walras's interest for the part played by money (and, of course, banknotes) in the course of the business cycle. His 1871 article is nothing more than a critical survey of the literature available at the time in Switzerland.[11] Part I is a detailed and lengthy discussion of the nature and origin of banknotes:

> Just as gold or silver are needed to strike coins, likewise, to issue banknotes, some raw material is needed: IOUs, bills of exchange, etc..., the ... quality as well as the ... quantity of which depend approximately on the circulation of capital. Thus, the question of the development of banknote circulation eventually boils down to the question of the development of capital circulation. How can the law promote this development? To what extent is one entitled to use it? What are the limits within which there is cause to hope it will succeed? Such is the aim of this study. (1871, p. 323)

Clearly, well before the first version of his capital theory (1877, Parts IV and V), Walras already ventured reflections on the impact of money-supply variations on capital accumulation. However, and building on the then current discussion on the question of whether banknotes (and credit in general) ought to be considered as money,[12] Walras reasserts again that only metallic currency is 'genuine money' (1871, p. 328).

That said, and at this stage of his argument, his 'theory of banknote' is no more than a slightly expanded version of Smith's well-known variations on the metaphor of the 'great wheel of circulation' (1871, p. 328): banknotes, like all credit operations, provide an economy with a 'sort of wagon-way through the air' (Smith 1776, I, p. 321). Short-term credit being used *par excellence* to finance investment in circulating capital (1871, p. 324) and banknotes being the shortest possible type of loans (p. 325),[13] banknotes can only be issued against circulating capital (p. 326). Finally, and very traditionally, Walras concludes that the total amount of banknotes in circulation has to be covered either by gold and silver or by short-term bills 'immediately negotiable' (p. 326): no maturity mismatch should be allowed to appear in the balance sheet of competing banknote issuers.

The next and central question for Walras is, of course, connected with the consequence of banknote issue (and/or short-term credit) on the *quantity* and the *velocity* of circulating capital.

Metallic currency being the only *genuine* money, a bill (against circulating capital) discounted *in cash* does 'increase the quantity of circulating capital' (p. 328). Savings in cash are 'genuine' saving that can be invested to increase the stock of circulating capital because someone 'has saved by keeping his consumption under his production' (p. 328). Discount against cash is thus a mere transfer of savings from one 'capitalist' to another.

Inversely, a bill discounted against banknotes does not and cannot increase the amount of current savings and thus the amount of circulating capital. Such an operation simply reflects a change in the structure of the banker's balance sheet. However, this transformation of a short-term bill into a 'sight bill' is clearly, for Walras, 'an increase in the velocity of circulation but not in the quantity of circulating capital' (1871, p. 328; 1875, *OEC*, VII, p. 207).

If Walras can thus readily paraphrase Smith's metaphor that 'the banknote provides a wagon-way through space by supporting a movement that owes nothing to highways on terra firma' (1871, p. 330), he nevertheless clearly departs from the master's opinion about the influence of 'fiduciary circulation' on 'monetary circulation'.

On the one hand, any increase in the banknote circulation does not send abroad part of the stock of precious metal as Smith would like to have it. Relying on Hume's *specie-flow* mechanism, Walras thinks rightly that such a move would ultimately decrease not the quantity but the *value* of metallic currency (1871, p. 331).

On the other hand, and going one step further, Walras asserts that there is no exact inverse relationship between the quantity of fiduciary paper and the value of money-metal so that when the first goes up the second always goes down 'in an exactly corresponding proportion' (1871, p. 331). For Walras, there is an asymmetry between 'normal' and 'crisis' conditions: 'Fiduciary circulation does not have the disadvantage in ordinary times of substituting itself to monetary circulation, and it has the advantage of taking its place in times of crises' (1871, p. 331). Walras has thus come full circle back to a monetary crisis during which 'the wagon-way through the air only takes over the travellers when the highway suffers from wear and tear, and only for the time necessary to mend it' (1871, p. 331).

However, and despite this temporary help brought to the production process in time of crisis,[14] Walras concludes on three occasions[15] his 'theory of banknote' by the leitmotiv that a banknote is *not* an instrument for creating additional circulating capital but only a way to increase 'the movement of circulating capital'.[16]

In general, and *even in the short run*, the left-hand side of Walras's equation of exchange has no effect on the real variables on the other side of the equality sign: the traditional quantity theory argument rules supreme. This was, however, soon to change with his seminal 1880 article on forced saving.

2 DEPRECIATION OF MONEY AND *FORCED SAVING*, OR THE 'INCREASE OF CAPITAL BY THE ISSUE OF BANKNOTES': WALRAS'S NEGLECTED CONTRIBUTION TO *PERIOD ANALYSIS* (1879)

Neither in his *Geldtheorie und Konjonkturtheorie* (1929, p. 131 n.), nor in the first edition of *Prices and Production* (1931, p. 20), does Hayek ever mention Walras. On the other hand, in his famous 'Note on the Development of the Doctrine of "Forced Saving"' (1932, pp. 131–2) in the second (revised and enlarged) edition of *Prices and Production* (1935, p. 22) and above all in the 1939 reprint of the article just mentioned (1939, pp. 195–6), Hayek lavishes praise on Walras and on his 'Théorie mathématique du billet de banque' (1880):

> More significant [than Marshall's views 'which add hardly anything to what had been evolved from Thornton to Tooke'] is the further development and perhaps independent re-discovery of the forced saving by Léon Walras in 1879. Although his contribution has been practically forgotten ... it is of

special interest because it is probably through Walras that this doctrine reached Knut Wicksell. (1935, p. 22)

Hayek goes one step further in the preamble to his 1939 discussion of this 1880 article:

> we find [Walras's] exposition of the theory of forced saving to which the modern developments can be pretty definitely traced ... That Walras inspired Knut Wicksell and, through Wicksell, all the later German authors who dealt with the problem, there can be little doubt. ... Indeed, Walras [in his article] gives more than his disciple Wicksell or any other author up to quite recent times. (1932, pp. 131–2; 1939, p. 195)

This sudden appearance of Walras as one of Hayek's foremost precursors finds its origins in one modest footnote inserted almost as an afterthought by Marget on the penultimate page of his 1931 paper on Walras's monetary theory: 'There is ... one aspect of Walras' work to which, so far as I know, nobody has yet called attention, which should certainly be cited in any history of doctrine which would undertake to trace the history of the notion ... [of] "forced saving"' (1931, p. 598, n.68).[17]

Eventually, another leading proponent of the interwar forced saving debate, Robertson, also quotes Walras approvingly (though second-hand from Hayek) as 'one of the early moderns' on that notion (1933, p. 81).

Given these remarkable assertions, it seems about time to fulfil Marget's wish and to examine Walras's model *per se*.[18] Accordingly, this section falls into three parts. After a brief discussion of what Walras's general intentions were and in what context and against which theoretical background he wrote his 'Théorie mathématique du billet de banque'[19] (Section 2.1), a detailed examination of his forced saving mechanism considers the exact working of the dynamic of that adjustment process on both the commodity and money markets (Section 2.2). The concluding Section 2.3 offers some remarks on the part played by that first piece of *period analysis* in Walras's overall monetary theory and assesses the influence it might have had on other economists, notably Wicksell.

2.1 The Background to the *Théorie Mathématique du Billet de Banque*

Walras's TMBB[20] is the centrepiece of a series of articles on credit and banking that Walras published between 1871 and 1898.[21] One main theme running through these papers is closely connected to a then current and heated debate in Swiss political and banking circles: the necessity of whether to establish a Central Bank. Walras's position is rather subtle[22] and runs mainly along two lines. On the one hand, the very idea of a monopoly for the supply of money is so obviously alien to the whole logic of his theoretical framework that Walras goes as far as to assert:

> Why should government interfere with the issue, the circulation of banknotes? Why should it interfere in that field more than in any other sector of industrial production? *Either the question is settled, or the whole of political economy has to be re-written.* (1871, p. 332; italics added)

On the other hand, neither a monopolistic nor a competitive supply of money could satisfactorily eliminate the fear that, whatever the market structure, the issuer would use banknotes not as a 'means of circulation' but as an 'instrument of credit'. For Walras, the danger of cyclical disturbances that would result from such a confusion about the nature of banknotes is *the central theoretical issue irrespective of the monopolistic or competitive structure of the money supply.*[23] If an unregulated issue of banknotes is, on these very grounds, obviously out of the question, Walras does not trust, either, a monopolistic Central Bank to perform such a task to guarantee the quality of the money supply.[24] Walras built his forced saving proposition precisely during a detailed discussion of that question. Put in other words, in the process of analysing what he considered to be the disastrous consequences of using banknotes as long-term (or in a later version even short-term) credit instruments to justify regulating their supply, Walras offers his original analysis of the stimulating, albeit temporary, effects of an increase in the money supply on capital and money markets: 'The *permanent* facts are these: a contraction of the *value* of money and an increase in the *quantity* of capital' (1879, II).

Before turning to the model Walras built to reach conclusions such as these, one last remark about their theoretical antecedents is in order. Cantillon (1755, pp. 97–100), Thornton (1802, pp. 239–41), Bentham (1804, I, pp. 239–40), Ricardo (1815, III, p. 91 and 1817, I, pp. 363–4) and Mill (1844, p. 118 and, above all, in a famous footnote added to the revised Book III, Chapter XI of the sixth 1865 edition of his *Principles* (1848, p. 512)), are usually mentioned as the major pre-marginalist forerunners of the forced saving doctrine.[25] Surprisingly, none of these classic references is mentioned by Walras: Cantillon, Thornton and Bentham are names that do not even appear in the whole of Walras's writings. Ricardo and Mill, though mentioned often notably in connection with the theory of rent, are not referred to with respect to monetary or interest theories.[26] A single and lengthy quotation from Adam Smith (on which more below) is the only reference to earlier forced saving doctrine that Walras seems to have been aware of. Even more intriguing, this extract from the *Wealth of Nations* is not used as a starting-point for the argument but only mentioned *in fine* as if

Walras were looking over his shoulder for some sort of blessing on his argument.

2.2 Walras's *Forced Saving* Analysis

Walras's central forced saving argument is developed in three stages. An increase in the supply of banknotes (money) triggers (1) a drop in the value of money; (2) an increase in the quantity of fixed capital; and (3) with quasi-certainty ('very high risks') ends up in a 'liquidation crisis'. Even if several difficult theoretical problems are, for the first time, satisfactorily tackled and solved, the risks for Walras of such a process are so high that in general 'the issue of banknotes has more drawbacks than advantages' (1880, p. 592; *OEC*, X, p. 341).

The depreciation of money
As in the first edition of the *Eléments*, the determination of the value of money is discussed with a fixed quantity of precious metal, A, considered both in its commodity and in its monetary uses (Q'_a and Q''_a). Considering, then, an exogenously given and fixed demand for *real* balances (H/P),[27] Walras's diagram reflects all the possible market-equilibrium situations resulting from various allocations of A between monetized and non-monetized demands for precious metal. The value of money, of course, varies inversely with the quantity of monetized metal. Changes in the quantity of banknotes are only added as an afterthought. In particular, if 'the use of fiduciary money has a certain influence on prices' (1874, p. 201; *OEC*, VIII, p. 524), nothing more is said about the exact nature of that influence.

In his TMBB, this whole argument is re-worked to take into account the full consequences of a change in the supply of banknotes on the value of money in particular, and on the whole economy in general. Such an approach that substitutes a non-produced medium of exchange for produced precious metal can no longer be conducted within a comparative static framework. Walras *has* to offer some sort of stability analysis of a dynamic type. And it is precisely with such an intention in mind that within a sequence of 'periodical markets', Walras works out a tentative and early cumulative-process-like argument. He seeks to explain how and why the depreciation of money resulting from an increase in the supply of banknotes is not of an explosive nature; that is, that changes in the money supply do not alter the stability of the system defined by his general equilibrium equations.

Simplifying somewhat the original formulation discussed in the *Eléments,* and thus turning the price curve for money into an exact rectangular hyperbola,[28] Walras begins his demonstration with the following equation:

$$Q_a = F(P_a) + \frac{H}{P_a} \quad .^{29} \tag{2.1}$$

Fully convertible banknotes, valued in terms of A and payable at sight to the bearers are then introduced into the demonstration. The quantity of money in circulation (Q''_a) is now split between metallic money (monetized A) M_m and banknotes M_p. Clearly, and as observed by Walras, 'what we call *issue stricto sensu* [M_p] is the excess of total issue over metallic reserves' (1880, p. 558; *OEC*, X, p. 315).

It then follows that the quantity of metallic money is equal to the difference between the available quantity of A and the demand for its commodity use:

$$M_m = Q_a - F(p) \tag{2.2}$$

and the quantity of paper money is equal to the amount of money in circulation in excess of metallic money:

$$M_p = \frac{H}{P} - [Q_a - F(p)]. \tag{2.3}$$

The obvious conclusion Walras draws from this set of equations is an inverse relation between the volume of paper money and the price level.

The introduction of paper money and the discussion of the limits of the influence of banknotes on the price level hardly amount to a full-blown dynamic analysis of the depreciation of money. However, and in view of later developments, notably by Wicksell, four remarks on Walras's argument may help clarify at this stage the results reached so far.

- A *given* increase of paper money causes a *given*, and not a continuous, depreciation of money. Walras's treatment is accordingly well within the so-called direct mechanism. Bank and 'real' rates of interest as well as discrepancies between them have not yet appeared: there is no explanation of why banks expand or contract their issue of banknotes.
- However,[30] the full-convertibility principle sets a clear ceiling and (with profit-maximizing competitive banks) a floor[31] to the issue of paper money: the risks of an internal drain of banks' metallic reserves that would immediately follow an over-issue do curb drastically the banks' ability to increase beyond very precise limits the volume of banknotes, and thus the depreciation of money. Heir to the good old French anti-*assignats* tradition, Walras always remained ferociously opposed to inconvertible paper currency, refusing to be drawn even out of purely theoretical interest into a Wicksellian 'pure credit' economy.

- As in the first edition of the *Eléments*, Walras admits explicitly that the demand for real balances (H/P) is exogenously given (1880, p. 561; *OEC*, X, p. 317).
- Finally, it is of considerable interest to note at this stage that the theoretical framework presented in TMBB (depreciation of money as well as forced saving) will remain intact throughout the various editions (including the final 1898 end version) *despite the radical changes brought by Walras to his pure theory of money* from the 1880s onwards. Apart from minor and mainly stylistic alterations, the replacement of 'circulation à desservir' (1880, p. 561; *OEC*, X, p. 317) by 'encaisse désirée' (1898, p. 347; *OEC*, X, p. 317) in connection with the determination of the size of the demand for real balances is the only substantial modification brought by Walras to a text that survived otherwise unscathed the major developments that took place in his monetary theory between the first and last editions of the *Eléments* (1954, p. 38). In other words, while the analysis conducted on the 'once-and-for-all market' was thoroughly reworked, the quantity theory type of argument carried on the 'periodical market' remained unchanged.

The forced saving process I: 'the increase of capital by the issue of banknotes'

A rise in the price level (or alternatively a depreciation of the value of precious metals) is not the only consequence of an issue of banknotes. More important for Walras is the influence such an issue may or may not have on the volume of fixed and/or circulating capital: 'to tell the truth it [is] the capital point of our contribution' (1880, p. 591; *OEC*, X, p. 340). TMBB marks in that respect not only a complete about-turn regarding Walras's previous treatment of the problem (1871, 1875) but is also the very first attempt by a marginalist economist to tackle this theoretical riddle.

The first question to be solved by Walras is that of the nature of an issue of banknotes with respect to credit. On the one hand, Walras refers sarcastically to 'Law, the Socialists ... and other utopists' exaggerations' (1880, p. 563; *OEC*, X, p. 319; 1879, II)[32] for whom printing money is synonymous with creating physical capital. On the other, he mentions equally ironically economists who, in reaction, utterly refuse to consider that a change in the supply of banknotes could in any way increase the volume of credit and capital. Coquelin, one of the leading French banking economists of the time, is roundly criticized for arguing – in terms practically identical to those used four years earlier by Walras himself! – that an issue of banknotes does not create additional circulating capital but only increases its velocity of circulation.

In terms anticipating Wicksell's and those of the debate around the loanable-funds theory of interest, Walras cuts boldly through this Gordian knot: 'the issue of banknotes extends the limits of credit allowing banks and bankers to lend to entrepreneurs without borrowing from capitalists' (1880, p. 563; *OEC*, X, p. 319; 1879, II). Banknotes being a form of credit after all, the total supply of savings (loanable funds) is now made up for Walras of the supply out of 'capitalists' savings' and of a supply through net credit creation (banknotes). In other words, credit creation through an issue of banknotes does alter the volume of savings offered for investment. Taking this introductory statement one step further, Walras offers at the very beginning of his argument the central conclusion to which will eventually lead his painstaking demonstration: 'It is indisputable that: The issue of banknotes for a certain amount allows an increase in the *quantity* of capital by an equal sum' (1880, p. 564), with the proviso immediately added that 'this increase in the quantity of capital is not the direct result but is only made *possible* by an issue of banknotes' (1880, p. 565).

These two central assertions remain, of course, to be analytically demonstrated and all their theoretical consequences to be drawn. Accordingly, Walras is faced with the necessity of building a dynamic model which, on both method and theory, breaks entirely new ground. With such changes in the issues of banknotes, money comes to the forefront of a model that, by definition, has to be *sequential*. By way of a 'period analysis'[33] conducted on the 'periodical market', the founder of general equilibrium analysis lays down as a framework to his forced saving process some of the methodological and theoretical stepping-stones that will reappear only half a century later with the 'monetary equilibrium' approach inaugurated by Wicksell and refined by the Swedish School, Hayek, Hicks, Robertson and Keynes up to the *Treatise*[34]:

> under such an hypothesis [that is, forced saving resulting from an issue of banknotes] there is ... an *issuing period* during which the past [process of] production of goods consisting of [current] consumable incomes and new capital goods are entirely disturbed. During that period, the demand for new capital goods [that is, investment] resulting from the issue is added to the previous demand for capital goods and for consumable incomes [that is, consumption]. Two main consequences follow: on the one hand, the proportion in the [current] production of consumable incomes and of new capital goods is changed; there is a contraction of the former and an increase of the latter; and, on the other, the price of all these goods [that is, the price level] is changed because, under the assumption that the contraction of the final demand is proportional to the rise in prices, their total [nominal] value is raised by an amount equal to the issue of banknotes. (1880, pp. 565–6; *OEC*, X, p. 320)[35]

Walras is clearly arguing here in terms of full-employment output: the propensity to consume/save being constant, the increased demand for investment goods can only be made available through a forced saving process resulting from the rise in the price level initiated by the issue of banknotes. The redistribution of a constant full-employment output between consumption and savings/investment is only made possible through a rise of nominal output: 'In the case of the issue of banknotes, there is an increased demand on one side without a decrease on the other side, and, thus, an increase of the total [nominal] value of output' (1880 p. 566).

This inflationary process has, however, clear and inbuilt limits measured by the size of this issue of banknotes:

> During the whole of the issuing period, the issue of banknotes for a certain sum brings about a rise in both the prices of consumable goods and of new capital goods approximately measured by the ratio of the size of the issue to the size of the previous [period's] social product. This process is transitory: once the issue has come to an end, the price rise in question disappears and that linked to the depreciation of precious metal is the only one left. (1880, p. 566; *OEC*, X, p. 321)

It is precisely during that 'issuing period' that the 'creation of [new] capital' is taking place: 'One sees how favourable to the production this issue of banknotes is' (1879, II).

Walras having thus offered the general outline of his argument, it remains for him to offer a step-by-step demonstration of the results reached at the end of this 'period of issue'. The mathematical demonstration of his intuitive argument revolves, of course, around two main propositions that are of the essence of the forced saving process: the distinction between real and nominal magnitudes; and the distributional effects and their consequences on the real growth rate of the social product.

K is defined as the total amount of fixed and circulating capital valued in terms of A (including a quantity Q_a of A) when the price of A in terms of B is P_a (that is, when the amount of banknotes in circulation is nil). In order to lower the price of A in terms of B from P_a to p, the amount of banknotes M_p to be issued is defined as

$$M_p = \frac{H - p\left[Q_a - F(p)\right]}{p}.$$
(2.4)

According to Walras's definitions, M_p is also equal to the 'supplement of capital to be obtained by the issue of banknotes' (1880, p. 567). However, to compare 'old' and 'new' capital stocks, the original amount of fixed and circulating capital K has to be valued at the new price level (to take precisely into account the depreciation of Q_a):

$$[K] = \frac{P_a(K - Q_a) + pQ_a}{p}. \tag{2.5}$$

The ratio of the 'supplement of capital' to the original capital stock can now be written as

$$\left[\frac{M_p}{K}\right] = \frac{H - p[Q_a - F(p)]}{P_a(K - Q_a) + pQ_a}. \tag{2.6}$$

This equation reaches a maximum when, of course, there is no longer any precious metal in monetary use ($M_m = 0$), that is, when, following an increase in the price of A in terms of B has fallen from P_a to p_a and that the whole of the 'circulation à desservir H' is made up of banknotes.[36]

Finally, defining R as the 'social income' (nominal GNP) before the issue of banknotes, adding to it the amount of banknotes issued to get 'the total value ... of consumable incomes and new capital goods' (1880, p. 568; *OEC*, X, p. 322), it is possible to measure the rise in price level *during* the issuing period:

$$\left[\frac{dp}{p}\right] = \frac{H - p[Q_a - F(p)]}{pR}. \tag{2.7}$$

This rise in prices linked to the ensuing increased demand for goods and the resulting conversion of (depreciated) monetized metal into commodity metal are the first twin consequences of the issue of additional banknotes. But more important, Walras is eventually able to show not only how the composition of output is changed *during* the issuing period in favour of the production of capital goods, but also that this process comes to an end as soon as the issue of banknotes grinds to a halt. His numerical example shows clearly that a new equilibrium price level is reached with a composition of output (income) reverting to the original ratio between consumption and investment goods as soon as the issue of additional banknotes falls back to zero: [37] 'the rise of prices during the issuing period is a transitory (and not a permanent) factor destined to stop when a new equilibrium for the prices of goods and productive service comes to be established' (1880, p. 586; *OEC*, X, p. 337).

However, Walras hastens to add that the exact proportionality postulated between the rise in prices and nominal income during the successive periods is only a simplifying assumption: 'there is [anyway] no great interest to make sure whether it is actually the case during that period' (1880, p. 572; *OEC*, X, p. 326). What is really interesting and crucial is to draw a clear-cut distinction between changes in nominal and changes in real income once the new equilibrium price level is eventually reached.

The forced saving process II: the two distribution effects

Clearly, the new equilibrium vector of prices reached after a change in the money supply not distributed equiproportionately[38] to the agents' initial money holdings would not be a multiple of the original set. In modern terminology, the real value of the increased money holdings of each agent (and hence his or her real wealth) will not be the same as in the original equilibrium position. In particular, and this is precisely Walras's argument, the amounts of market excess demands will also not be the same. The path followed by the economy *during* Walras's dynamic forced saving process is clearly dependent upon the way the excess supply of banknotes is distributed among individual agents.[39] The beneficiaries of the issues of banknotes being mainly entrepreneurs, the forced saving process will involve higher relative prices for capital goods (the goods most favoured by agents whose money holdings have increased more than proportionately) and lower relative prices for consumption goods (those most favoured by consumers whose money holdings have increased less than proportionately).

To put it in a slightly different way, other things being equal, a given economy will save more if the disequilibrium of the price system favours profits more than it favours wages.

The novelty of Walras's approach is to go one step further and to reflect on a second distributional effect between the various productive factors once the increased quantity of capital resulting from the forced saving process is available on the market for capital goods. What, then, is the consequence of such a redistribution effect on the three 'prices of productive services', wages, rents and, above all, the rate of interest?

Referring the reader to his *Eléments* (1877, p. 245; *OEC*, VIII, p. 301) Walras gives the following set of definitions:

T is the stock of land (landed capital);
P is the stock of labour (personal capital);
K is the stock of (fixed plus circulating) capital (proper);
i is the uniform (equilibrium) rate of *net* income on these productive factors;
ε is the depreciation charge and the insurance premium on both personal and capital goods.

The income R in terms of A in the initial equilibrium (before any increase in the banknote supply) is defined by the straightforward equation:

$$R_t = (T + P + K)i + \varepsilon \qquad (2.8)$$

When an increase in the supply of banknotes has reduced the price of A in terms of B from P_a to p, the new nominal income R' in terms of A is defined as

$$R' = \left(T' + R' + K'\right)i' + \varepsilon' \qquad (2.8a)$$

The whole question boils down eventually to an assessment of whether R' is equal or not to $(P_a/p)R$. Clearly, for Walras, $R' < (P_a/p)R$[40] and for two main reasons.

On the one hand, and there is here an explicit reference to the pure theory of interest and capital of the *Eléments* (para. 272, Lesson 45), 'we must remember ... that the *capital goods market*, that is, the market where capital goods are bought and sold, should not be confused with the *money market* [marché du capital] that is, the market where *money capital* is borrowed or lent' (1877, p. 277; *OEC*, VIII, p. 352). Walras emphasized time and again that these two markets are completely distinct. The rate of interest is determined on the market for *money capital*, that is, the market on which money is lent and borrowed for investment purposes. For its part, the *rate of net income* (that is, the ratio between the price of the service of a capital good, net of depreciation and insurance charges, and the price of the capital good itself) is determined on the market for new capital goods.

However, in the Walrasian system, these two markets are very closely related. The 'rate of interest' determined on the money market always 'tend[s] to equality' with the uniform 'rate of net income' determined on the capital-goods market. Furthermore, in equilibrium, this last rate must obviously be the *same* for all capital goods *and* at the same time be equal to the rate of interest on the money market where capitalists are lending their savings to entrepreneurs. There is definitely here a clear-cut analytical distinction between two markets and two rates – 'these two markets appear quite distinct from each other' (1954, p. 270). Walras suggests beyond doubt a distinction which closely anticipates Wicksell's natural-versus-market rate doctrine as well as Marshall's real-versus-discount rate argument (see Bridel, 1987, pp. 40–44). However, in the second and third editions of the *Eléments*, Walras makes it abundantly clear that this market for money capital 'is only of practical and not of theoretical interest'; and that, accordingly, the fundamentals of the analysis can concentrate on the market for capital goods only (1954, p. 289). In the *definitive* fourth edition, Walras will even go as far as to consider the money market 'however useful in practice, [to be] nothing but a superfoetation in theory' (1954, p. 290).

If there can thus be little doubt about the *un*importance of the money capital market in Walras's (long-run) *pure* theory,[41] in the realm of (short-run) *applied* economics on the periodical market, the entire forced saving argument and the inequality between R' and $(P_a/p)R$ rest precisely on the distinction between the interest rate on the money-capital market and the rate of net income on the capital-goods market:[42] '*The use of banknotes increasing the effective supply money-capital on the market for that capital brings about a drop in the rate of net income*. Thus, one gets *i'< i*' (1880, p. 573).

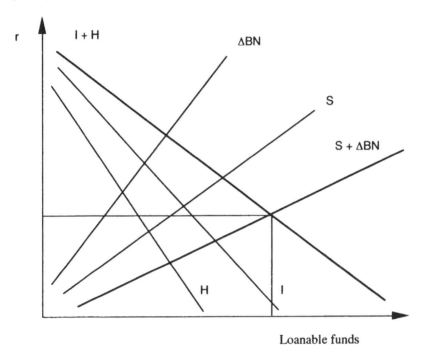

Figure 2.1 The loanable-funds theory of interest

Expressed with a slightly amended version of Lerner's famous graphic treatment of the loanable-funds theory of interest (1938, p. 281), Walras's argument can be summarized with Figure 2.1.

The (market) rate of interest is determined by the demand and supply of loanable funds. The demand for loanable funds consists, for Walras, of investment demand *plus* demand for cash balances to keep the real value of *H* constant. The supply of loanable funds consists of personal savings *plus* bank credit (the issue of banknotes in excess of the bank's metallic reserves). In equilibrium, the uniform rate of net income brings into equality planned saving and planned investment at a full-employment level of income characterized *inter alia* by a constant price level. This long-run equilibrium argument is obviously conducted as if borrowing and lending were conducted 'in kind', to use Wicksell's identical terminology (1906, II, p. 5).

Whenever a net issue of banknotes dBN/BN is added to planned savings, the total supply of loanable funds is equal to $S + dBN/BN$. On the other side of the market, dH/H being the necessary nominal increase in the demand for money for purposes of keeping the real value of H constant, the total demand of loanable funds is equal to $I + dH/H$. Without, however, explaining the *rationale* behind the banks' behaviour (in sharp contrast to Wicksell), Walras's forced saving process is clearly a disequilibrium cumulative process that will only grind to a halt when $I = S + dBN/BN - dH/H$ at a lower rate of net income.

Clearly, at the end of the issuing period when $dBN/BN = dH/H$, the price level is constant again and the stock of capital larger. This can only mean that the new rate of interest on the money market is equal to the new *lower* real rate of return on investment. Or, put in terms of price level, there is a positive correlation between prices and interest-rate *differentials*.[43]

If there is no rationale in terms of economic theory behind the bankers' decision to increase the supply of banknotes,[44] Walras is, however, clear about the bankers' ability to alter temporarily the rate of net income on real capital, and the growth rate of the economy by changing the growth rate of the money supply.

The second element to be examined is to assess whether $R' < (P_a/p)R$ is the balance that exists (or not) between 'the increase in the quantity of capital and the decrease of the value of monetised metal' (1880, p. 574) following an increase in the money supply. Or, in Walras's capital stock formulation why the value of the new stock of capital K' is different from $(P_a/p)K$.

The general relation between $(P_a/p)K$ and K' is defined as:

$$K' = \frac{P_a}{p}(K - Q_a) + Q_a + \frac{H}{p} - [Q_a - F(p)] \qquad (2.9)$$

which, for the sake of simplicity can be rewritten as

$$K' = \frac{P_a}{p}K + \frac{H}{p} + F(p) - \frac{P_a}{p}Q_a \qquad (2.10)$$

Clearly, K' differs from $(P_a/p)K$ on two accounts: the additional *quantity* of capital minus the drop in the value of monetized metal. Even if, to simplify his rather complicated argument, Walras assumes that 'they roughly compensate each other'.[45] in his numerical example he cannot ignore the remaining gap between K' and $(P_a/p)K$ that is nothing other than, 'the slight difference resulting from the lowering of the rate of net income from i to i'' (1880, p. 575; *OEC*, X, p. 328).

In other words, at the end of the forced saving process, though the physical quantity of capital has risen, the capitalists' share of total income has been reduced and the value of this stock of capital (at constant prices) has also diminished through a drop in its relative price.

However, since the rate of return on capital is lower 'on the market for capital' (1880, p. 575; *OEC*, X, p. 329), and since the supply and demand conditions on the labour and land markets are unchanged, Walras concludes that 'it is thus certain' that nominal wages and rents have been fully indexed to the rise in the level of prices; that is, that

$$\left(T' + P'\right)i' = \frac{P_a}{p}\left(T + p\right)i.$$ (2.11)

Accordingly, and since Walras assumes the depreciation charge and the insurance premium unaltered by the forced saving process, the increase of nominal income is not exactly inversely proportionate to the depreciation of money. Hence, since there is a 'larger quantity of cheaper capital [which allows entrepreneurs] to produce a larger quantity of cheaper goods' (1880, p. 576; *OEC*, X, p. 329), and since workers' and landowners' incomes are fully indexed while those of capitalists' are not, Walras concludes that the latter receive 'roughly' the same quantity of goods against a slightly reduced interest income while the former receive a larger quantity of goods for an unchanged amount of wages and rents: there is a distribution effect in favour of the classes of agents who did not benefit in the first place from the increased supply of money (banknotes).

To summarize the whole of Walras's second distribution effect in the author's very own words:

> Once the banknote issuing period is over and the new exchange and production equilibrium established, the amount of nominal social income has not risen proportionally to the increase in the price-level resulting from the reduction of the value of money, the difference resulting from the decline in the rate of net income brought about by the issue of banknotes. The real amount of this income has thus risen for landowners and workers who get a larger quantity of goods as rent and wages, but [this income has not risen] for capitalists who get roughly the same quantity [of goods] as interest payments. (1880, p. 575; *OEC*, X, pp. 329–30).

Walras clearly detects *real* effects of an increased supply of banknotes both on the level of output and on the distribution of income. *During* the forced saving process, there is a first distribution effect away from 'fixed incomists' in favour of the capitalists–investors benefiting from the additional supply of banknotes. Such an effect allows, of course, a rise in the volume of production/income to take place. However, when the system is back in equilibrium, that is, when the initial monetary shock has been fully absorbed, a second distribution effect is revealed. When, at the end of the forced saving process, the ratio of consumption goods to new capital goods is back to its original value, the consequence of a larger and cheaper production of consumption goods and a lower rate of net income on capital is, of course, a redistribution of income in favour of workers and landowners.

Clearly, Walras seems to admit beyond doubt that real variables may be altered by manipulating the money supply: money is not neutral after all.

But is this a temporary or a durable phenomenon? A discussion of this ultimate phase of Walras's demonstration reveals his position on the inevitability of liquidation crises.

The liquidation crisis

The extent to which Walras's argument displays similarities with the 'Austrian approach' to 'capital deepening/shallowing' and monetary crises is striking. Much earlier than Böhm-Bawerk and nearly half a century before Hayek, Walras discusses the inevitability of a liquidation crisis following an increase in the money supply in terms anticipating very much in spirit the former's 'length of the period of production' and the latter's 'capital shortage' ideas.

The first problem Walras tries to settle is whether the increased quantity of capital resulting from the forced saving process is going to take the shape of fixed or circulating capital. The stock of circulating capital being in fixed proportion to the level of income/output and the increased volume of output resulting from the forced saving process having induced a drop in the prices of consumption goods and circulating capital, 'the supplement of capital resulting from the issue of banknotes will necessarily be made up of fixed capital' (1880, p. 578; *OEC*, X, p. 330).[46]

Furthermore, Walras does not deem it necessary to make a distinction between the market for circulating and the market for fixed capital. Since 'the rate of interest tends towards equality on both markets' (1880, p. 578; *OEC*, X, p. 330), and since the additional demand for circulating capital following an increase in the money supply is either very modest or non-existent, Walras considers that the market for fixed capital bears the brunt of the adjustment process:

> It is a normal fact that, in most cases, [this adjustment] takes place in a disorderly fashion (though it could also happen in rare cases in a fixed orderly way) ... in the last analysis, banknotes stand for capital, whereas the supplement of capital they procure can be used in long term credit only. (1880, p. 581; *OEC*, X, p. 333).

Clearly, the reasoning involved is familiar to any student of the Austrian School from Böhm-Bawerk down to Hayek: the length of the period of production varies directly with real wages and inversely with the rate of interest.

The stage is thus set for Walras to demonstrate the inevitability of a liquidation crisis: if it is easy to transform circulating capital into fixed capital during the forced saving process, once the monetary expansion stops, the stability of the economic system is entirely in the hands of the banknote holders. Should they ask for a liquidation of these short-term credit instruments,[47] besides a classic circulation crisis, a credit crunch would first hit the circulating capital market and then, through a rapid and sharp rise in the rate of interest would play havoc with the fixed capital market. Unless a sudden increase in the agents' propensity to save takes place, the only possible way for Walras to avoid these twin crises is 'to decree the inconvertibility of banknotes' (*cours forcé*) (1880, p. 582; *OEC*, X, p. 334).

Thus, unless 'genuine savings' are substituted for forced savings (but why should they?), production will be 'partly stopped' and the economy will experience a long and protracted period of adjustment until the size of the stock of fixed capital is brought back to size. There is here more than a passing anticipation of the interwar forced saving doctrine, notably Hayek's. During the period of extension, when the (money) market rate of interest is clearly lower than the real (marginal productivity) rate, a monetary expansion leads to forced saving, raising the prices of capital goods relative to those of consumer goods (the first redistribution effect). Production of fixed capital would thus rise, but because Walras assumes an initial state of full employment, the only way in which the capital stock can be increased is through a phenomenon akin to Hayek's lengthening of the period of production: demand for labour being, in the short run, very inelastic, the adoption of a capital-intensive process is the only logical result of an expansion of the supply of banknotes. To the drop in the rate of interest (coupled, of course, with an increase in the quantity of capital) corresponds Walras's second distribution effect: the lower marginal productivity of (a larger quantity of) capital is synonymous with a drop in the capitalists' share in national income.

However, when monetary expansion stops, forced saving ceases, too, and total savings return to their previous levels, thus raising the market rate of interest. The price of consumption goods then rises relative to that of production goods. This rise in the rate of interest, and the associated shift in relative prices, makes unprofitable the longer production processes started during the boom; they will be shut down, thus releasing labour and lowering real wages. Shorter production processes will be expanded but this will, of course, take time as stocks of fixed capital goods have to be turned into circulating capital goods: during this adjustment period, even if Walras refers to the production process as being 'partly stopped' (1880, p. 582; *OEC*, X,

p. 333), clearly there will be unemployment. These disruptions[48] brought to production result from the impossibility of quickly turning fixed capital goods released from capital-intensive processes initiated by forced saving into the necessary capital goods to be used in the shorter, less capital-intensive, processes that need to be started up.

Eventually, Walras reverts to his main argument. Using Smith's analogy between paper money and 'a sort of wagon-way through the air',[49] he draws the central conclusion to his entire forced saving argument:

> According to A. Smith, issuing banknotes has one advantage: the possibility of increasing the quantity of capital, compensated [however] by one drawback: the probability of a circulation crisis resulting from a dearth of money. In our opinion, the issue of banknotes has two advantages and two drawbacks ... the probability of a circulation crisis resulting from a scarcity of money is correlative to the possibility of transforming money metal into commodity metal; and to the possibility of increasing the quantity of capital corresponds the probability of a credit crisis following a lack of circulating capital. But the advantage of being able to transform money-metal into commodity-metal as well as that of increasing the quantities of capital correspond very well to [Smith's] advantage of turning into cultivated lands a country's main highways; and, above all, the drawback of running the risk of a financial crisis, as well as that of risking a monetary crisis, is perfectly adequately represented by the inconvenience of being hurled down from high up in the air. (1880, pp. 587–8; *OEC,* X, pp. 337–8)

Walras's position is thus clear. Anticipating the interwar 'forced saving process' by half a century, his detailed step-by-step analysis has one aim and one aim only: to demonstrate that, though tampering with the money supply does have short-time real effects favourable to the economy's growth rate, the inevitability of a liquidation crisis and the no-less inevitable return to a structure of production determined by real magnitudes only make amply clear that, again, 'the issue of banknotes has more drawbacks than advantages' (1880, p. 592; *OEC,* X, p. 341).

Walras's policy recommendations are accordingly straightforward and very much akin to Fisher's 100 per cent money. A *laissez-faire, laissez-passer* competitive supply of banknotes by multiple issuing banks is, under such conditions, out of the question. Not that a monopolistic Central Bank controlled by the government 'would offer more reassuring perspectives'. In both cases, issuing banknotes involves '[entering] into an engagement that one cannot fulfil short of bringing social and political upheavals' (1880, p. 591; *OEC,* X, p. 341).

2.3 Place of 'Period Analysis' and 'Forced Saving' in Walras's Overall Monetary Theory

Walras's monetary theory clearly contains many a theme that would only begin to appear two decades later in Wicksell's early writings. As far as forced saving and the inevitability of a liquidation crisis are concerned, economists would even have to wait until the early 1920s for similar results to be attained. However, one thing is certain. For all practical purposes, the theoretical argument of TMBB was hardly to be mentioned again, let alone seriously considered, until the 1920s.[50]

Faced with such an interesting case of persistent neglect, it remains to suggest some explanation for the reasons why TMBB had such a small impact on the development of monetary theory. Two types of explanations are possible: circumstantial and theoretical.

Thanks to the three *Correspondence* volumes (1965), it is possible to trace with accuracy the names and reactions of the 'happy few' deemed important enough by Walras to receive off-prints of TMBB. Though thirteen names,[51] some very prestigious indeed, can be linked with certainty to TMBB, this article led to very little analytical discussion (in sharp contrast to books and articles in pure theory). The most surprising case is that of Jevons. Specifically provided by Walras with a copy of TMBB and a request for comments,[52] Jevons only acknowledged on a postcard the receipt of Walras's letter and article with the promise that 'I shall have pleasure in returning an answer in a little time when I am free from some engagements on hand at present' (Jevons, 1972–81, V, p. 98; letter dated 11 April 1880). But nothing ever followed. It was, of course, a serious set-back for Walras. Jevons was one of the leading English authorities on money and the opinion of the only other mathematical economist known to Walras at the time was certainly of great importance to him. Jevons's early death sixteen months later probably goes some way towards explaining this lack of reaction.

Altogether, only three correspondents were ready to discuss at various lengths different aspects of Walras's argument: Foxwell, Gide and Wicksell.

In a first comment on the role of cheques in the monetary system (1965, I, pp. 737–8), Foxwell criticizes TMBB for giving too much importance to banknotes as opposed to cheques and other instruments of credit. Obviously troubled by Foxwell's remark, Walras altered his text in the 1898 reprint without, however, showing that he ever mastered the straightforward deposit – credit mechanism. Though important on practical grounds, Walras's lack of understanding of this analytical instrument did not alter the essence of his forced saving mechanism.

In his second query (1965, I, p. 737), Foxwell shows an inability to understand clearly that Walras's argument does not imply a mere one-for-one substitution of metallic currency for banknotes: a *net* increase of the stock of money through an issue of banknotes is obviously necessary to induce the inflationary process on which the drop in consumption, synonymous with forced saving, is precisely based.

Less interesting are Gide's comments (1965, I, pp. 668–9). Non-committal about the 'new and interesting' forced saving argument (which seems anyway to be beyond his modest analytical competence), Gide questions Walras's 'war on banknotes' on rather naive grounds. For Gide, the substitution of metallic money by banknotes should be strongly encouraged: the workforce made redundant in goldmines would obviously be available to produce in other sectors more useful goods or services. Gide obviously misses completely the logic of Walras's argument in terms of a dynamic adjustment process.

Last but not least, Wicksell can also be connected with TMBB, but with the 1898 reprint only. Although typically eager to give due credit to others, in the realm of money, credit and banking, Wicksell's references to forerunners are surprisingly few and scattered. In the case of Walras, particularly important for his pure theory of money, and, above all for his cumulative process, Wicksell never took up Walras's position for an extended and detailed discussion. In his correspondence with Walras, however he makes some very precise comments about the importance of Walras's monetary theory for his own model. In a letter dated 26 August 1898, thanking Walras for a copy of *Etudes d'économie politique appliquée*, besides mentioning that 'the largest part of the articles' contained in this collection were already known to him, Wicksell devotes the best part of this letter to monetary theory:

> As you know I published myself lately a monograph on monetary theory [probably *Interest and Prices*, 1898] ... my theory only displays slight differences from yours and can be considered more or less as a direct derivation from yours .... It might well be that eventually [our] two theories are in fact the same – *i.e.*, yours. (as in Walras, 1965, III, p. 30)

Although a large part of this letter is devoted by Wicksell to a comparison of the influence of Walras's *billon régulateur* on the discount rate with his own 'trailing bankrate' doctrine, it is not possible to link specifically that discussion of their respective adjustment/cumulative process to TMBB. However, Wicksell is unmistakably referring to such a step-by-step monetary approach, and not to the Walrasian pure theory of money: 'Any theory of money worthy of the name' writes Wicksell 'must be able to show how and why, in given conditions, the monetary or pecuniary demand for goods exceeds or falls short of the supply of goods' (1906, II, p. 160). A very sharp and condensed summary indeed of Walras's intentions in TMBB.

Finally, Walras's argument is submitted to a slightly more precise critique in Wicksell's review of *Etudes d'économie politique appliquée*. In his review article, Wicksell concentrates his argument on a comparison of Walras's dynamic of the price level with his own cumulative process. Of course, one cannot be certain that Wicksell knew of TMBB and of Walras's forced saving argument before 1898 or that his monetary theory was influenced by Walras's earlier writings on money with the evident exception of the first edition of the *Eléments*.[53]

Wicksell concentrates the part of his review devoted to money on the *modus operandi* of Walras's cumulative process. Although well aware that Walras's article was twenty years old, Wicksell displays a marked displeasure at Walras's approach:

> An ... important question is ... whether every increase or decrease in the money supply [*Münzvorrat*) would influence with sufficient speed [or not] the value of money and the prices of goods ... . In this respect, Walras's demonstration seems to me not very satisfactory. He [not only] pretends that the first as well as any subsequent emission of inconvertible banknotes ... would have a definite influence on the value of money but also asserts that he has mathematically 'proven' that under such circumstances the price level would rise and fall *proportionally* with every increase or decrease of monetised money. (1899, p. 827; italics in original)

Referring the reader to his then recently published *Interest and Prices* (1898), Wicksell leads a two-pronged attack against TMBB. On the one hand, developing unknowingly Foxwell's earlier remarks, he criticizes Walras for considering far too primitive a banking system and restricting his argument to changes in the supply of banknotes only. Despite Walras's alterations, the 1898 version of TMBB suffers from the same major flaw as the original article. According to Wicksell, the monetary, banking and financial framework is so primitive as to render Walras's 'chain of reasoning [that is, his cumulative process] somewhat fragile' (1899, p. 827). Walras's 'adoption of a rigid quantity theory of money', almost exclusively based on the so-called direct mechanism, excludes to a large extent the rate of interest that is for Wicksell the essence of any study of 'real world' monetary theory. If the rate of interest is clearly present in TMBB, and even if, as shown above, Walras's treatment anticipates many an aspect of the 'two-rate' doctrine, the absence of a theory of credit around which one could articulate the link between the rate of interest and the price level is, for Wicksell, *the* major weakness of Walras's theory:

> should the Walrasian scheme try ... to raise interest rates when prices are high and lower it when prices tend to drop, then an increase or decrease in the money supply would have, under similar conditions, a tendency to

decrease/increase the rate of interest; but at what speed? This is precisely *the* question. (1899, p. 828; italics in original)

To sum up: for Wicksell, Walras fails completely to integrate the rate of interest and the price level within a cumulative process; and the speed at which this adjustment is taking place ('*the* question') is infinite. Hardly the most helpful of hypotheses! But is it not the logical consequence of Walras's 'periodical market' technique?

Eventually, and curiously, Wicksell has very little to say about Walras's forced saving process except that 'he is not very surprised' (1899, p. 828) by the consequences of issuing inconvertible banknotes. In fact, Wicksell falls victim to the same analytical weakness that he has just accused Walras to be guilty of: in jumping to his comparative static conclusions, he completely neglects Walras's step by step dynamic analysis. In other words, if Wicksell rightly admonishes Walras for his lack of a dynamic credit theory integrating the rate of interest and the price level, he is completely blind to the originality of Walras's own cumulative process in terms of forced saving.[54] The merit of interwar theorists such as Keynes, Robertson and Hayek rests precisely on their ability to move some way on the road towards an integration of the two halves of that difficult theoretical nut.[55]

The theoretical explanations of the neglect suffered by TMBB are of course of a more speculative nature. With the notable exception of a series of papers on price-level stabilization and the necessity of monetary reform, Walras *never* returned in as much detail as in TMBB to the dynamic of the adjustment process following a monetary shock. In fact, and as already discussed earlier, in the realm of 'applied monetary theory', the forced saving argument remained *unchanged* for the rest of Walras's life. While his pure theory underwent a succession of upheavals, the thrust of his applied theory was almost exclusively aimed at preventing monetary shocks, *not* at explaining any further the adjustment process (and the negative conclusions about the influence of changes in money supply on the economy) developed in 1879–80.

In that respect, Walras's agenda for research in the field of monetary theory is not much different from that of other first-generation marginalist theorists; though he clearly took the various strands of his argument much further than most.

In the field of pure monetary theory, Walras clearly considered the logical inclusion of money within his *static* general equilibrium as *the* main analytical challenge to be met. Chapters 3 and 4, below, show that, despite Walras's efforts to insert money in the utility function, this analysis never displayed a proper dynamic stability analysis. The diagrammatic as well as the algebraic versions of the equation of exchange are market-equilibrium conditions fulfilled on the 'periodical' market only. Anticipating somewhat the present book's main conclusions, and to put things even more bluntly, Walras never suggested a possible mechanism (either in the money or in the commodity market) which, following a monetary shock, would bring the economic system back to equilibrium.

Having shown in TMBB the 'evil consequences' of manipulating the money supply by means of paper money, his preoccupation in the realm of applied monetary theory would be, besides working on index numbers, to devise institutional mechanisms to prevent such 'monetary crises' and stabilize in the medium and long run the general level of prices. Hence the fate of TMBB. Theoretically well ahead of its time in its articulating, in a precise and well-argued model, the short-run consequences of the then universally shared quantity theory, this seminal article was completely left aside by Walras himself, and, of course, by most of his contemporaries and immediate followers;[56] it had served its objective by showing 'les inconvénients de la variation de la valeur du numéraire et de la valeur' (1886, p. 50; *OEC*, X, p. 96).

The preceding analysis of TMBB has clearly shown that anticipation of many components of the modern post-Hicksian approach to monetary theory, even if not fully developed, is already at least clearly hinted at by Walras. However, Walras was *not* interested either in elaborating an analysis in terms of a temporary market-clearing monetary equilibrium or in a detailed analysis of stability theorems within a dynamic framework. His general strategy is a clear sign that, like all other marginalist founding fathers, Walras kept value and monetary theories in two separate boxes. The progressive blurring of this frontier will start with Wicksell and is, if at all possible, far from being achieved, even today.

In order to support hypotheses such as these, a return to Walras's central contribution to the pure theory of money is now clearly called for.

NOTES

1. Walras's pre-1870 knowledge in banking was surprisingly good. Well read in contemporary literature and equipped with his own (disastrous!) attempt at practical banking, Walras had also analysed in an unexpectedly clear and detailed fashion some of the main issues of the day in the field of banking and cycles. The influence of his father's 1849 booklet is, at times, unmistakable; in particular in his lengthy discussion of Proudhon's fallacy of 'free credit' (1860, pp. 88–100 and 105–7).
2. Equation (1.5) discussed above in Chapter 1, Section 2, $\alpha''Q_a'' + F = \alpha'Q_a' + \beta Q_b P_b + \gamma Q_c P_c + \delta Q_d P_d + ...$ is the fullest version of Walras's equation of exchange. The left-hand side includes not only quantity and velocity of money but also F standing for 'fiduciary circulation'.

3. The slightly different 1874 notation is used here to make the argument compatible with equations (1.3) and (1.5) above. The original 1872 version can be found in *OEC*, XI, p. 458.
4. Walras's parallel with illness or disease dates back at least to Quesnay and the Physiocrats.
5. 1871, pp. 321–2; 1872, *OEC*, XI, p. 463; 1875, *OEC*, VII, pp. 203–5.
6. For example, the 1870 Swiss case mentioned by Walras when, at the beginning of the Franco-Prussian war, French gold *Napoléons* all but disappeared from circulation as Switzerland's main supply of metallic currency.
7. Should v_a go up, $p_b = v_b / v_a$ would obviously go down.
8. 1871, pp. 321–2; 1872, *OEC*, XI, pp. 463–4.
9. A mechanism Walras will start analysing in earnest only in the early 1880s.
10. In opposition to a monetary crisis, the drop in prices results here from lower v_a, v_b, v_c, v_d with a fixed v_e.
11. Even if, on theoretical grounds, Walras argued firmly against such a Central Bank, he is 'ready to acknowledge that a State intervention may be necessary to break away from inveterate vagaries and to prevent troublesome errors from occurring again' (1871, pp. 341–2).
12. Mill had even added in 1857 an entirely new Section 7 to Book III, Chapter XII of his *Principles* devoted exclusively to a four-page discussion of that issue.
13 By definition, at sight.
14. 'Let us suppose that for a reason or another the available quantity of metallic currency has been reduced' (1871, p. 331), if compensated by an increase of the supply of banknotes, such a contraction of metallic currency would not translate itself into a contraction of the demand for goods and services. The monetary crisis would thus be avoided.
15. 1871, pp. 331–2; 1874, pp. 198–9 as in *OEC*, VIII, 301–2; 1875, p. 207.
16 One of Walras's main arguments against a state-owned Central Bank is his fear of seeing this new monopoly turning banknotes into long-term credit (see Bridel, 1991).
17. See also Marget (1935, p. 150) for a witty footnote 12 about Hayek going 'as far as to displace the name of Wicksell, which has held the post of honour in the original German version of 1929 ... by the name of Walras, as the "founder" of the theory of "forced saving"'. See also Marget (1938–42, II, pp. 71 and 315) where forced saving is even considered to be synonymous with 'cumulative process'. Wagner (1937, pp. 359–64) suggests parallels between Walras and earlier English and French credit-cycle theorists such as Wilson (1847) and, above all, Victor Bonnet (1859, 1865, 1866, 1870).
18. See, however, brief references to Walras's forced saving argument in James and Lecoq (1961, pp. 628–31); L'Huillier and Guggenheim (1971, pp. 440–41) and Cirillo, (1986, p. 218).
19. Henceforth TMBB.
20. Besides being reprinted in three different places with relatively minor textual alterations (1880, 1883 and 1898), TMBB also appeared in an abridged and simplified version in the Swiss daily *Gazette de Lausanne* (2 and 3 December 1879), hardly a month after Walras first read it before the *Société vaudoise des Sciences naturelles*.
21. 1871, 1875 and 1898.
22. See Bridel (1991).
23. This argument will grow more and more strident in the successive versions of TMBB (compare, for example, 1879, II; 1880, p. 585; 1883, pp. 169–70 and 1898, pp. 368–9). This is the only notable alteration brought by Walras to his main argument throughout the various versions of his original TMBB (see *OEC*, X, pp. 311–42 for the collation of the various editions of this text).
24. Despite this fairly strongly-worded opposition to any Central Bank, like many theoretical proponents of the free banking doctrine, Walras concludes, however, by admitting that 'the issue of banknotes cannot be left to the rule of *laissez-faire, laissez-passer*' (1880, p. 588).

25. In the case of Mill, see also further development in Book III, Chapter VIII, pp. 491–2 and Chapter XXIII, pp. 645–6 in terms of a loanable-funds theory of interest.

26. Furthermore, the edition of Mill's *Principles* used by Walras is the 1861 French translation of the 1852 English third edition. The 1865 footnote much acclaimed by Hayek as 'a remarkably clear statement' (1939, p. 194) of the doctrine of forced saving was clearly unknown to Walras.

27. The exogenously given *circulation à desservir* discussed in Chapter 1, Section 2.

28. By eliminating 'the negligible term α'/α'' ', that is, the ratio of the velocity of circulation of Q'_a to the velocity of circulation of Q''_a. This rectangular-hyperbola diagram was drawn the same year (1871) as Marshall's but published much earlier (1874) (see *OEC*, XI, p. 457). See above, Chapter 1, Section 2.

29. In which, of course, $Q_a = Q'_a + Q''_a$ when $Q'_a = F(P_a)$ is the demand for non-monetized precious metal and $Q''_a = H/P_a$ is the demand for monetized A.

30. And this argument does anticipate Wicksell's treatment of the limits set to banks in their ability to expand credit.

31. Corresponding to the two limiting cases where $M_p = 0$ and $M_m = H/P$; and where $M_p = H/P$ and $M_m = 0$.

32. A thinly disguised reference to Proudhon and to his 'free credit' doctrine already savaged by Walras in a book-length review article in 1860.

33. Note the use of these very words by Walras (1880, p. 565).

34. And specifically claimed today by Lucas (1981, p. 215) and his epigones.

35. With this line of argument, Walras goes for the first (and only) time one step further than the purely static approach to capital formation adopted in the *Eléments* (1st edn, Lessons 51 and 52). While he had resisted all temptations to dynamize even slightly his general equilibrium system in his account of the pricing of new capital goods, in the realm of applied economics, he seems prepared, for his argument's sake, to drop his hypothesis of constancy in the capital stock.

36. That is, when $H/\left[P_a \left(K - Q_a \right) + p_a Q_a \right] = \left(M_p / K \right)$.

37. Walras also introduces an implicit one-year lag between the increased supply of banknotes and the rise in the price level linked to the increased demand. His numerical example is nothing other than an extension of the computational technique used in the lesson devoted to the periodical market.

38. See above, Chapter 1, Section 2.

39. This is nothing other than the good old 'Cantillon effect'!

40. Or, put another way, $pK' < P_a R$.

41. See below, Chapter 4.

42. Patinkin's opinion, according to which 'Walras makes little, if any, analytical use of the distinction between these two markets' (1965, p. 563, n. 71), and Walker's similar idea, according to which in his theory of capital Walras 'did not develop a true theory of credit ... because he did not introduce credit extended by banks'(1987a, p. 857), are both clearly correct in the realm of the pure theory of money. Furthermore, it is equally true that the same symbol '*i*' is used by Walras sometimes to refer to the rate of net income (Lessons 24 and 25) and sometimes to define the rate of interest (1954, pp. 242, 332 and 333). The opposite is, however, true in TMBB, as is shown below. In the 1898 reprint, Walras will add a very telling foootnote: 'Il y a bien une baisse du taux de l'intérêt résultant de l'émission de billets de banque, mais momentanée et servant à produire la hausse des prix après laquelle elle cesse' (1898, p. 358, note 1; *OEC*, X, p. 327, note 1).

43. What Keynes will later dub the *Gibson Paradox* (1930, II, pp. 177–86). See also Bridel (1992b, pp. 239–40).

44. In his cumulative process, Wicksell links the drop in the market rate either to the discovery of new goldfields or, more generally, to the bankers' inability to perfectly shadow with changes in their money market rates oscillations of the real rate of interest (an early version of the interwar 'trailing rate doctrine'). Wicksell's review of TMBB (1899) revolves essentially around Walras's inability to introduce a genuine theory of

credit to explain the link between the rate of interest and the price level (see below, Section 2.3).

45. Under the hypothesis that $pK' = P_o K$.

46. Among others, Conant quotes this passage approvingly (1906, I, p. 412).

47. Quoting Walras's TMBB precisely on this point, Mises might well be the link between Walras and Hayek (1912, p. 321; see also p. 357).

48. Or 'concertina effect', to use Kaldor's terminology.

49. *Wealth of Nations*, Bk. II, Chapter 2, 1776, I, p. 321.

50. Even today, books and articles specifically devoted to Walras's monetary theory do not even mention the existence of TMBB (see, for example, Patinkin (1965); Morishima (1977); Witteloostjuin and Maks (1990); and Walker (1994a, 1994b).

51. G. Boccardo, H. Cernuschi, E. Cheysson, H.S Foxwell, Ch. Gide, H. de la Goupillière, S.D. Horton, W. Lexis, C. Menger, V. Pareto, P. del Pezzo, L. Say and K. Wicksell.

52. 'Je serais particulièrement heureux d'avoir votre avis sur ce sujet' (1965, I, p. 647).

53. The first-known exchange of correspondence between Walras and Wicksell dates back to 1893 and a copy of Walras's first edition was all that Wicksell knew of the *Eléments* until Walras presented him in 1898 with a copy of the third edition (1965, II, p. 596 and III, p. 37). No wonder why, when reviewing *Études d'économie politique appliquée* Wicksell was not familiar with the development in pure monetary theory Walras introduced in subsequent editions of the *Eléments*.

54. The absence of a discussion in terms of forced saving in Wicksell's work has already been noted by several authors (see, for example, Uhr, 1960, pp. 139–43).

55. Despite the critique levelled at TMBB, Wicksell is, however, still ready to conclude his review by asserting that 'Walras is doubtless the greatest synthesizer of his time; and may be of all times' (1899, p. 829).

56. However, in various applied monetary articles, Walras alludes briefly to a TMBB-like argument to support his central policy aim of stabilizing the price level by way of his *billon régulateur*: see, for example, in the *Théorie de la monnaie* (1886, pp. 50–52; *OEC*, X, pp. 96–7) and in his 1893 'Le problème monétaire anglo-indien' (*OEC*, X, p. 157) from which the following characteristic quotation is drawn: 'In effect as the quantity of money increases ... producers gain, while workers and other consumers lose. On the other hand, when the supply of money diminishes, entrepreneurs suffer, while landowners, workers and capitalists gain. In either case, economic equilibrium is destroyed. The crisis will last until a new equilibrium is established'.

3. From *Théorie de la monnaie* to the *Etudes d'économie politique appliquée*: More Variations on the Same Themes (1886–1898)

[I]n both eds. 2 and 3, the monetary theory was still not effectively integrated with [Walras's] general equilibrium theory. (Jaffé in Walras, 1954, p. 601)

Even if during these twelve years, no breakthrough took place in Walras's pure monetary theory, this period witnessed a slow but steady reorganization of his monetary thought. Various existing stepping-stones are redefined and rearranged in a different order; important new notions replace old ones; interesting additions are brought into the discussion of pure and applied theories but, fundamentally, Walras clings fast to his 1874 monetary logic centred on a straightforward equation of exchange: a solution to the delicate incorporation of money into general equilibrium equations is still a long march away.

First and foremost, the Fisherian *circulation à desservir* is replaced in 1886 by a cash-balance-like *encaisse désirée*. This move from an aggregate demand for money to individual demands for desired cash balances is, however, left unexplained: linked with the postulate of monetary exchange, the size of these desired balances is simply *assumed* . To quote Schumpeter: 'the concept of the "amount of cash people desire to hold" (*encaisse désirée*) was not made part and parcel of his pure general equilibrium – not fully amalgamated with it – before the fourth edition (1900)' (1954, p. 1020).

Second, the structure of the *Eléments* is completely reworked from the 1889 second edition onwards. For the sake of the overall logic of the general equilibrium model, the money section is shifted after exchange, production and capital formation. For the first time, as an add-on notion, money is considered as part of circulating capital.

Third, interesting additions are brought to the analysis of the working of the money market, in particular the definition of the rate of interest as a measure of the opportunity cost of holding money. However, the line between pure and applied monetary theory is not yet clearly drawn. In the second edition, the four lessons in applied monetary theory (subsequently transferred to the *Etudes d'économie politique appliquée*) are still present and on the same analytical level as the lessons on the pure monetary equations.

This lengthy process of theoretical *tâtonnement* is examined in detail below. Section 1 is built around the *Théorie de la monnaie* and Section 2

79

examines in detail the second and third editions of the *Eléments*. The racecourse is being progressively built up but the monetary horse is still left at the gate.

1   THE *THEORIE DE LA MONNAIE* (1886)

By any standard, the title of Walras's volume on money is among the greatest misnomers in the history of monetary theory. Of one hundred and twenty-three pages, ten at most deal with what is today considered as monetary *theory*: the bulk of this slim volume is in fact devoted to the defence and illustration of Walras's pet scheme for monetary reform. In addition, the theoretical argument contained in the three crucial paragraphs 8 to 10[1] improves only marginally on Section III of the 1874 first edition of the *Eléments*. Section 1.1 offers a brief survey of the *rationale* behind a pamphlet designed to support a particular scheme of *monetary reform* and not as a novel contribution to pure theory of money. Section 1.2 is devoted to the modest changes Walras introduces in the equation of exchange carried over from the *Eléments*. Finally, it is argued in Section 1.3 that, despite the inclusion of fiat money and 'compensation' in his *théorie de la quantité*, Walras fails to go beyond an impeccable but perfectly static quantity theory and to deduce his equation from the principle of utility maximization.

1.1   A Pamphlet for Monetary Reform

The *Théorie de la monnaie* is, according to Walras himself, the crowning of eight papers on the *applied* theory of money published between 1867 and 1885.[2] In these various articles, Walras reiterates time and again the two main aims of the line of research leading to this book:[3]

- first and foremost to submit a workable scheme for a semi-managed currency in order to stabilize in the medium and long run the general level of prices;
- second, and no less important for Walras's grand scientific design, to demonstrate that such a scheme is the logical result of his contribution to pure economics epitomized by marginal utility (*rareté*) and general equilibrium analysis.

Given the difficulties Walras will be facing when trying to find room for money (and not simply for *numéraire*) in his general equilibrium framework, these two objectives clearly have to be examined in some more detail.

Like all marginalist founding fathers, Walras was trapped in the whirlwind of the bimetallism debate of the second half of the nineteenth century; and like most marginalist theorists,[4] working against a similar theoretical background, Walras reached similar conclusions. Since, as Walras puts it, 'le mécanisme économique naturel [étant], jusqu'à un certain point automoteur et autorégulateur', [5] money should not obstruct but reinforce the self-adjusting forces at work in the economy:

Il faut absolument renoncer à l'optimisme qui a régné jusqu'ici et qui règne encore dans ... l'économie politique. ... le système des phénomènes économiques tend de lui-même à l'équilibre sous le régime de la libre concurrence, comme le système des phénomènes astronomiques sous l'influence de l'attraction universelle; mais, au lieu que les corps célestes gravitent régulièrement et paisiblement le long de leurs trajectoires, les services et les produits subissent des changements de prix brusques et violents dont il faudrait connaître bien plus à fond que nous ne les connaissons les causes et les conséquences afin de les prévoir et peut-être de les prévenir. (1886, pp. 81–2; *OEC*, X, p. 115)

Clearly, the sophisticated results of his pure economics do not lead Walras into the optimism of *laissez-faire* policies. Quite the opposite: competitive equilibrium is a normative benchmark near which actual economies should be maintained by way of an active economic policy. However, Walras stops well short of suggesting a policy aimed at ironing out all fluctuations, crises or 'economic tides'. The author wants, more modestly, to offer a scheme allowing for the stabilization of the price level by way of a monetary policy aimed at preventing 'monetary disorders':

comme ... les crises sont un phénomène régulier et, en un sens, normal, il est essentiel de respecter les hausses et les baisses de prix qui marquent le cours de la marée économique[6] et il faut seulement faire en sorte que, d'une marée à l'autre, la moyenne des prix n'aille pas en s'élevant ou s'abaissant indéfiniment. (1886, p. 21; *OEC*, X, pp. 74–5)
   La monnaie doit être d'une valeur réelle égale à sa valeur nominale; elle doit être, en outre, d'une valeur aussi régulièrement variable que possible. C'est là ce qu'elle doit être. Et si, pour la rendre telle, il est besoin que l'Etat intervienne ... la monnaie ne doit pas être et ne sera pas automatique. (1886, p. 83; *OEC*, X, p. 116)[7]

The structure of the *Théorie de la monnaie* exactly reflects Walras's main strategy. In Part I (*Principles*), and with the help of his price theory, Walras works out a slightly amended version of his 1874 equation of exchange; in Part II, he submits to the criticism the various existing monetary systems and suggests his own 'étalon-or avec billon régulateur'; in Part III, he discusses the 'statistical *desiderata*' (that is, index number issues) linked to the working of his monetary scheme.[8] Short-run oscillations of the price level around a *horizontal* axis[9] are best minimized neither by monometallism (gold or silver) nor by bimetallism but through the implementation of a gold-exchange standard *cum billon régulateur*: the natural oscillations of the price of the gold standard have to be dampened by way of an active open market policy conducted with silver coins (*billon d'argent régulateur*) the value of which is partly fiduciary (that is, not necessarily equal to their intrinsic metallic value).

On many occasions, Walras is keen to emphasize that policy conclusions such as these are clearly built upon his pure theory of money. In that respect, the introductory sentence to Part II of the *Théorie* leaves no doubt about this connection: 'En possession d'un idéal monétaire bien défini, voyons jusqu'à quel point les divers et nombreux systèmes existants ou proposés le réalisent' (1886, p. 57; *OEC*, X, p. 101).

Even more to the point is a passage from a letter addressed to Gide: 'Je m'attache à cette question de la monnaie ... parce qu'elle m'offre l'occasion d'une merveilleuse application de mes théories d'économie politique pure' (Walras, 1965, II, p. 114).[10] Walras's grand design to use pure economics to provide 'rational solutions' to practical issues of great social importance is here obviously at stake. To assess the feasibility and the success of such a strategy, it is necessary to appraise now to what extent the *principles* of monetary theory contained in the *Théorie de la monnaie* (1886) improve on those of the *Eléments* (1874).

1.2 Marginal Amendments to the Equation of Exchange

In sum and substance, the theoretical chapter of the *Théorie de la monnaie* has nothing really new to offer. However, the framework in which Walras offers his slightly amended equation of exchange is methodologically extremely interesting. Faced for the first time with the necessity of bridging the gap between pure economics and a solution to a practical problem, consciously or not, and despite allegations to the contrary, Walras is much more measured in his claims for a direct and operational link between pure and applied economics. He has to admit explicitly that his general equilibrium framework is of a purely static nature: characteristically the *tâtonnement* on the money market has to be instantaneous and his pure theory of money (Quantity Theory) has nothing to say on the dynamic of the adjustment process following a change in the money supply. Struggling to inject some (monetary) realism into his formal model, Walras is constantly torn between his 'once-and-for-all' market and his more realistic 'periodical'/continuous markets; between microeconomic rigour and macroeconomic relevance.

Sections I and II of the *Théorie*'s Part I contain a potted and semi-intuitive version of Walras's general equilibrium. In 1886, a mere twelve years after his seminal contribution, Walras is still clearly seizing every opportunity to promote his main theoretical findings: in a state of general competitive equilibrium (exchange and production), prices are proportional to marginal utilities. In one sentence, he also reminds his reader about the purely abstract nature of this result: 'Cette vérité est une vérité rationnelle; l'expérience ne saurait la confirmer' (1886, p. 34; *OEC*, X, p. 82).

In other words, for Walras, to question the realism or the falsifiability of his general equilibrium model is not to be hard-headed, positivistic or even rigorous. It is to be utterly confused about its nature. The whole question remains, of course, to assess how much the understanding of real-world situations can gain from such a purely rational analysis. Monetary theory is clearly for Walras one of the earliest acid tests of his pure theory.

In the first paragraph of Section III, Walras reworks briefly the standard distinction discussed at length in the *Eléments* between *numéraire* (unit of account) and money (medium of exchange), adds a few remarks on what will subsequently be called Walras's law and restates with great clarity the cash-in-advance hypothesis already introduced in the *Eléments*:

> nous vendons nos services à des entrepreneurs qui ne fabriquent pas les produits dont nous avons besoin, et nous achetons des produits à des entrepreneurs qui n'emploient pas nos services. D'où la nécessité d'un intermédiaire d'échange ou d'une monnaie. (1886, pp. 38–9; *OEC*, X, p. 86)

Again,[11] and a century before modern theorists, Walras postulates that only money buys goods. Money should thus have an *essential* part to play in the transaction technology. Unfortunately, and despite this very lucid statement, Walras's model will again reveal itself unable to support such a hypothesis: Walras's procedure simply *assumes* what should be explained, that is, a positive exchange value for money.

As already noted by Marget more than sixty years ago (1931, p. 580), the analytical paragraphs 9 and 10 witness the first appearance of the Walrasian idea of *encaisses*. While in the first edition of his *Eléments* Walras discussed the demand for money in terms of a *circulation à desservir* determined at the macro-level using a Fisherian equation of exchange,[12] from his *Théorie de la monnaie* onwards Walras works out equations that are similar to Cambridge-like '*real*-balance' or cash-balance equations. Every individual agent displays individually a demand for real (not nominal) money balances. However, at this stage, Walras is not yet able to connect these individually-determined *encaisses* with the principle of utility maximization: nowhere is the word *encaisses* linked in the *Théorie de la monnaie* with the notion of *désirées*. Despite Walras's later claim to the contrary,[13] in 1886, he only makes use of the wordings of *encaisse nécessaire* (1886, p. 40; *OEC*, X, p. 87), *encaisse monétaire* (1886, pp. 39, 45; *OEC*, X, pp. 86, 91) or *encaisse d'équilibre* (pp. 43–4; *OEC*, X, p. 90).[14] Indeed, in the *Théorie*, Walras makes no use of marginal-utility analysis except of course, as in the first edition of the *Eléments*, to deal – in a partial analysis framework and only *after* he has first arbitrarily posited the monetary equation – with the case of money that is also a commodity. In Walras's own words:

> Without investigating the natural circumstances that may require land-owners, workers, capitalists, and entrepreneurs to hold, *at a given moment,* a cash balance of varying size to carry out purchases of varying sizes, we posit that, for simplicity, the value of this cash balance and of these purchases depend not only on the [current] situation, but also on the character and habits of each individual ... . What must now be understood is that when a consumer or a producer requires to have in his possession a certain store of ... money, he is concerned not with the [nominal] quantity of this money – which as such is a matter of indifference to him – but solely with the quantity of other goods, commodities or services, that he will be able to obtain in exchange for his money. Let ... (*A*) then represent a commodity that is also the unit of account and the medium of exchange; let Q'_a be the existing quantity of this commodity; let $\alpha,\beta,\gamma,\delta$ represent the respective quantities of the commodities (*A*),(*B*),(*C*),(*D*), whose money value individuals require, at any given moment, to hold in the form of cash. The quantity of money Q''_a needed to satisfy these requirements is then

$$\alpha + \beta p_b + \gamma p_c + \delta p_d + ...$$

[where $p_b,p_c,p_d,...$ are the prices of (*B*),(*C*),(*D*) ... in terms of (*A*)]. (1886, pp. 40–41; *OEC*, X, p. 87; italics added)

As in the first edition of the *Eléments*, this passage deals only with the case of money that also has a normal commodity use.[15] Walras obviously has gold in mind. The term marginal utility of money refers only to the utility added to the commodity used as money by the simple fact that it has been chosen as a means of exchange:

> la marchandise monnaie a, par elle-même et comme marchandise, une certaine valeur; mais la loi qui la désigne pour l'usage de monnaie ajoute pour ainsi dire à cette première valeur une seconde valeur d'où résulte la valeur totale et définitive. (1886, p. 40; *OEC*, X, p. 86)

Clearly, for Walras, the *service of money* has, as such, a *direct* utility even if there is admittedly no rationale behind this assertion, no room for it in the utility function. Walras can thus rework his 1872–74 equations to have them fit his new cash-balance approach:

$$Q_a = Q'_a + Q''_a$$
$$= Q'_a + \alpha + \beta p_b + \gamma p_c + \delta p_d$$

in which Q_a is the total quantity of the money-metal (A); Q'_a, the quantity of this metal that is used as an ordinary commodity and Q''_a, the quantity of this money-metal used as money. Obviously, therefore, the demand for money is, in equilibrium and at a given moment, defined as

$$Q''_a = \alpha + \beta p_b + \gamma p_c + \beta p_d + \ldots$$

Accordingly, resulting from the decision to use a particular commodity (that is, gold) as money, the ratio of the total quantity of metal to the quantity of this metal used as an ordinary commodity is defined as $n = Q_a/Q'_a$. Cash balances have to be created at the expense of agents' total holdings of money-metal, the marginal utility of which will naturally increase by a factor n and the consumption decrease by the same factor n. To demonstrate the validity of the quantity theory for a money that is also a commodity, Walras has naturally to prove that, simultaneously, all other nominal prices $p_b, p_c, p_d, \ldots$ [16] have to decrease n-fold to keep the value of *real* cash balances constant. To this end, Walras restricts his demonstration to the case where (i) the marginal utility of the commodity money is inversely proportional to its quantity, and (ii) the nominal value of the *encaisses monétaires* is directly proportionate to the prices of other commodities (1886, p. 42; *OEC*, X, p. 88).

These three conditions being laid down, Walras explicitly admits that the existence and the stability of such equilibrium conditions[17] remain to be proved: 'il s'agit de faire voir d'abord que l'équilibre existera sous tous les rapports dans ces conditions comme dans les précédentes, et ensuite que cet équilibre tendra à se réaliser de lui-même sous le régime de la libre concurrence' (1886, p. 42; *OEC*, X, p. 89).

Clearly, under 'the hypothetical regime of perfect competition', to demonstrate the exact proportionality of nominal prices to the quantity of money, Walras is well aware of the necessity of offering an *existence*[18] and a stability theorem. The 'proof'[19] of the existence of a new vector of equilibrium prices is straightforward: if all nominal prices are divided by n and the marginal utility of the numéraire-money multiplied by the same factor n, the exchange, production and monetary equilibrium conditions stay exactly the same: the price of every commodity remains equal to its marginal utility. In Walras's own algebra:

$$\frac{p_b}{n} = \frac{R_b}{nR_a} \ ; \quad \frac{p_c}{n} = \frac{R_c}{nR_a} \ ; \quad \frac{p_d}{n} = \frac{R_d}{nR_a} \ \ldots$$

in which *R* stands for *rareté*, that is, marginal utility (1886, p. 42; *OEC*, X, p. 89).

As far as the stability of the system is concerned (specifying again the perfect competition hypothesis), Walras – torn between rigour and realism – has no other way but to opt for the once-and-for-all market approach: he has to make the *tâtonnement* on the money market congruent with the rules laid down for the real sector. As long as actual cash balances are higher/lower than equilibrium cash balances, money-metal (*A*) would be turned into commodity (*A*) and vice versa in order for the price of commodity (*A*) to be equal to the price of money-metal (*A*). Since this *tâtonnement* on the money market is simultaneously conducted *at a given point in time* with the *tâtonnements* on the other (*n* − 1) commodity markets, it has to be durationless, instantaneous and to exclude any trading out of equilibrium even if a virtual adjustment process takes place in logical time.

> Ces ... prix courants d'équilibre ... résultent, *à un moment donné*, de ce vaste tâtonnement qui a consisté à crier d'abord des prix au hasard, puis à faire la hausse quand la demande était supérieure à l'offre et la baisse quand l'offre était supérieure à la demande, puis aussi à augmenter la quantité des produits quand leur prix de vente était supérieur à leur prix de revient en services et à diminuer cette quantité quand le prix de revient était supérieur au prix de vente, puis enfin à transformer de l'(*A*) marchandise en (*A*) monnaie ou de l'(*A*) monnaie en (*A*) marchandise suivant que la valeur de (*A*) était plus grande comme monnaie que comme marchandise ou comme marchandise que comme monnaie; *cette triple série d'opérations se faisant d'ailleurs **simultanément** et réagissant les unes sur les autres. Enfin l'équilibre est atteint.* (1886, pp. 50-51; *OEC*, X, p. 96, italics and emphasis added)

Walras's argument is unequivocally a straightforward extension of his *tâtonnement* procedure on the commodity markets (where money is only a *numéraire*[20]) to an economy in which money is supposed to have an essential part to play in the exchange process. At this stage of the development of his monetary thought, Walras is obviously unable to reconcile money as a medium of exchange with an imaginary procedure conducted in terms of *numéraire* in a purely static framework. By definition, the *tâtonnements* conducted *simultaneously* on all markets (including the money market) *at a given point in time* is only congruent with the once-and-for-all market. Besides, thanks to this 'instantaneous' interdependence between the *tâtonnement* on the money market and those taking place on the other markets, Walras's model seems to avoid the trap of the classical dichotomy: nominal prices are determinate and the quantity theory vindicated. However, by collapsing the future into the present, this simultaneous *tâtonnement* procedure rules out any dynamic analysis, any essential role for money. Clearly, without sequences, there is no monetary theory; and without monetary theory, there is no demonstration of the positive exchange value for money.

Finally, probably unaware of this subtlety, Walras fails to recognize that the apparently simple inverse relationship between money and nominal prices inherent to the quantity theory is accurate only when the money supply is exogenous (that is, made up of fiat money only): this is obviously not the case for gold.

1.3 Fiat Money and 'Compensation'

The understanding of the difficulties faced by Walras can be brought one step further by considering two additional 'complications' added in his paragraph 10 (1886, pp. 44–7; *OEC*, X, pp. 91–4): the introduction of fiat money either in the form of banknotes or through a compensation scheme in a clearing system. For Walras, these two 'complications' have no influence whatsoever on the 'theorem of proportionality between money-metal and [nominal] prices' (1886, p. 46; *OEC*, X, p. 93). In contrast to TMBB, the thrust of Walras's argument is here primarily aimed at the long-run, comparative static validity of his equation of exchange – not at a real-time dissection of a step-by-step adjustment process. Introducing paper money P to cover both bank notes and 'compensations', Walras rewrites his cash-balance equation in the following fashion:

$$Q_a + P = Q_a' + \alpha + \beta p_b + \gamma p_c + \delta p_d + \ldots$$

Even if cash balances Q_a'' are getting smaller and smaller replaced as they are by paper money, *at a given moment*, or at the end of an adjustment process started by an increase in the volume of P, nominal prices are *still* directly proportionate to the volume of money-metal Q_a, the only 'true' money: 'je soutiens que, *à un moment donné*, ou *d'un moment à l'autre* toutes choses restant égales d'ailleurs, si la quantité de la marchandise monnaie augmente ou diminue, les prix hausseront ou baisseront en proportion' (1886, p. 46; *OEC*, X, p. 93; italics added).

Clearly, Walras is working here either in his once-and-for-all market or in comparative static. In his answers to critics added to the book version of *Théorie de la monnaie* (1886, pp. 3–22; *OEC*, X, pp. 63–75) Walras rejects more specifically a remark made by Cheysson and Juglar according to which the proportionality theorem is rendered ineffectual by the introduction of paper money:

Son importance ne change rien à la position et *sa connaissance est inutile à la solution du problème qui nous occupe*. La quantité Q de la monnaie, le prix p de cette monnaie en quelque autre marchandise, le montant H [21] des échanges à régler et le montant *C* des échanges qui se règlent par compensation étant reliés entre eux par l'équation

$$Qp = H - C,$$

laquelle devient, au bout d'un certain temps,

$$Q'p' = H' - C',$$

quels que soient, dans l'avenir, les perfectionnements du crédit, c'est-à-dire quel que soit le développement de *C* par rapport à *H*, il y aura toujours lieu et il y aura toujours moyen de ramener *p'* à *p* par un changement de *Q'* en *Q''* effectué selon la formule

$$Q'' = Q' \frac{p'}{p}$$

et qui ne suppose que la seule connaissance de *p*, *p* et *Q'* (1880, p. 13, *OEC*, X, p. 70)

In other words, since Walras postulates a *fixed* relationship between paper money (banknotes plus 'compensations') and 'true' money Q_a'', should agents ask (as they were entitled to in Walras's time) for a full conversion of fiduciary money into metal money, the proportionality theorem between money and prices would be once again vindicated. Paper money and 'compensations' are mere illusions that should not blind the theorist to the fact that only a commodity can be money. Clearly, Walras's idiosyncratic understanding of the nineteenth-century French financial system was of considerable help in strengthening his homogeneity postulate.

However, as in TMBB, Walras is not blind to the short run influence of *P* on the price level. After reiterating his proportionality theorem, he adds – as a realistic afterthought – a proviso couched in terms of a dynamic period analysis:

je concède parfaitement que, *d'un moment à l'autre*, toutes les données du problème se modifiant, il n'y a plus de rapport nécessaire de proportionalité entre la quantité de la marchandise monnaie et les prix; que, par exemple, la quantité de marchandise monnaie diminuant, mais la monnaie de papier suppléant de plus en plus la monnaie métallique, ou les compensations se développant de jour en jour, les prix se maintiendraient au lieu de baisser. (1886, p. 46; *OEC*, X, p. 93; italics added)

But these are temporary intra-period incidents only: there is no room for them in the pure theory of money.[22] These are matters best dealt with in the applied theory of money under the headings of Banking and Credit (as they are, for example, in TMBB).

All in all, and despite an ambitious title, the sum total of the theoretical improvements brought about by *Théorie de la monnaie* are extremely modest.

2 THE SECOND EDITION OF THE *ELEMENTS* AND AFTER: THE *ENCAISSES DESIREES* WITHOUT THE UTILITY FUNCTION, OR GROPING TOWARDS A NEW FORMULATION (1889–1898)

Walras submitted the second edition of the *Eléments* (1889) to some fundamental structural changes. In contrast to the first edition, the treatment of money is preceded by the discussion of exchange, production and capital formation. The capital formation model is then enlarged in Part V by the equations relating to the theory of money. At that stage, this new configuration is of importance not so much for Walras's monetary theory *per se* as for the optional role now explicitly granted to money in general equilibrium. In the second edition, monetary phenomena are not yet an integral component of the overall general equilibrium model. In fact, this important alteration set the analytical structure within which theorists have been trying to fit money for at least a century. However, Walras will only strive to offer the first such derivation of the agents' demand functions for money from the utility-maximization principle[23] in the 1900 fourth edition.

Short of displaying such a theoretically crucial integration of money into value theory, the second edition concentrates on a vivid – though theoretically feeble – intuitive description of various issues linked to monetary disequilibria. Again, oscillating between analytical rigour and 'realistic' assertions, Walras this time chooses the latter at the expense of the former. In particular, in his monetary chapters, Walras's use of the *Eléments* time structure is hardly satisfactory if not very confusing: to graft the description of a dynamic adjustment process in terms of interest rate on a perfectly static equilibrium model of 'real' markets without finding room for money in the utility function is hardly a convincing procedure. In short, and despite the remarkable insight about the rate of interest as the opportunity cost of holding money, this second edition is no more than *Hamlet* without its prince, the *encaisse désirée* without the utility function. To use Kuenne's gibe (1956, p. 244), the new extension to Walras's mansion is still essentially stocked with old pieces of monetary furniture.

Accordingly, the reasons and consequences of the new ordering of the *Eléments* are briefly discussed in Section 2.1. In Section 2.2, the modifications brought by Walras to his monetary theory to fit this new niche are examined and contrasted with the remarkable intuitive accounts of the short-run workings of the money and capital markets. The various and repeated rearrangements of the same monetary deck-chairs performed during the following decade in various (mostly applied) articles are discussed finally in Section 2.3.

2.1 The Structural Reorganization of the 1889 Second Edition

In the preface to his second (and third) edition, Walras stresses vigorously the reason why the reordering of the first five parts of his *Eléments* is theoretically important:

> En vue d'introduire le résultat de mes recherches [sur la question de la monnaie], j'ai reporté après la notion de la capitalisation et du crédit la section de la monnaie. ... On a dans les quatres leçons de théorie pure [de la monnaie], la solution du quatrième grand problème qui se présente en économie politique pure après ceux de l'échange, de la production, de la capitalisation et du crédit: celui de la monnaie. ... j'ai [donc] considérablement développé la section consacrée à la monnaie. (1889, pp. ix–x; *OEC*, VIII, pp. 4 and 6)

Furthermore, and quite surprisingly, Walras insists again on what he sees as substantial changes in this pure theory itself:

> J'ai substitué, en la complétant convenablement, pour la solution du problème de la valeur de la monnaie, à la démonstration fondée sur la considération de la 'circulation à desservir' que j'avais empruntée aux économistes dans la première édition de ces *Eléments d'économie politique pure*, la démonstration fondée sur la considération de l'"encaisse désirée' dont je me suis servi dans la théorie monétaire. (1889, pp. ix–x; *OEC*, VIII, pp. 4 and 6)

For the reasons already discussed in Section 1, above, this assertion is somewhat misleading. Nowhere does the notion of 'encaisse désirée' appear in the *Théorie de la monnaie*; and, in 1889, the substitution of the phrase 'encaisses désirées'[24] for 'encaisses nécessaires' does not herald in the least a formal attempt at finding room for money within the agent's utility function. The 1889 lessons in pure theory are a straightforward rewriting (often word for word) of the relevant sections of *Théorie de la monnaie*. Thus, and even if, with the idea of a demand for a stock of money without direct utility but linked to its *service d'approvisionnement*, Walras clearly works in a cash-balance framework, he has not yet elaborated any cash-balance theory.

Most of the alterations brought in 1889 to the analytical sections of the 1886 *Théorie* are in fact meant to adapt them to a model in which capital and credit are present: money is for the first time considered as a circulating capital providing a *service d'approvisionnement* traded on the money market the price of which is the rate of interest:

> lorsqu'un consommateur ou un producteur a le désir d'avoir par devers lui une certaine provision ... de monnaie, ce qu'il considère uniquement, c'est non la quantité de cette monnaie, qui lui est tout à fait indifférente en elle-même, mais la quantité des autres marchandises, produits, services ou capitaux qu'il pourra obtenir en échange de sa monnaie. ... L'intérêt du capital circulant paie le service de la monnaie pendant qu'on la garde [tout comme] celui des approvisionnements en matières premières. (1889, pp. 378 and 380; *OEC*, VIII, pp. 454 and 464)

However, at the very beginning of his demonstration and borrowing the very paragraphs used in the *Théorie de la monnaie*,[25] Walras warns the reader that the agents' demand functions for money are simply *empirically* given: thus, any integration of monetary and value theory is excluded *ex definitio*.

Furthermore, in 1889, money is not only a numéraire and a means of exchange but also, and for the first time a reserve of value linked to savings in the form of money:[26]

> Une marchandise en laquelle se forme l'excédent du revenu sur la consommation et se prête le capital fixe et circulant, sur le marché du capital-monnaie, et qui sert de *monnaie d'épargne*. ... Nous formons nos épargnes en monnaie et nous prêtons cette monnaie aux entrepreneurs, D'où la nécessité d'un intermédiaire de crédit. (1889, p. 376; *OEC*, VIII, pp. 442–4)

Walras is here dangerously flirting with production and capital theories, the rate(s) of interest, time and what appears to be a dynamic model discussed about the *periodical* and *permanent* market hypotheses. However, and despite a first attempt at describing a simplified and intuitively 'realistic' *tâtonnement* process in terms of fiat paper money involving a market for *capital goods* and a market for *money-capital*, the sum total of Walras's effort does not go beyond a comparative static version of his quantitative equation. The exact technology of exchange – and the part played (or rather not played) therein by money – is beginning to emerge but will have to wait until 1899–1900 to come out with greater clarity.

2.2 *Encaisses Désirées* Without Utility Maximization

The structural reorganization of the 1889 second edition of the *Eléments* indicates a shift in Walras's 'vision' in the Schumpeterian sense of the word. And for once, all main commentators seem to agree.[27] In the exchange, production and capital formation theories (discussed in Parts II–IV), prices are all expressed in terms of *numéraire* and the vector of equilibrium prices is determined by *tâtonnement* on the durationless once-and-for-all market.[28] What place, then, could Walras possibly find in such a timeless equilibrium model for money characterized by its three usual functions? This most difficult of all problems raised in the *Eléments* will have to wait until the fourth edition to receive the beginning of an (unsatisfactory) answer (see below, Chapter 4, Section 1). However, at this stage, Walras's preliminary attempt at tackling this crucial issue in the second and third editions deserves full attention.

In 1889, the novel part of Walras's monetary analysis begins with a theoretically remarkable innovation. For the first time, money is supposed to be an object without any utility of its own: 'nous supposerons d'abord qu'on prenne pour monnaie de circulation et d'épargne une chose bien définie, de quantité déterminée, mais inutile et qui, par conséquent, n'ait pas de valeur d'échange par elle-même' (1889, p. 377; OEC, VIII, p. 448).

Walras considers this analysis of fiduciary money as much more than a mere pedagogical device. In the pure theory of money, the positive marginal utility of money is independent from the nature of the instrument used as a means of exchange and store of value. Walras even goes as far as to admit that his cherished analysis of commodity money (as the only 'real' money)[29] is a 'considération de théorie appliquée' (1886, p. 377; *OEC*, VIII, p. 448). In other words, the whole (and lengthy) exercise conducted by Walras in terms of commodity money and bimetallic standard can be safely neglected without any loss to the fundamentals of his pure theory of money: 'For pure theory, it is obviously advantageous to investigate how something gets value when it becomes money, before exploring how this value as money has to be combined with value as a commodity' (1889, p. 377; *OEC*, VIII, p. 452).

Again, and as in the *Théorie de la monnaie*, Walras starts his demonstration from a situation where exchange, production and capitalization equilibrium conditions are fulfilled,[30] that is, the vector of (relative) equilibrium prices is already defined on the provisional assumption that the economy is one of barter. Money is then introduced as a mere optional add-on, not as an integral component of the mechanisms of exchange, production and capital accumulation. (U) is defined as the worthless 'thing' (that is, not commodity) chosen to play the part of money. Q_u is the total given amount of (U) available in the economy. To leave open the possibility of taking at a later stage commodity (A) as money, (B) is chosen as the *numéraire*. Without resorting at any point to marginal utility analysis, Walras then considers the agents' demand functions for money[31] as empirically given, that is, the proportion of the value of the respective goods and services agents wish to hold in money are given parameters of the model: 'Soient a, b, c, d ... T ... P ... K, K', K'' ... t ... p ... k, k', k'' ... m, m' ... les quantités respectives des ... marchandises[32] dont les échangeurs ont le désir d'avoir en caisse, dans ces conditions, la contre-valeur en monnaie' (1889, p. 378; *OEC*, VIII, p. 456).

In the second edition, the 1886 equation for the aggregate cash balance valued in (B) is accordingly slightly amended as

$$ap_a + b + cp_c + dp_d + \ldots + TP_t + \ldots + PP_p + \ldots + KP_k$$
$$+ K'P_{k'} + K''P_{k''} + \ldots + tp_t + \ldots + pp_p + \ldots \qquad (3.1)$$
$$+ kp_k + k'p_{k'} + k''p_{k''} + \ldots + mp_m + \ldots = H.$$

On the right-hand side of this equation (3.1), the exogenously given H reappears under a different guise from in the first edition[33] as the total value in (B) of the money agents' need for transaction or investment (saving) purposes. Since Q_u of (U) is given, the price (value) of money p_u simply follows from equation (3.2)

$$Q_u p_u = H \qquad (3.2)$$

To obtain eventually the prices of goods and services in terms of (U), all prices in terms of (B) have to be divided by $p_u = H/Q_u$. Walras's cumbersome algebra involves a conversion of all prices in equation (3.1) into prices in terms of (U) to get the equilibrium conditions on the money market:

$$a\pi_a + b\pi_b + c\pi_c + d\pi_d + \ldots + T\Pi_t + \ldots + P\Pi_p + \ldots$$
$$+ K\Pi_k + K'\Pi_{k'} + K''\Pi_{k''} + \ldots + t\pi_t + \ldots + p\pi_p + \ldots \qquad (3.3)$$
$$+ k\pi_k + k'\pi_{k'} + k''\pi_{k''} + \ldots + m\pi_m + \ldots = Q_u.$$

At this stage, and without a word of warning or explanation, Walras makes an interesting (though uncoordinated) analytical move: he links the cost of holding cash balances with the rate of interest. In Walras's own words, the rate of interest is simply the opportunity cost of holding money:

> In a society where one holds money in cash from the moment when one receives it until the day when one gives it out in payment or lends it out, money renders few services, and those who hold it, producers or consumers, pointlessly lose the interest on the capital that it represents. (1889, p. 382; *OEC*, VIII, p.474)

The cost of holding the stock of money Q_u is, indeed, $Q_u i$ where i is, in equilibrium, both the rate of net return on capital goods and the rate of interest. Equation (3.3) simply reflects that, at this equilibrium rate, agents would hold cash balances exactly equal to their *encaisses désirées*[34] (equal in turn to the exogenously given supply of money Q_u). The gaping hole in Walras's new and interesting analysis is that nothing is said about how these *encaisses désirées* are determined in the first place. However, for Walras, the proportionality theorem is validated. Should Q_u rise (fall), money prices would rise (fall); alternatively, should the exogenously given H rise (fall), equilibrium would be maintained by a fall (rise) of all money prices.[35] Clearly, variations in the absolute price level have no influence on the other markets; changes in Q_u have no effect on real variables: there is a dichotomy between money and relative prices; and money is neutral.

If this conclusion is a well-worn one, the casual appearance of *i* as the cost of holding money is a pregnant innovation even if this variable completely disappeared from Walras's 1900 attempt at integrating money into general equilibrium. Odd as it may seem, it is only when demonstrating how this cash-balance equation is solved by a *tâtonnement* on the rate of interest, that Walras suddenly sees the need for clarifying the connection between the rate of interest, the net rate of return and the *encaisse désirée*.

Again, and given the hypothesis used in positing equation (3.3),[36] Walras's bid at introducing a dose of realism in his *tâtonnement* process will not be more convincing than the undertaking offered in the *Théorie de la monnaie*. To use the pseudo-realism of an adjustment process on the money market to demonstrate the *undefined* existence theorem of a monetary equilibrium is hardly a sound theoretical procedure. The constant vacillation between the strictly static conditions implied by the once-and-for-all market and the pseudo-realism of the periodical/continuous markets comforts the nagging conjecture that, in the realm of pure theory, Walras had not much, if anything, to offer in terms of a dynamic monetary adjustment process. Again, the only way to save his proportionality theorem is, for Walras, to adopt a periodical market approach in which time periods (that is, days) are strictly theoretical[37] and do not reflect any real-world adjustments taking place in historical time.

[Il] reste à faire voir comment cette proportionnalité directe des prix à la quantité de la monnaie et cette proportionnalité inverse des prix à l'encaisse désirée tendent à se maintenir d'elles-mêmes sous le régime de la libre concurrence. (1889, p. 379; *OEC*, VIII, p. 460)

In a nutshell, the main tenor of Walras's 1889 presentation revolves around the inclusion of money into circulating capital. As shown earlier, money is conceived as a good yielding no utility in itself. However, by furnishing a *service d'approvisionnement* of an inventory nature, the possession of money allows agents (consumers and entrepreneurs alike) to order goods when there is a lack of synchronization during a given period between the receipt of income and its outlay. Agents equate the marginal utility of these services to that of all other goods to determine their net demand for cash balances. In equilibrium, the rate of interest on the money market (or alternatively as shown below the market for money-capital) being the price of holding *encaisses désirées* is equal to the net rate of return on all other assets.

The market on which the *tâtonnement* on the rate of interest is to be conducted has first to be clearly defined. Brushing aside ('for the sake of the pure theory of money') all differences between fixed and circulating capital,[38] Walras recalls his triple distinction between the market for capital goods, the market for *numéraire*-capital and the market for money-capital. So long as the theorist is abstracting from money, Walras entitles him to speak not of money-capital but of *numéraire*-capital. The capital goods market is the market where capital goods are theoretically bought and sold 'in kind'. From the point of view of 'practical convenience', capital goods are usually hired in the form of money-capital in the money market ('marché du capital') which is merely an annex to the service market. In other words, the rate of interest on circulating capital is the cost of the *service d'approvisionnement* of money just as it reflects the costs of the services of all fixed or circulating capital.

> Nous supposerons donc un seul marché que nous appellerons dorénavant *marché du capital monnaie* ... sur lequel les entrepreneurs viennent demander tous les jours de la monnaie en vue de constituer, compléter, entretenir leur capital fixe ... et leur capital circulant .... L'intérêt du capital circulant paie le **service** de la monnaie pendant qu'on la garde et celui [the service] des approvisionnements en matières premières et produits fabriqués, exactement comme l'intérêt du capital fixe paie le **service** des machines, instruments, outils. (1889, p. 380; *OEC*, VIII, pp. 462–4; italics in original, bold emphasis added)

This demand function is then generalized to include the *encaisses désirées* of all agents, producers, sellers of productive services as well as consumers to which is added the demand for money saving.

A hypothetical time-lag allegory has to be introduced at that stage to accommodate the circular flow of this stock of money with the purely static exchange, production and capital models. Walras submits a little parable about the working of the money market. The turnover of the given stock of (U) coincides exactly with a one-day period; in other words, at the end of the day (in the narrow sense of the word!) the entire stock of money flows back into the pockets in which it was originally kept:

> Nous supposerons donc les propriétaires fonciers, travailleurs et capitalistes venant tous les jours, comme les entrepreneurs, sur le marché du capital monnaie, demander la monnaie dont ils ont besoin pour constituer, compléter et entretenir leur capital fixe et circulant. Ils achèteront dans la journée avec leur monnaie les meubles, vêtements, objets d'art et de luxe et les objets de consommation à ce destinés; et les vendeurs rapporteront, eux aussi, le lendemain sur le marché la monnaie qu'ils auront reçue.

Qu'on joigne à cette double demande de monnaie celle qui sera faite par des créateurs d'épargnes en vue d'acheter des capitaux neufs pour les louer en nature, on aura la demande journalière de monnaie qui se fait sur le marché du capital monnaie. Et qu'on joigne la monnaie rapportée par les vendeurs de ces capitaux neufs à celle rapportée ... par tous les autres entrepreneurs qui l'auront reçue la veille en échange de produits et par tous les propriétaires fonciers, travailleurs et capitalistes qui l'auront reçue en échange de services, on aura l'offre journalière de monnaie, égale à la quantité existante de la monnaie, qui se fait sur le marché du capital monnaie. (1889, pp. 380–81; *OEC*, VIII, pp. 466–8)[39]

On this money market which is at the same time the market for money-capital, the *tâtonnement* is conducted on the rate of interest to adjust day after day the *encaisses désirées* to the supply of money-capital. The highly intuitive version of this blow-by-blow adjustment process on the money market is worth quoting in full:

Supposons qu'un jour la quantité existante de monnaie Q_u ait diminué ou que l'encaisse désirée H représentant l'utilité [du service] de la monnaie ait augmenté, après la détermination d'un taux courant de l'intérêt égal au taux du revenu net. L'équilibre ne s'établirait, le lendemain, sur le marché, qu'à un nouveau taux de l'intérêt plus élevé auquel l'encaisse désirée se réduirait. Mais, par suite de cette réduction de l'encaisse désirée, tous les prix [nominaux] des produits, capitaux, services et matières premières, baisseraient; par suite de cette baisse, l'encaisse désirée pourrait redevenir ce qu'elle était; et, le surlendemain, l'équilibre pourrait s'établir au taux courant de l'intérêt égal au taux du revenu net. (1889, p. 383; *OEC*, VIII, pp. 476–8)

The analytical rigour of the exchange–production–capital model is clearly in sharp contrast with this 'let us assume' *descriptive* account of how such a monetary *tâtonnement could* [40] take place in the 'real' world. The nagging suspicion about this schizophrenic antithesis is strengthened by three very revealing considerations made by Walras during the discussion of his *tâtonnement* process on the money market.

Foremost, Walras makes it explicitly clear that this *tâtonnement* process takes place on the *permanent* and not on the theoretical once-and-for-all market, or on the periodical market:

La demande journalière [de monnaie] qui se fait [sur le marché de la monnaie] n'est autre chose que la demande de cette fraction du capital fixe et du capital circulant de la société qui se renouvelle tous les jours, comme nous l'avons expliqué (§ 271) *en parlant du marché permanent*. (1889, p. 381; *OEC*, VIII, p. 470; italics added).

The *tâtonnement* process on the money market is clearly of a completely different nature from the timeless 'no trade out of equilibrium' method applied to 'real' markets. In fact, Walras uses here a dynamic succession of periodical disequilibrium situations (today, tomorrow, the day after tomorrow, and so on) framed into the historical time of a continuous market. In that respect, the reference to paragraph 271 (1889, pp. 316–17; *OEC*, VIII, pp. 579–80) is of crucial importance. Unchanged throughout all editions, this paragraph[41] specifies clearly (see above, Chapter 1, Section 3) that the adoption of the continuous market hypothesis coincides with a move 'from the static to the dynamic state' in which production and consumption 'hitherto represented as a constant magnitude for every moment of the year under consideration, change from instant to instant, along with the basic data of the problem' (1889, p. 316; *OEC*, VIII, p. 579; 1954, p. 380). Furthermore, the necessary congruence mentioned earlier between the periodical market and the quantity equation essential to the working of the proportionality theorem does not hold any longer on a permanent market where all data (and not only the money supply) are subject to changes.

In particular, and this is the second difficulty raised by Walras's *tâtonnement* process, it appears clearly from the penultimate quotation that the rate of interest on the money-capital/money market is fluctuating around a *fixed* rate of net return of the market for capital.[42] Again, this hypothesis – pivotal for the proportionality theorem – is not the least compatible with a *tâtonnement* taking place explicitly in a dynamic 'permanent' market in which all data are variables. Specifically, and as abundantly shown in Walras's forced saving argument, the rate of net return on capital (that is, the real rate of interest) is not inelastic to changes in the rate of interest on the money market.

Finally, the substitution effects introduced by Walras within the *encaisses désirées* between transaction and saving balances imply changes of all sorts to real variables (for example, propensity to save and growth rate of the economy) which are not compatible with the fixed data hypothesis linked to the instantaneous *tâtonnement* on the once-and-for-all market.

To crown his constant hesitation between a once-and-for-all market model necessary to the validity of his main static general equilibrium theorems and a dynamic *tâtonnement* on the money market in terms of interest rate, Walras refers readers interested in the 'détails multiples et complexes [de] ce mécanisme' to Walter Bagehot's *Lombard Street*. Hardly the best theoretical treatise on the existence and stability of a monetary equilibrium!

Having reached this stage of his argument, Walras then abruptly reverts to his purely static commodity-money analysis first introduced in 1872 and 1874. Since this 1889 version of this mechanism is only marginally different from the original statement, it is possible to be mercifully brief. It is, however, important to realize that this version will remain strictly *unchanged* in editions 2 to 5.[43]

One of the n commodities (A), chosen as money, is assumed to be endowed with both money and commodity uses. Q_a is the total existing quantity of this good (A), of which Q'_a is kept in the commodity form and $Q''_a = Q_a - Q'_a$ in the form of money. Equations (3.1) and (3.2) above are reworked as

$$Q''_a P_a = aP_a + b + cp_c + dp_d + \ldots + TP_t + \ldots + PP_p + \ldots$$
$$+KP_k + K'P_{k'} + K''P_{k''} + \ldots + tp_t + \ldots + pp_p + \ldots \qquad (3.4)$$
$$+kp_k + k'p_{k'} + k''p_{k''} + \ldots + mp_m + \ldots = H + a(P_a - p_a).$$

P_a is the price of (A), in terms of *numéraire* (B). (A) cannot be the *numéraire* since, in that case, it would be impossible to study the effect of changes in the price of money. P_a is written with a capital letter to differentiate it from p_a in equation (3.2) where money is a strictly fiat money. The *encaisses désirées H* are, of course, still exogenously given; that is, they are independent of P_a. Changing slightly his 1874 notation, Walras writes what he calls the equation of the demand curve for monetized (A),

$$q = \frac{H}{P} \qquad (3.5)$$

and the equation of the demand curve for (A), in its ordinary commodity use:

$$q = F_a(p). \qquad (3.6)$$

In a pq plane, and for the same reason as in the 1874 version, equation (3.5) *tends* 'si l'on néglige un terme négligeable'[44] to be a rectangular hyperbola, that is, this curve illustrates the inverse relation between the value of money and its quantity. In Walras's own terms:

> It is a curve such that the product of its ordinates, representing quantities of (A), in monetary use, multiplied by its abscissas, representing the corresponding prices of the monetised (A) in terms of (B), is a constant and is equal in magnitude to H, the *encaisses désirées* reckoned in terms of (B), which is assumed to be predetermined. (1889, p. 384; *OEC*, VIII, p. 482)

In the same pq plane, equation (3.6) is a straightforward downward sloping demand curve for commodity (A) in ordinary use. Adding the two demands, one gets the total demand for commodity (A) in both its uses as a commodity and as money. This curve is expressed in equation (3.7):

$$q = F_a(p) + \frac{H}{p}. \qquad (3.7)$$

As in 1874, Walras grandly concludes that these 'curves give effectually a geometric solution of the problem of the determination of: (1) the price of commodity money; (2) the quantity of (*A*) in commodity use; and (3) the quantity of (*A*) in monetary use' (1889, p. 385; *OEC*, VIII, p. 484).

Furthermore, and crowning this 'existence theorem', Walras even goes so far as to add his familiar leitmotiv about the selfsameness between the theoretical and the market solution to his equilibrium equation: 'This is precisely the solution which is reached by *tâtonnements* in the real world' (1889, p. 385; *OEC*, VIII, p. 484). Wishful thinking has never made good economic theory!

To recapitulate: even if, in 1889, Walras suggests a first *description* of an adjustment process on the money market involving the rate of interest, he has no *rationale* behind the *encaisses désirées*: they are what they are because they are what they are! In other words, how could one possibly devise a satisfactory stability analysis for an unspecified *exogenously posited* equilibrium? Such a procedure involves a head-on clash between the purely static general equilibrium model (exchange, production and capital formation) framed in a timeless once-and-for-all market and a dynamic adjustment process on the money market conducted under the so-called continuous market hypothesis. Finally, in the theory of the 'price of money', when reverting from a fiat-money to a commodity-money analysis, Walras again falls victim to a purely static quantity theory failing completely to offer a proper stability analysis of the equilibrium absolute price level. In a nutshell: in 1889, Walras submits no choice-theoretic underpinning to the individual demand for money and thus leaves the determination of the price level indeterminate.

2.3 Towards the 'Equations de la Circulation'

The decade[45] following the publication of the second edition witnessed no real progress in Walras's monetary theory. Nevertheless, spread throughout various articles and sundry writings, some components of Walras's 1899 'Equations de la circulation' are begining to emerge. In parallel, and sometimes in the same articles, variations on the forced saving period analysis are suggested in Walras's various contributions to applied economics.[46] However important this accretion phenomenon may look retrospectively, during this decade (at least up until the winter of 1898), Walras was certainly more interested in demonstrating once again his quantity equation than in making room for money in the agents' utility functions. However, it should appear no less clearly that these lengthy, and often clumsy manipulations of a cash-balance equation and exogenously given *encaisses désirées* were the necessary prelude to a first attempt at integrating monetary theory into a pre-existing theory of value.

There is no definite indication of the date on which Walras started to revise his monetary framework. Certainly not before 1896, since the relevant 1889 chapters are reproduced verbatim in the 1896 third edition of the *Eléments*. Furthermore, busy working simultaneously on the *Etudes d'économie sociale* also published in 1896, Walras had probably little time for such a thorough and sustained analytical work. Leaving aside various articles on the Indian currency problem, bimetallism and other policy issues,[47] the 'Note sur la théorie de la quantité' (1897) is the first indication that Walras had decided to go back to monetary theory.

This 'Note' has a curious history. Originally written in the summer of 1897 for the American Economic Association, it was never published[48] in English and was eventually added to the *Etudes d'économie politique appliquée* (1898). The correspondence exchanged between Walras, Fisher and Taussig (Walras, 1965, II, pp. 759–62 and III, pp. 4–5) reveals that Walras spontaneously offered his 'Note' under the impression that this would lead the American economists to adhere to mathematical economics.[49] Once again, Walras was convinced that his pure economics and his monetary theory would stand or fall together. Some American economists having apparently shown an interest in his various schemes of monetary reform,[50] Walras was clearly hoping to gain new converts to mathematical economics through the back door of monetary theory:

> J'ai la conviction que la méthode mathématique peut seule faire cesser ces derniers et légers dissentiments [on monetary reform], et je vais l'employer encore une fois pour identifier de telle sorte la théorie de la quantité avec la théorie de la rareté qu'il faille renverser celle-ci pour avoir le droit de nier la première. (1898, p. 153; *OEC*, X, p. 146)

And Walras adds that the notion of *encaisse désirée* is by far the most convenient way to define the marginal utility of money:

> 'Il s'agit ... de dégager et de mettre en évidence ce qu'on pourra appeler le *degré final d'utilité* ... ou la *rareté* de la monnaie. Et c'est ce que permet de faire aisément la considération de l'encaisse désirée' (1898, p. 153; *OEC*, X, p. 146).

Unfortunately, the core of the 'Note' does not live up to expectations. Not only does Walras stick to his previous definition of *encaisses désirées*, but he also uses marginal-utility analysis to validate the quantity theory in the case of a money which is also a commodity. The algebraic demonstration follows the *Théorie de la monnaie* with one single novelty taken over from the second edition of the *Eléments*: the proportions $\alpha, \beta, \gamma, \delta$ of the values of the respective goods and services agents wish to hold in money, that is, the *encaisses désirées* are given parameters of the model *at a given interest rate i*.[51] The opportunity cost of the *service d'approvisionnement* is for the first time formally linked to the size of the *encaisses désirées* but, *i* being exogenously given, both variables are eventually left unexplained. Hence, Walras's proportionality theorem is vindicated: the marginal utility of money is inversely related to its quantity.

Allowing for the possibility of adding paper money and 'compensation' to his commodity money, Walras reworks and develops the argument first offered in the preface of the *Théorie de la monnaie*. Such a complication leaves unchanged the comparative static conclusions of his quantity theory. With or without paper money and/or 'compensation', the marginal utility of commodity money, and hence the price of this commodity money is inversely related to its quantity. Not a very original conclusion or a particularly eloquent explanation of the dynamic process leading from one position of equilibrium to the next! The reader is not even referred to the forced saving demonstration of TMBB.

The first edition of the *Etudes d'économie politique appliquée* and the editing process leading to this publication in August 1898 compelled Walras to revisit his *Théorie de la monnaie* and certain applied texts in monetary theory which he wanted to include in this volume.[52] Eventually, reactions to this volume, notably from Wicksell, set Walras on the road to a complete overhaul of his monetary theory.

The textual alterations brought to the analytical paragraphs 8 to 10 reflect more an exercise in merging the original text with fragments taken over from the second edition of the *Eléments* and the 'Note sur la Théorie de la quantité' than an attempt at rethinking anew the whole argument. No theoretical advance is in sight. The cost of the *service d'approvisionnement* rendered by the *encaisses désirées* is clearly expressed by the rate of interest; but the size of these desired cash balances is still exogenously given; there is no retroaction of the *tâtonnement* on the money market on the other markets which, mysteriously remain in equilibrium and the quantity equation is set for a case in which money is also a commodity. The crucial new paragraphs run as follows:

When a landowner, worker, capitalist or entrepreneur desires to have in his possession, at a given moment, a certain store of ... money, it is evident that he is not concerned with the [nominal] quantity of this money, but only with the quantity of goods, commodities or services, that he wants to buy with it. In other words, the need one has for money is nothing but the need one has for goods that one will buy with this money. This need stems from the necessity for storage [*besoin d'approvisionnement*]; it is satisfied at the cost of interest, and that is why the effective demand for money is a decreasing function of the rate of interest.

Let a general equilibrium be established on the basis of $1, p_b, p_c, p_d, \ldots$ prices of $(A),(B),(C),(D)\ldots$ in terms of (A) which is already the *numéraire* and should become money. Let i be the rate of interest. And let $\alpha, \beta, \gamma, \delta$ be the respective quantities of $(A),(B),(C),(D)\ldots$ that consumers and producers would like to buy in order to maintain their fixed and circulating capital at this given rate [of interest]. Then the quantity of money

$$H_a = \alpha + \beta p_b + \gamma p_c + \delta p_d + \ldots$$

would be the *encaisse désirée*. (1898, pp. 94–5; *OEC*, X, pp. 86–7)

As mentioned earlier, a few days after publication, Walras sent Wicksell a copy of his *Etudes* for review. If Wicksell's article appeared only in December 1899 and was centred on Walras's applied scheme and his forced saving argument,[53] the correspondence between the two men is of interest more for Walras's answers on his theory of money than for Wicksell's queries. Referring to his own *Interest and Prices*, Wicksell assures Walras that his monetary 'theory can be considered more or less as a derivation from yours'. Always worried about possible misinterpretations, Walras, however, deems it necessary to make sure that, in view of the planned book review, Wicksell has properly understood the essence of his pure theory of money. Accordingly, by return of post, Walras provides his correspondent with the clearest summary so far of his pure theory of money as of August 1898: 'Ma théorie *pure* de la monnaie est assez simplement résumée dans l'Etude sur la *Caisse de Vienne* [54] aux lignes 8–20 de la page 378 [*OEC*, X, pp. 344–5] dans l'équation du bas de la page 388 [p. 353] et aux pages 390–1 [pp. 355–6] (1965, III, p. 32).

The first excerpt sets the problem in terms of exogenously given *encaisses désirées* as parts of the agents' circulating capital and providing a *service d'approvisionnement*. Money is clearly seen as a reserve bridging through time possible discrepancies between payments and receipts. The time structure of the model is still very vague: nothing is said about the length of the period during which money is to be held against such possible contingencies; besides, are there other contingencies? Are there other occasions for uncertainty? Do the agents hold money out of choice or out of the necessity to replenish their stocks in the future with an already known quantity of goods? Walras is still clearly light years from his articulate final monetary model.

Tout être économique est consommateur et doit avoir, en cette qualité, un fonds de roulement comprenant des approvisionnements en objets de consommation *et la monnaie* nécessaire pour renouveler ces approvisionnements au fur et à mesure qu'ils s'épuisent en attendant les rentrées en salaires, fermages et intérêts. Un certain nombre d'êtres économiques sont entrepreneurs et doivent avoir, à ce titre, un fonds de roulement comprenant des approvisionnements en matières premières, des produits fabriqués en vente à l'étalage *et la monnaie* nécessaire pour payer les services producteurs et pour renouveler les approvisionnements en matières premières au fur et à mesure qu'ils disparaissent en attendant les rentrées en paiement de produits vendus. (1898, p. 378; *OEC*, X, pp. 344–5; italics added)

The second excerpt recalls Walras's crucial *equilibrium* equation of the demand for fiat money (U):

Soit (U) une chose quelconque, inutile par elle-même, existant seulement en quantité déterminée Q_u, et susceptible par cela même de servir de numéraire et de monnaie. Soient, à l'état d'équilibre de la production et de l'échange ... $\alpha, \beta, \gamma, \delta$ ... les quantités de $(A),(B),(C),(D)$... dont les producteurs et consommateurs désirent avoir en caisse la représentation en monnaie, la valeur v_u de la monnaie (U) sera déterminée par l'équation d'équilibre de la circulation.

$$Q_u v_u = \alpha v_a + \beta v_b + \gamma v_c + \delta v_d + ...$$

(1898, p. 388; *OEC*, X, p. 353)

The text of Walras's letter to Wicksell reworks this equation and formulates with great clarity the *consecutive tâtonnement* processes on the money and real markets following a change in the supply of (U): a first *tâtonnement* in the money market determines the equilibrium rate of interest (which makes its first appearance); this first adjustment process then reacts back on the equilibrium initially achieved on the other markets where a second *tâtonnement* takes place in order to determine the new set of equilibrium nominal prices:

Puisque vous êtes mathématicien, il me semble que vous ne devez avoir aucune peine à comprendre qu'étant donnée l'équation

$$Q_u = \alpha p_a + \beta p_b + \gamma p_c + \delta p_d + ...$$

dans laquelle $Q_u, p_a, p_b, p_c, p_d, ...$ sont déterminés, et $\alpha, \beta, \gamma, \delta$ ... sont des fonctions de i, on arrive d'abord à une *première* détermination de $\alpha, \beta, \gamma, \delta$ ... par la variation de i, puis ensuite à une *seconde* détermination de ces mêmes quantités par la variation proportionnelle de $p_a, p_b, p_c, p_d, ...$ Cette seconde détermination se fait sur le grand marché de services et de produits. Quant à la première elle se fait sur le marché où le capital monnaie se prête à courte échéance. (1965, III, p. 32; italics added)

Finally, the third excerpt summarizes in a very intuitive way the definition of a monetary equilibrium and the adjustment process linking two such equilibrium positions. After all, there is no dichotomy in the pricing process; there are market forces which bring back real balances to their original level and, this time, the absolute level of money prices is determinate:

> Théoriquement, la monnaie, réelle ou fictive, existe journellement sur le marché, entre les mains des détenteurs, comme un capital dont le service est demandé suivant une courbe décroissante et offert suivant une courbe successivement croissante et décroissante en fonction du prix de ce service qui est le taux de l'intérêt. Le prix d'équilibre est celui d'égalité de l'offre effective et de la demande effective. A ce prix, la monnaie se partage entre les consommateurs et les producteurs; ce qui ne va pas aux uns va aux autres ... Mais ces transactionneurs ont basé leur demande ou leur offre sur l'utilité du service, c'est-à-dire sur l'approvisionnement de marchandises que représentait l'approvisionnement de monnaie en raison des prix de ces marchandises résultant d'une certaine quantité existante de monnaie. *Si cette quantité a varié d'un jour à l'autre, entre les mains des détenteurs, pour équilibrer l'offre et la demande, après la variation, il a fallu une baisse du taux de l'intérêt en cas d'augmentation, une hausse en cas de diminution. Les échangeurs ont ainsi augmenté ou diminué leur encaisse désirée; mais quand ils vont ensuite sur le marché des produits et des services ... ils ne trouvent toujours que la même quantité de toutes ces marchandises, et c'est alors qu'ils font la hausse ou la baisse des prix en raison de l'augmentation ou de la diminution dans la quantité de l'instrument d'échange.* Telle est la théorie de la monnaie. (1898, 390–91; *OEC*, X, pp. 355–6; italics added)[55]

Clearly, for the first and last time, Walras offers here the embryo of an explanation about the agents' behaviour when faced with, say, a doubling of their *encaisses désirées*[56] following a drop in the rate of interest resulting from a doubling of the money supply on the money market. After the quantity of money supply has been doubled, there exists *at the current price level* an excess supply of money: there is a real-balance effect in the money market. At these nominal prices, the agents' real-money holdings are twice as high as in the original equilibrium position. But an excess supply of money means an excess demand for commodities. People plan a *flow* of extra expenditures because they feel their *stock* of money is too high. Therefore, at the current price level Walras shows clearly that there are pressures in the markets for goods and services to drive up the price level, and hence drive down the value of money until real balances are back to their desired level.

In other words, and to paraphrase Walras's summary:

- an increase in the supply of money disturbs the optimum relation between the *encaisses désirées* and the agents' expenditures;
- this disturbance generates an increase in the planned volume of their expenditures on the commodity market (a real-balance effect);
- this increase creates upward pressures on the price level until it has risen in the same proportion as the quantity of money;

- the vector of relative prices determined on the commodity market remains unchanged: money is neutral.

Walras considers that, accordingly, his *équation de la quantité* is vindicated. However, and despite the vividness of this *intuitive description*, his argument falls well short of a full-blooded analysis of the stability of a monetary equilibrium; let alone of a theoretically rationalized integration of money into value theory via the utility function. In fact, in 1898, this task still lies in front of Walras. However, and faithful to the strictly static approach of his general equilibrium, Walras's only attempt to solve an issue central to the internal consistency of his model will be achieved at the cost of emasculating money of most of its functions and depriving it finally of its *raison d'être*.

Giving up completely the main intuition behind this mere description of the real-balance effect, in 1899, Walras switched to a completely different (and static) approach to money in a model characterized by the introduction of money into the utility function and by decision-taking under certainty. Accordingly, Chapter 4 is entirely devoted to this ultimate 1899–1900 monetary model.

NOTES

1. The first two parts of Walras's *Théorie de la monnaie* were first published in the *Revue scientifique*, 37, April 1886. In June 1886, Walras adds to the offprint of his article an Introduction, in which he answers some of his critics. With the addition of a Preface and of Part III, the *Théorie de la monnaie* appears in bookform in November of the same year. This last version (with substantial alterations in Part I) is eventually republished in *Etudes d'économie politique appliquée* (1898). In Chapter 3, Section 1, references are made to the original 1886 volume and to *OEC*, X, pp. 57–145 where all textual variations are carefully recorded.

   A year earlier, Launhardt had devoted a chapter of his *Mathematische Begründung* (1885a, pp. 140–48) and a 75-page leaflet (1885b) to monetary theory. Presented earlier by Walras with a copy of *Théorie mathématique de la richesse sociale*, Launhardt sent in return his two publications. Excited first at the idea of breaking into the 'German market', Walras retreated rapidly when faced with Launhardt's anti-quantity theory approach and his quasi-Marshallian trick of positing a constant marginal utility for money: 'Nous appliquons tous deux la méthode mathématique, mais il se trouve que notre conception du système des faits économiques est très différente, de sorte que nous aboutissons à des conclusions tout à fait opposées. Nous ne pouvons évidemment songer à nous convertir l'un l'autre. ... Heureux celui d'entre nous qui sera reconnu être économiste autant que mathématicien' (Walras, 1965, II, p. 131; see also pp. 78 and 192–3). Apart from his failure to set up a network of mathematical economists in Germany, and in ways similar to those experienced during his dispute with Edgeworth, Walras begins (already!) to realize that a common mathematical language is not enough to sort out disagreements on the 'system of economic facts'. On Launhardt's weak monetary theory, see Del Vecchio (1933, pp. 665–71) and Niehans (1987, pp. 141–42).

2.   The references are given by Walras in the introduction to the *Théorie* (1886, pp. 3–6; *OEC*, X, pp. 63–5: 'Les erreurs du système monétaire français' (1867); 'Des billets de banque en Suisse' (1871); 'Note sur le 15 1/2 légal' (1876); 'Théorie mathématique du bimétallisme' (1881); 'De la fixité de valeur de l'étalon monétaire' (1882); 'Théorie mathématique du billet de banque (1880); 'Monnaie d'or avec billon d'argent régulateur' (1884); and 'D'une méthode de régularisation de la valeur de la monnaie' (1885).

3.   See, for example, *Correspondence* (1965, II, p. 93) and *Théorie de la monnaie* (1886, pp. 21–2, 57 and 83–4; *OEC*, X, pp. 74–5, 101, 116–7.

4.   Jevons and Marshall are the best examples of famous theorists investing tremendous amounts of energy in devising similar monetary schemes to stabilize prices.

5.   *Correspondence* (1965, II, p. 254). In the same letter to Gide, Walras links explicitly this main 'thesis' to Smith and to 'les économistes [qui] l'ont produite il y a quelque cent ans'. However, Walras hastens to add that 'toute mon ambition a été de donner à cette thèse une valeur qu'elle n'a jamais eue en la *démontrant* scientifiquement' (italics added).

6.   Quite independently from Marshall (and much later Keynes and Robertson) Walras makes use of the same analogy with the 'ebb and flow' of the 'economic tide' to illustrate the inevitability, even the necessity, of ʊⁱ⁰ᵘᵇᵘⁱ Oₙ ₜₕᵢₛ fᵢⁿᵐᵘₗₐₜᵢₒₙ ₛₑₑ ₐₗₛₒ Jₐₗᵢₙₖ (1994).

7.   On Walras as a monetary activist see Jaccoud (1994).

8.   Not surprisingly, this trilogy is common to most, if not all monetary economists, at least down to Keynes's *Treatise on Money*: a pure theory linked to some version of the quantity theory more or less satisfactorily connected with price theory; lengthy discussions on the choice of the best index numbers to estimate changes in the price level; and eventually, the economic policy propositions to implement price stability.

9.   Or, alternatively and once again, Walras uses the water-level analogy made in the lesson of the *Eléments* devoted to the continuous market (1954, p. 380): 'le monde économique oscille perpétuellement sans jamais l'atteindre, comme un lac autour de l'horizontalité de son niveau' (1886, p. 28; *OEC*, X, p. 79).

10. See also a similar statement in a letter addressed to del Pezzo (Walras, 1965, II, p. 73).

11. See above, Chapter 1, Section 1.

12. See above, Chapter 1, Section 2.

13. In the words of the Preface to the 1900 fourth edition of the *Eléments*: 'In the first edition, this solution [of the problem of the value of money], was founded on the consideration of the "circulation to be cleared" [*circulation à desservir*] which I had borrowed from the economists. In the second and subsequent editions, however, I based the solution on the concept of the "desired cash balance" [*encaisse désirée*] which I had already used in my *Théorie de la monnaie*' (1954, p. 38; *OEC*, VIII, p. 9; see also Patinkin, 1965, pp. 542–3 for a discussion of Jaffé's translation of this particular passage). In 1900, Walras was in fact suffering from a delusion extremely common among scientists when reflecting on their scientific achievements: they frequently overestimate their theoretical precociousness! In fact the first mention of the concept of *encaisses désirées* appears in the second 1889 edition of the *Eléments* (1889, pp. ix–x; *OEC*, VIII, p. 6) *but still without any attempt to integrate money into the utility function*: the terminology is coined in fact ten years before the 1900 utility-maximization analysis. To be absolutely fair to Walras, one has to admit the presence of the expression *encaisses désirées* in the final 1898 reprint of *Théorie monétaire* in *Etudes d'économie politique appliquée* (see, for example, *OEC*, X, pp. 87 and 89); but, once again, as in TMBB, the introduction of these crucial words is not yet connected with any type of utility-maximization analysis: the demand function for money is based on considerations extraneous to Walras's main general equilibrium argument. As will be made abundantly clear in Chapter 4, Walras's first attempt to bridge that gap in order to integrate money in the utility function coincides with the publication of his 1899 memoir on 'Equations de la circulation'.

14. Expressions that could be translated as *balances, cash balances* and *equilibrium balances*.
15. See, however, above p. 28 and below p. 154 for the unessential introduction of banknotes and other fiat money in this equation.
16. By replacing this vector of nominal prices with a price index weighted by the quantities $\alpha, \beta, \gamma, \delta \ldots$ the connection with a straightforward Cambridge equation would be obvious.
17. In other words that $Q_a = Q'_a/n + \alpha/n + \beta p_b/n + \gamma p_c/n + \delta p_d/n + \ldots$
18. After all, the very word is present!
19. Implicitly contained in the hypotheses mentioned above.
20. See above Chapter 1, Section 1.
21. Already used in 1874 to represent the *circulation à desservir*, H reappears here for the first time to express the *encaisses monétaires* made up of Q''_a and C (for compensation).
22. In his review of *Théorie de la monnaie*, Lexis casts doubts on the use of what he calls such an abstract quantity theory of money. Prices might vary proportionately with the quantity of money, but only if all other quantities and relationships remain constant. In reality, other things do not remain equal because they are intimately linked with changes in the quantity of money (1886, p. 115). In his answer to Lexis, Walras has no other solution but to resort to the purely comparative static version of his quantity equation: 'je connais ... toute la "Verwickelte Mannigfaltigkeit" des phénomènes économiques dans la réalité. Mais je ne vois pas que cette circonstance nous interdise absolument d'en faire la théorie exacte ... S'il est vrai que, *toutes choses égales d'ailleurs*, les prix haussant ou baissant proportionnellement à l'argent, on le doit à la quantité de la monnaie, il s'ensuit qu'on peut *à un moment donné* agir sur le niveau général des prix en agissant sur la quantité de la monnaie' (Walras, 1965, II, p. 145; italics added).
23. For various reasons (explained at length by the editor of the variorum edition of the *Eléments, OEC*, VIII, p. 809), the second and third editions are for our purposes practically identical. As far as Part V is concerned, Lessons 33 to 36 on the so-called pure theory of money from the second edition are left rigorously unchanged in the third edition. As far as the applied theory is concerned, Lessons 37 to 40 are simply eliminated and moved to the 1898 *Etudes d'économie politique appliquée*.
24. The first mentions of these very words occur in the second edition (1889, pp. ix, 378–9, 381–3; *OEC*, VIII, pp. 6, 456, 460, 468, 472, 476 and 478).
25. See above, Chapter 3, Section 1.
26. 'Monnaie de circulation ou d'épargne' (1889, p. 376; *OEC*, VIII, p. 442) translated as 'money [earmarked] for transactions or investment [purposes]' by Schumpeter (1954, pp. 1000, n. 5 and 1023) and Patinkin (1965, p. 553) and 'cash or money savings' by Jaffé (in Walras, 1954, pp. 321).
27. See Kuenne (1963, pp. 311–25); Patinkin (1965, pp. 546–8); Jaffé (1980, pp. 361–4); Walker (1987a, pp. 858–9).
28. As far as capital formation is concerned, the 'tâtonnement sur bons' appears in 1899 only. The technique used by Walras to avoid the consequence of disequilibrium production in the first three editions is less elegant but leads to the same as-if *ab ovo* equilibrium result (1889, pp. 234–5; *OEC*, VIII, p. 308).
29. See above, the analysis in Chapter 1, Section 2, which was kept intact in all editions.
30. '[D]ans les conditions *précédemment* définies d'équilibre de l'échange, de la production et de la capitalisation' (1889, p. 378; *OEC*, VIII, p. 454; italics added).
31. As a result of the shift of the theory of money from Part III to Part V, the demand functions for money of the *Théorie de la monnaie* are generalized to include the *encaisses désirées* of producers and sellers of productive services, as well as of consumers.
32. $(A),(B),(C)$ are defined as consumer goods; $(T)...(P)...(K),(K'),(K'')$ as 'capital goods' and 'services'; and $(M),(M')$ as raw materials. Their prices are all equilibrium prices in terms of B and i is the equilibrium rate of net return for all capital goods and, of course, the rate of interest.

33. See above, Chapter 1, Section 2.
34. '[E]t enfin on aurait l'équilibre de la circulation, vu que les échangeurs auraient l'encaisse désirée au taux de l'intérêt annoncé' (1889, p. 379; *OEC*, VIII, p. 460).
35. '[S]upposons qu'un jour la quantité existante de monnaie Q_a ait diminué ou que l'encaisse désirée H représentant l'utilité de la monnaie ait augmenté, après la détermination d'un taux courant de l'intérêt égal au taux du revenu net. L'équilibre ne s'établirait, le lendemain, sur le marché, qu'à un nouveau taux de l'intérêt plus élevé auquel l'encaisse désirée se réduirait. Mais, par suite de cette réduction de l'encaisse désirée, tous les prix ... baisseraient; par suite de cette baisse, l'encaisse désirée pourrait redevenir ce qu'elle était; et le surlendemain, l'équilibre pourrait s'établir au taux courant de l'intérêt égal au taux du revenu net' (1889, p. 383; *OEC*, VIII, pp. 476 and 478).
36. Notably the competitive equilibrium assumption and the crucial supposition that money is introduced in the model when the vector of relative prices on all other markets has *already* been determined (hence the classical dichotomy and the indeterminacy of the price level).
37. See above Chapter 1, Section 3, for a detailed discussion of Walras's notion of periodical market.
38. The former is only partly – and the latter wholly – hired in money. In his demonstration, Walras considers that both are entirely hired in the form of money.
39. For a similar text used to describe a real-world money market in an applied economic context, see *OEC*, X, p. 168.
40. The whole passage is written in the conditional tense.
41. Characteristically, in the second and third editions of the *Eléments*, this paragraph 271 appears well *before* the lesson on the pure theory of money (paras 319–25). That, in the fourth edition, this (unchanged) paragraph is relegated *after* the section on money seems to indicate again Walras's ambivalent attitude about the role of money in his general equilibrium model. As readily shown, in 1889 and 1896, and despite claims to the contrary, Walras seems to consider money as a mere add-on appendage to his model. In 1900, his attempt at forcing money into this static model without, however, changing anything to its time structure, is hardly satisfactory from an analytical point of view. This difficult issue is discussed in detail in Chapter 4, Section 1 below.
42. See also 1889, p. 381; *OEC*, VIII, pp. 470–72 for similar evidence: 'ces deux taux tendent à l'égalité par la raison que, suivant que le premier est supérieur ou inférieur au second, les créateurs d'épargnes et les emprunteurs ont également intérêt à laisser ou à prendre du capital monnaie sur le marché'
43. As shown below, this procedure introduces a contradiction in the fourth edition where H is, in the same Lesson 30, both endogenously and exogenously determined.
44. 1889, p. 384; *OEC*, VIII, p. 481. Actually, as it is abundantly shown above in Chapter 1, Section 2, this demand curve for money is in fact a market-equilibrium demand curve for money. Since, for Walras, a is very small, the term $a(P_a - p_a)$ is negligible in equation (3.4); that is, the proportion of the value of the demand for (A) in its uses as a commodity agents wish to hold in money is, according to Walras, realistically (?) insignificant.
45. Besides retiring from his chair in 1892, moving twice, losing his mother, suffering from rapidly deteriorating health, publishing nearly twenty articles, bringing to the press the third edition of the *Eléments* and his two volumes of *Etudes* (1896 and 1898), Walras kept an extraordinarily busy correspondence with all the great theorists of the day. In particular, he took a crucial part in the famous (and heated) debate on the marginal productivity theory of distribution involving Wicksteed, Pareto, Barone, Clark, Wicksell and, of course, the 'pauvre M. Edgeworth' (see Jaffé (1964) for an excellent introduction to this famous quarrel).
46. As argued earlier, the convention of disregarding articles/contributions devoted to reforms of the monetary system and index number issues is upheld in this chapter, unless, of course, arguments relevant to monetary theory *stricto sensu* are offered therein by Walras.

47. See the relevant years in Walker's bibliography (Walker, 1987c).
48. For a detailed history of this 'Note', see the editor's footnotes in *OEC*, X, pp. 464–7. Irving Fisher and William Taussig were involved in Walras's failed attempt to have his text published in the AEA's *Economic Studies*.
49. 'Et, pour aider à ce mouvement, j'adresse aujourd'hui au ... président de la "American Economic Association" ... une 'Note' *sur la "théorie de la quantité"*' (Walras, 1965, II, p. 760).
50. See the various references in the first paragraph of his 'Note' (1898, p. 153; OEC, X, p. 146).
51. $\alpha, \beta, \gamma, \delta$ are nevertheless considered as decreasing functions of i (*OEC*, X, p. 147).
52 In particular, the 'Théorie mathématique du billet de banque' and the 'Caisse d'épargne postale de Vienne et le comptabilisme social' (see *OEC*, X, pp. 311–61).
53. See above, Chapter 2, Section 2.
54. This article published in the March 1898 issue of the *Revue d'économie politique* has already been mentioned earlier in connection with the theory of forced saving.
55. In his answer, Wicksell quotes approvingly the passage in italics and concludes: 'C'est presque mot pour mot ma théorie' (Walras, 1965, III, p. 39). Wicksell's only reservation (and thus the word 'presque') is connected with what will later be called the trailing rate doctrine of interest. Walras is simply chided here by Wicksell for concentrating exclusively on changes in the money-market rate of interest to the detriment of changes in the 'real' rate of interest: 'selon moi, c'est dans le plus grand nombre des cas la variation même du taux de l'intérêt *naturel* ... qui sont [sic!] la cause du changement des prix' (Walras, 1965, III, p. 40). In other words, the gap between real and money rates of interest which initiates changes in the price level is for Wicksell the result of the bank rate always trailing behind changes in the real rate of return; and not, as for Walras, the result of a deliberate decision of banks to modulate their money/credit supply. This is none other than an important component of Wicksell's cumulative process outlined a few *months* earlier in *Interest and Prices*.
56. The validity of this conclusion clearly depends on the assumption discussed at length in Chapter 2, Section 2, that agents' initial money holdings are all doubled *in the same proportion*.

4. The Last Monetary Model (1899–1900), or the Ultimate Triumph of Internal Consistency

> We shall see in this fourth edition how the inclusion of the '*encaisse désirée*' made it possible for me to state and solve the problem [of circulation and money] within this *static* framework in exactly the same terms and in precisely the same way as I solved the preceding problems. L. Walras, September 1900 (1954, p. 42; original italics)

In order to put in perspective the fundamental and final revision of his theory of money, Walras offers in the preface to the fourth edition of his *Eléments*, a particularly lucid overview of his thirty-year theoretical evolution:

> Chiefly, however, it was my theory of money that underwent the most important changes as a result of my research on the subject from 1876 to 1899. In the first and second editions [of the *Eléments*] the Lessons on money were made up partly of pure theory, and partly of applied theory; but the latter having been eliminated from the third and fourth editions I shall speak only of the former, and particularly of the underlying idea of this theory, namely, the solution of the problem of the value of money. In the first edition, this solution was founded on a consideration of the *circulation à desservir*, which I had borrowed from the economists. In the second and subsequent editions, however, I based the solution on the concept of *encaisse désirée* ... Nevertheless, I continued in the second and third editions, as in the first, to write the equation of offer and demand for money apart from the other equations and as empirically given. In the present edition this equation is deduced rationally from the equations of exchange and maximum satisfaction as well as from the equations showing equality between the demand and offer of circulating capital goods. (1954, p. 38)

Of course, such a procedure – if successful – would allow Walras to fulfil a lifelong dream by eventually closing his general equilibrium system:

> In this way, the *theory of circulation and money*, like the *theories of exchange, production, capital formation and credit*, not only posits, but solves the relevant system of equations. The six Lessons in which this theory is developed give the solution of the fourth major problem of pure economics, that of circulation. (1954, pp. 38–9; original italics)

This chapter is devoted entirely to a careful assessment of Walras's claim to have eventually found room for money in the agents' utility functions. This is a difficult and hazardous junction. While early developments of Walras's monetary theory have raised little interest outside a small band of historians of thought, the ultimate 1900 monetary model has been, and still is, regularly (re)visited by modern economists.[1] It is after all the first genuine attempt to explain the still unsolved riddle of the positive marginal utility of money.[2] The size of the literature directly, or much more important, indirectly inspired by Walras's last monetary model is enormous. Interpretations vary, of course, from one extreme to the other. Victims of a disease well known to historians of thought, many commentators, critics or contemporary economists are understandably more interested in calling the blessing of the founding father of general equilibrium on their own nth reformulation of his model rather than in actually trying to understand what exactly Walras's intentions were. Proceeding sometimes blissfully unaware of what Walras's primary aim was in building his general equilibrium, some of them feel genuinely surprised not to find their favourite argument in the *Eléments*: how could one expect to get a correct answer from a model devised to tackle a question other than that being asked?[3] Given the crucial part played by general equilibrium in modern economic theory, it might not be completely pointless to grapple again with this problem. In particular, and this is one of the central conjectures of this chapter, the extremely restrictive (static) conditions under which Walras manages to include a transaction demand for money in the utility function, if properly understood, should have warned subsequent authors against any deceptively simple dynamic solution to the frightfully difficult issue of 'money and general equilibrium'. Walras clearly left gaping holes in his monetary theory but, at least, held insights about the limits and the relevance of his model several orders more profound than most of his successors[4] and recent critics.

As discussed in Chapter 3, Section 2, Walras started to revise his monetary framework during the winter of 1898–99. Little evidence to document this crucial period is left. Besides the 'Equations de la circulation', the summary written for the *Giornale degli Economisti* (*OEC*, XI, pp. 583–8) and Lessons 29 and 30 of the fourth edition of the *Eléments*, only a handful of letters to various correspondents refer to the theoretical 'crowning' of his model by a sixty-five-year-old sick man.[5]

In this correspondence, one main theme of crucial importance to this transition period is worth mentioning. On several occasions, Walras maintains with insistence that his general equilibrium is a purely *static* theory of relative prices. For example, referring Hermann Laurent to his 1899 article, Walras asserts that his pure theory of money has brought 'la statique économique jusqu'aux confins de la dynamique' but not beyond (1965, III, p. 80). Similarly, in a letter to Montemartini, Walras describes his new monetary section as marking the boundary between economic static and the dynamics of the *marché permanent* (1965, III, p. 86). Winiarsky is equally informed that in the fourth edition 'la théorie monétaire viendra s'intercaler entre les *Lois d'établissement et de variation du prix des capitaux* et le tableau du *Marché permanent*, toute la dynamique ... étant ainsi nettement rejetée après la statique' (1965, III, p. 89; original italics). The clearest mention of this distinction, and by far the most relevant for monetary theory, is worth quoting in full:

> Dans quelques semaines, j'aurai refait la 33è leçon[6] de mes *Eléments d'économie politique pure* ... en introduisant les équations rigoureuses de l'encaisse désirée et du capital circulant dans le système des équations de l'équilibre général. J'aurai ainsi complètement achevé la **statique économique**, c'est-à-dire que j'aurai complètement résolu le problème qui consiste, en partant de certaines *utilités* et de certaines *quantités possédées* de toutes les espèces de la richesse [including money] pour et par un certain nombre d'échangeurs, à établir rationnellement un équilibre complet de la société économique **à un moment donné**. (1965, III, p. 66; original italics; bold emphasis added. See also pp. 43 and 80)

This hypothesis will be of pivotal importance when examining in Sections 1 and 2 the conceptual framework and the working of the *équations de la circulation*, their connection with the simultaneous appearance of the *tâtonnement sur bons* in the capital market and the all important reassessment of the time structure of the *Eléments*. That Walras eventually went as far as possible in a purely static framework to take account of the positive value of money while resisting all temptations to dynamize his system has been misunderstood for too long. The consequences of such a misinterpretation are far-reaching for Walras's monetary theory as well as for a proper grasp of the stringent limits of his static general equilibrium model. A more circumspect reading of Walras's intentions would probably have saved many critics, followers and recent theorists from the highly disappointing results reached after a century of toil and labour, particularly in the fields of stability analysis and monetary theory.

1   THE CONCEPTUAL FRAMEWORK OF THE 'EQUATIONS DE LA CIRCULATION': MONEY, UNSYNCHRONIZED EXCHANGE, DECISION-TAKING UNDER CERTAINTY AND THE '*TÂTONNEMENTS* SUR BONS'

To understand in Section 2, below, the strictly technical problems raised by Walras's avowed intention to include money into his equilibrium equation system, it is necessary to examine first and foremost the alterations brought in 1899–1900 to the conceptual framework and time structure of his model as well as the links established with capital theory and the *tâtonnements sur bons*. After some general introductory comments (Section 1.1), the three components of this conceptual framework are examined in turn (Section 1.2).

1.1 Preliminary Remarks

Many commentators of Walras's last monetary model have been, and some still are, amazed by its complexity and simultaneously by its highly compressed form. Jaffé finds Walras's exposition 'skeletal' (1981, p. 362); Lange calls it 'somewhat obscure' (1938b, p. 179); Kuenne describes it as replete with 'ambiguities, carelessness, and sheer error' (1963, p. 337); Patinkin asserts that Walras 'failed to clothe his elaborate mathematical framework with adequate economic meaning' and considers that his monetary theory 'has not been thought through to its logical end' (1965, pp. 570–71); van Daal and Jolink regard it as 'a nearly incomprehensible mass of formulae' (1993, p. 105); Marget is the only critic to consider reassuringly that 'Walras's presentation of the theory of money appears much more complicated than it really is' (1931, p. 581, n. 29).

Any cursory reading of the *Eléments* would convince anyone that Walras is the archetype of Archilochus' hedgehog: he knowns one big thing – the interdependence of all prices and quantities – and is ready to go to any extreme to defend and illustrate it. Accordingly, any sympathetic reader who has cared to follow so far the present discussion can probably agree with Kuenne's following statement: 'Walras's ... presentation of his monetary theory ... emerged from a "vision" of economic processes which its authors employed with consistency when thinking in terms of equation systems. From this "vision" and its rigorous formulation emerges an internal logic which interpretations must not contradict' (1963, p. 311). Hence, Walras's last monetary model has to be elucidated with reference to this lifelong attempt to preserve the symmetry of his system – even if the introduction of money in a purely comparative static piece of analysis was bound to be a sheer exercise in pyrotechnics.

The alterations brought by Walras in 1899–1900 to the time structure of his model is the thread one has to grasp firmly to understand the substance of his demonstration. The whole exercise amounts to a clever adaptation of the relationship between the once-and-for-all market and the periodical market *in order to make room for money considered as circulating capital*. The once-and-for-all market (including, for the first, time money) is kept as 'the preliminary phase of timeless *tâtonnement* ... with equilibrium [including money] established *in principle*' (1954, p. 378; original italics): equilibrium prices are *instantaneously* reached and disequilibrium exchange and production are, of course, ruled out *ex definitione*. In the fourth edition, the periodical market now coincides with 'the phase [where] the static equilibrium has actually commenced, so that equilibrium is established *in fact*' (1954; p. 378; original italics): equilibrium exchanges and production defined on the once-and-for-all market are actually taking place in a fully 'monetized' economy. In other words, the fiction of the once-and-for-all market is augmented with the fiction of a periodical market on which Walras supposes 'the basic data [7] [determined on the once-and-for-all market] to remain fixed' (1954, p. 378): this parable allows Walras to cultivate the illusion that he has succeeded in squeezing money into his equilibrium equations while keeping dynamics strictly separated from statics.

The sum and substance of Walras's demonstration is already contained in his article entitled 'Equations de la circulation'. Moreover, Section 2 and the all-important 'Note' added as a mere postscript go beyond the contribution to monetary theory *stricto sensu*: they offer the first outline of the revised time structure but also the first ever appearance of the *tâtonnement sur bons*. A careful scrutiny of this article (and of the minor changes introduced in the *Eléments*[8]) should convince the reader that Walras's famous recantation about groping on the capital market is the *consequence* (not the cause) of the introduction of money into the system of equilibrium equations.

In a first step, Walras refers the reader back to the thirteen-equation model outlined to illustrate the complete mechanism of production (see above Chapter 1). For the purpose of this analysis, Walras had imagined 'the process of economic production in a given country to be momentarily arrested' (1954, p. 218). Paradoxically, to dispose of all income goods including money, that is, headings 8 to 13, in order to set up his theory of production and capital formation, Walras had to suppose that this 'process of economic production ... is set in motion again' (1954, p. 219). Clearly, *ex definitione*, the presence of money in Walras's 'system of economic equilibrium' (1954, p. 315) is only conceivable from a strictly static point of view. In other words, to reintroduce at the beginning of his monetary theory the eight categories of the element of production discarded earlier, Walras has to revert to a purely static analysis. Using various stratagems[9] to eliminate the markets for new capital goods (seventh category) and the markets of income goods held by producers (ninth and tenth categories), Walras is left with the crucial categories of circulating capital (11), (12) and (13): consumers' *cash holdings*, producers' *cash holdings* and *money savings*. These slots provided in 1877 for money as part of the circulating capital had remained empty, or at least had been exogenously filled throughout editions 1 to 3. To reactivate these three headings he had so far neglected, Walras is eventually faced with the difficult task of filling them with a monetary theory properly integrated within the logic of his overall static 'vision'. In other words, what Walras calls money is only compatible with a strictly static construction; or, alternatively, to save the validity of his purely static equilibrium equations of exchange, production and capitalization, Walras has to perform the unusual deed of depriving money of most, if not all, of its dynamic properties.

Walras is clearly conscious of the need to offer his readers more than a passing explanation for this curious analytical procedure:

> further explanation is required in order to make clear how we intend to formulate the problem of circulation ... and link it with the problems of exchange, production and capital formation already treated, **without abandoning the** *static* **point of view, but at the same time bringing ourselves as close as possible to the** *dynamic* **point of view.** (1954, p. 316; original italics; bold emphasis added)

In a second step, and to foot such a tall bill, Walras offers a new, rich and highly original reading of his original time structure in which he attempts to accommodate his general equilibrium model cum money.

1.2 A New Reading of the Original Time Structure

Merging[10] Section 2 of 'Equations' and the remarkable 'Note' appended at the end of this article, it is possible to sum up under three headings the gist of Walras's demonstration: the preliminary *tâtonnement* in principle; the *static* phase in which equilibrium is established *ab ovo* and the *dynamic* phase.

The phase of preliminary *tâtonnement* **to define equilibrium prices** *in principle* **(phase 1; once-and-for-all market)**
In his first three editions, Walras considered the theories of production and exchange as reaching equilibrium prices and quantities by way of a virtual disequilibrium process through 'logical' time. However, the 'false quantities' 'produced' during this virtual disequilibrium-*tâtonnement* mechanism left the agents' budget constraints, utility and production functions unchanged. In other words, the so-called disequilibrium quantities and prices could not alter the parameters of the model: the pseudo-realistic hypothesis of allowing virtual disequilibrium production was exactly counterbalanced by the hypothetical elimination of their influence on equilibrium prices.[11] The logic of this approach implied, of course, that all prices were expressed in terms of *numéraire*: by definition, money was kept out of the picture.

Given the strictly static hypothesis under which he wants to subsume his theory of circulation/money, Walras is clearly in need of a way out of this quandary. Money *as part of circulating capital* cannot be reconciled with a model in which even 'virtual' disequilibrium exchange and production are possible. Disequilibrium transactions (even virtual), particularly disequilibrium production, have formally to be dispensed with. In other words, Walras's final attempt at introducing money in his set of equilibrium equations compelled him to tidy up the loose ends previously left in his capital theory. Hence, the first appearance of the *tâtonnement sur bons* in the 'Equations de la circulation': 'Once equilibrium [is] achieved in principle, upon completion of the preliminary process of *tâtonnement* by means of *bons*, the actual transfer of service will begin immediately' (1954, p. 316).

This 'hypothetical use of bons' (1954, p. 319)[12] allows thus an *ex ante* formal reconciliation of the agents' intentions before actual production/transactions take place. One has to underline once again that this *preliminary tâtonnement sur bons* necessary to define equilibrium prices *in principle* appears for the first time in the theory of money. Subsequently, nearly a year later, Walras had to rework his theory of production for the fourth edition of the *Eléments*, to bring it into line with his theory of money.[13] Hence, for the sake of introducing money into equilibrium equations, Walras has to force a drastic revision on the theories of exchange, production and capitalization in order to save the internal consistency of his entire theoretical approach. Oddly enough the introduction of money into Walras's general equilibrium model deprives it of the little dynamics it apparently displayed in previous editions.

In summary, together and simultaneously with the three other sets of markets, the equilibrium price of money is first theoretically determined *in principle* and defined in terms of *numéraire*. However, Walras has not yet suggested any *rationale* for the demand of money. Phase 2 of his time structure, and its connection with the equilibrium *in principle* offers just that: the equilibrium price of money determined *ex ante* through a *tâtonnement* in principle on the money market in phase 1 is a function of the *expected* supply and demand for money during phase 2. In Walras's framework, agents know with absolute certainty the exact amounts they must make and receive in payments in phase 1, and the exact dates on which these payments must take place during phase 2. Even if they are purely formal, even virtual, these two phases clearly confirm the necessity of introducing (even in logical time) a *sequential* framework for handling money. Once again, and to quote Hahn, 'no monetary theory without sequences and no sequences without expectations' (1982b, p. 3). Agents know, therefore, the exact amount of money needed to cover the temporary gaps between outlays and receipts. Money is conceived as a good yielding no utility in itself, but, by providing 'services' of an inventory nature (it is part of circulating capital, after all), its possession allows consumers and entrepreneurs to bridge the fully anticipated future gaps between expenditures and receipts. As an intermediary in exchange, money is thus a desirable asset which gives utility not because it acts as a precautionary stock in the presence of uncertainty, but because it allows trades to be unsynchronized in the case of perfect knowledge. Even in a world in which everything were perfectly foreseen, a lack of synchronization would give rise to a demand for money.[14] In this conceptual framework, money, like bread in the larder, soap in the pantry, firewood in the garden shed or any other stock of circulating capital, has to be held in quantities that are assumed to be perfectly known along perfectly predictable time patterns of consumption during phase 2. Just as the consumer derives satisfactions from the holding of good inventories, he or she can also be viewed as deriving utility from holding command over future goods *in money form*. Agents equate the marginal utility of these services of money divided by the price of a unit of the service in *numéraire* to a similar ratio for all other goods to determine their demand for cash balances. This is the crux of Walras's explanation behind his theory of money. This is how money is formally introduced into the utility function.

The *static* phase in which equilibrium is effectively established *ab ovo* (phase 2; periodical market)
Given the crucial importance of this analysis, a lengthy quotation from the original 'Equations de la circulation' does not seem out of place here. In Walras's own very pregnant words:

> Once equilibrium has been achieved in principle, upon completion of the preliminary process of *tâtonnement* by means of *bons*, the actual transfer of service will begin immediately and will continue *in a given manner* during the whole period of time considered. The payment for these services, evaluated in *numéraire*, will be made *at fixed dates*. The delivery of the products will also begin immediately and will continue *in a given manner* during the same period [phase 2]. And the payments for these products evaluated in *numéraire*, will also be made in money *at fixed dates*. It is readily seen that the introduction of these conditions makes it necessary, first so far as consumers are concerned, that they have on hand a fund of circulating capital or working capital consisting of:
>
> (1) certain quantities of final products ... and
> (2) a certain quantity of cash on hands ... mathematically determined by the ... attainment of maximum satisfaction ...
>
> and, secondly, so far as producers are concerned, that they have on hand a fund of circulating and working capital, consisting in this case of:
>
> (1) certain quantities of raw materials held in stock for future use and certain quantities of finished products places on display for sale ...
> (2) a certain quantity of cash on hand which is mathematically determined, under identically the same conditions as above ...

This conception is drawn from reality, but is here given rigorous expression for purposes of scientific analysis.
In a real operating economy, every consumer, whether landowner, labourer or capitalist, has at every moment a fairly exact idea of: (1) what stocks of [final] products he ought to have for his convenience and (2) what cash balance he ought to have, not only in order to replenish these stocks and make current purchases of consumers' goods and services for daily consumption while waiting to receive rents, wages, and interest payable *at fixed future dates,* but also to acquire new capital goods. There may be a small element of uncertainty which is due solely to the difficulty of foreseeing possible changes in the data of the problem. If, however, we suppose these data constant for a given period of time [phase 2] and if we suppose the prices of goods and services and also the dates of their purchase and sale to be known for the whole period, *there will be no occasion for uncertainty.* (1954, pp. 317–18; original italics, bold emphasis added)

Walras duplicates the same demonstration this time for the entrepreneurs' cash balances, in order to reach a similar conclusion:

Here again there may be some uncertainty because of the possibility of changes in the data of the problem and because of the difficulty of foreseeing these changes. But if, as before, we remove this possibility of change for a given period of time [phase 2], and if we suppose the prices of goods and services and also the dates of their purchase and sale to be known for the entire period, *we eliminate all occasion for uncertainty.* (1954, pp. 317–18; italics added)

This extremely clever conceptual framework, and, of course, its limitations, bring immediately to mind a host of theoretically interesting problems. However, before examining them in turn, a note of caution does not seem out of place. Actually, the reader should be warned against reading Walras's analytical framework 'through' later monetary models. Any serious historian of thought knows well that his or her standards of judgement are by definition those of the modern economic theory within which he or she has been brought up as a schoolchild. However, judging a prestigious forerunner such as Walras by the canons of modern monetary theory is a dangerous exercise indeed. In particular, the idiosyncrasies of his monetary model may justly appear so odd to a modern critic that he or she may be tempted to commit the old sin of reformulation instead of trying to understand the author's primary aim. Without measuring up to the problems of interpretation raised by Ricardo's theory of value, Walras's last monetary model is, nevertheless, a good case at hand.

Clearly, Walras seems to provide in this text no *rationale*, in the modern sense of the term, for the holding of money. In Walras's economy, consumers and producers alike know with absolute certainty the exact amounts they must make and receive in payments as well as the exact dates on which these payments must take place in phase 2. As Hicks remarked long ago (1933, pp. 446–8), why should agents hold unproductive cash balances during the gap between receipt and outlay when they can instead hold interest-yielding assets? In modern parlance, Walras already found it difficult to build a model that formally explains why money is used in transactions when it is dominated as a store of value. Moreover, in a model characterized by decision-taking under certainty and market-clearing prices, all commodities, not only money, are perfectly liquid. Consequently, and like most modern theorists, Walras took a short cut and started with the assumption that money *must* be used in some transactions: unknowingly, and once again, he is already faced with an early version of the cash-in-advance constraint.

For Walras, as mentioned earlier, the explanation lies somewhere else, presumably in the field of the transaction technology.

Accordingly, and in full agreement with Patinkin's interpretation, the preceding passages give ample evidence that 'Walras was *not* an exponent of the cash balance approach to monetary theory in the accepted [Cantabridgian] sense of the term' (1965, p. 549; original italics).[15] As a matter of fact, and as widely agreed,[16] the sum and substance of this approach is that agents choose to hold money as a *reserve* against *possible* discrepancies between receipts and outlays or against any other *unforeseen* discrepancies or contingencies. The excerpts quoted above clearly exclude such a notion of precautionary monetary reserve linked to uncertainty. *In Walras's economy, agents hold money not out of choice but out of a technological necessity.* Planning in phase 1 to buy (strictly cash on delivery)[17] a given quantity of goods at given prices in phase 2, and given their perfect knowledge in advance of any lack of synchronization between receipts and outlays, they are compelled by the working of the system to hold money until it is needed.[18]

The obvious corollary of these two remarks is that Walras has no need to provide a conceptual framework to introduce the *service d'approvisionnement* of money in the utility function in today's usual sense of the term. Once again, the transaction technology, not the direct utility of money, explains the holding of money. Money is needed in phase 1 to make payments which are planned with certainty in advance and the cost of this money service is simply the rate of interest on the loan needed to bridge this gap. In other words, money is used to bridge a known number of unsynchronized transactions and the desired money stock is a function of this quantity of transactions and interest rates. In a roundabout way, Walras's theory displays after all a cash balance approach to monetary theory but these *encaisses désirées* are only wanted for *transactions* purposes (conducted under perfect certainty). As Negishi puts it:

> Since disequilibrium transactions are ... excluded and there is no uncertainty, there is no room here for money as a store of value. We have to assume, therefore, that people only demand money for the sake of convenience in transactions. Since all actual transactions are carried out at general equilibrium after the preliminary *tâtonnement* is over, however, this rationale for the demand for money is not at all convincing. (1989, p. 275)[19]

Once again, and despite his theoretical efforts, Walras seems unable to escape from his early version of the modern cash-in-advance constraint to the demand for money.

Such a conceptual framework calls for some further discussion of a more speculative nature. First, what remains in Walras's model of the three traditional functions of money? Money as a unit of account (*numéraire*) raises no problem and the difficulties connected with money as a medium of exchange have already been discussed.[20] But what of money as a store of value in a model in which no uncertainty inherent in the passage of time is allowed? Once again, in a strictly static framework characterized by decision-taking under certainty, and like stores of circulating or fixed capital, each unit of the *encaisses désirées* decided upon in phase 1 is earmarked for a particular use and held in lieu of one monetary unit's worth of the circulating or fixed capital it is destined to purchase. Hence, money is as good a store of value as any other piece of circulating capital: its marginal utility, and therefore its value, is positive. Hence, even in a world of perfect knowledge, money – in the Walrasian sense – is a store of value.[21] In this sense, and in this sense only, Walras's indirect utility of money does not fall victim to the infamous *circularity charge*:[22] the rules of the game laid down by Walras imply that the *encaisses désirées* indirectly derive their utility from the utility of the particular goods which they *will* buy on fixed dates and at given prices and not from the liquidity advantages of holding money *per se*.[23] Clearly, and to use Hahn's terminology, 'the money of this construction is only a contingent store of value' (1984, p. 160).

Second, the pure logic of Walras's analytical framework anticipates many characteristics of what is now called a spot economy.[24] The economy delineated by Walras is a market held in phase 1 (Hicks's 'Monday') at which all transactions are arranged that involve delivery during phase 2 (Hicks's 'week').[25] In order to stick to the central static characteristics of his model, Walras is clearly not considering a sequence of markets, a succession of temporary equilibrium, but only one of them, that is, phase 2. Markets are not reopened. Uncertainty being excluded *ex definitione,* expectations are irrelevant; or more properly speaking, plans for future trades being reconciled in phase 1, the expectations of prices and quantities are held with certainty within the finite horizon of a single period. The 'future' formally depicted by phase 2 is simply collapsed into the present corresponding to phase 1; that is, equilibrium prices and quantities determined in phase 1 hold unchanged in phase 2. Besides, there is no relevant analytical future beyond phase 2; hence there is no intertemporal planning by producers and consumers even if, in his overall model, Walras makes (better than most of his successors) the distinction between current consumption and resources reserved for the support of consumption in future periods. Investment is after all taking place during phase 2: since the cost of investment goods will depend on the level of investment, a high level of investment will raise the prices of the productive services needed to produce them and thus the prices of investment goods themselves. The future creeps back into the picture through the back door. The spirit of Walras's static analysis cannot be strictly upheld in each and every circumstance. On the other hand, to avoid an obvious temptation in the realm of capital theory, Walras carefully excludes any use of new capital goods during phase 2: 'The *new capital goods* ... which are made available during the second phase at costs of production equal to selling [market-clearing] prices ... are not put to use until the third phase. This should be clearly understood' (1954, p. 319; original italics).

After being established *in principle* during phase 1, the equilibrium in capital formation is established *effectively* during phase 2 by the exchange between savings and new capital goods. However, no change in the data is permitted; one has to stay within the static logic of phase 1. If phase 2 postulates duration, it is only duration in logical, not historical time. In Walras's own subtle words: 'Although the economy is becoming *progressive*, it remains *static* because of the fact that the new capital goods play no part in the economy until later in a period subsequent to the one under consideration' (1954, p. 281; original italics).

The general tenor of this demonstration is very clear even if Walras has obviously bitten off more than he could reasonably chew. Jaffé comments vividly on Walras's heroic efforts to stay on the high ground of his static model while at the same time gazing at the promised land of dynamic analysis:

> Walras indulged in a brinkmanship that might well have excited the envy of John Foster Dulles. ... [His] formal analysis brought him to the very brink of economic dynamics where, without ever overstepping the brink, he stood tiptoe to report in digressions ... what he glimpsed beyond. (1980, pp. 366–7)

Likewise, McKenzie, one of the three founding fathers of modern general equilibrium analysis, is prepared to acknowledge that 'Walras provides the most complete and detailed model of [stationary] temporary equilibrium that has ever been given' (1987, p. 503).

Eventually and similarly, Blaug agrees fully with the spirit of this interpretation of Walras's ultimate monetary model:

> What Walras did was to go as far as possible in a purely static framework ... while resisting all temptations to dynamise his system even slightly. In fact, what is really unique about Walras in the entire history of economic thought was his amazing grasp of the absolute gulf between statics and dynamics, between equilibrium analyses defined without reference to time and those that take seriously the passage of historical time. He was the first economist to be continuously aware of this gulf, and certainly the first to follow it through in the treatment of every economic problem. (1984, p. 481)

Though money is the trickiest question of all to be dealt with without reference to time, Walras's attempt, if not totally convincing, is a pretty impressive achievement.

The *dynamic* phase in which equilibrium is constantly disturbed by changes in the data (continuous market)

> Our economy will then be ready to function, and we shall be in a position, if we so desire, to pass from the static to the *dynamic* point of view. In order to make this transition we need only suppose the data of the problem, viz. the quantities possessed, the utility of wants curves, and so on.., to vary as a function of *time*. The fixed equilibrium will then be transformed into a *variable* or *moving* equilibrium, which re-establishes itself automatically as soon as it is disturbed. (1954, p. 318; original italics).

The parallel with the 'continuous' market introduced in 1877 is perfect. Between the lines, and under the implicit hypothesis of perfect competition, the reader is referred to the homeostatic properties of 'the surface of a lake ... incessantly seeking its level without ever reaching it' (1954, p. 380). This time, however, money and circulation have been explicitly, and for the first time, formally included in phases 1 and 2. However, in phase 3, whenever realism, time and dynamics not so much creep in as pour in, formal economic theory comes to a standstill. One is referred back to the continuous market type of macroeconomic analysis. And Walras concludes solemnly: 'In this way we bring to completion our rational synthesis of economic *equilibrium* founded on the equation of exchange and maximum satisfaction' (1954, p. 319; italics added). Once again, Walras clearly refuses to be drawn on to the slippery slopes of dynamic analysis with his rigorously static tools. The strictly technical problems linked to the introduction of money into these static general equilibrium equations remain now to be carefully examined.

2   THE INTEGRATION OF MONEY IN THE UTILITY AND PRODUCTION FUNCTIONS: EXISTENCE AND *TÂTONNEMENTS*

Keeping in mind the transaction role played by money as circulating capital in the 'logical' time structure discussed in Section 1, it is now possible to turn to the strictly technical problems raised by the inclusion of money in Walras's equilibrium equations. In Section 2.1, the mechanisms of the inclusion of the money equation are examined in detail; Walras's utility analysis and his definition of an 'existence' theorem for a monetary equilibrium reveal a complete lack of reference to historical time. Section 2.2 provides a discussion of the instantaneous character of the *tâtonnement* 'mechanism'. Since the market system simultaneously reaches equilibrium *in principle* on all markets (including the money market), the trial-and-error *tâtonnement* 'process' to solve general equilibrium equations is at long last formally acknowledged by Walras as being a mere convenience of analytical exposition – not an attempt to describe how it actually happens on real markets. All in all, despite the introduction of money (or at least what he considers as money), Walras is able to keep unchanged the purely static nature and conclusions of his model. This eventual and formal unification of his comprehensive system is, of course, bound to be realized at the expense of its realism. Section 2.3 examines the discussion between Walras and Albert Aupetit on the strictly static properties of the latter's *Théorie générale de la monnaie* published in 1901. Finally, Section 2.4 offers some concluding considerations of a more methodological nature: the treacherous question of the antagonism between formal development and interpretative contents is re-examined in connection with the evolution of Walras's monetary theory between 1870 and 1901.

2.1 The Integration of the Money Equation

Walras's point of departure is fiat money (U), understood as circulating capital in *optima forma*.[26] Fiat money as such has no utility; only its *service d'approvisionnement* is useful. As discussed at length above, the demand for money balances is a special case of the agents' demands for circulating capital. The *services d'approvisionnement* of this circulating capital and hence of cash balances are related to the goods themselves just as productive services are related to the capital goods which help produce them. Money balances should thus be analysed in the same way that fixed capital goods are.

$(A),(B),(C),(D),...(M),...(T),(P),(K)$ are final products (commodities), raw materials and productive fixed capital (land, personal capital and capital proper). $1, p_b, p_c, p_d, \ldots$ are their prices expressed in terms of the *numéraire* (A). $(A'), (B'), (C'), (D'), \ldots (M'), \ldots (T'), (P'), (K')$ are the *same* products, raw materials and capital goods considered as circulating capital rendering a *service d'approvisionnement* 'either in the larders and cupboards of consumers or in the storerooms and salesrooms of producers' (1954, p. 319). i being the rate of interest, the prices of these services are just as the net prices of productive services are equal to the value of the capital good rendering such a service multiplied by the rate of interest.

Eventually, in the fourth edition, Walras introduces savings (E), the price of which in terms of (A) is $p_e = 1/i$; (E'), is, of course, part of the circulating capital rendering a *service d'approvisionnement;* it is defined as a perpetual net income, not in kind but in *money,* that is, the part of the *encaisse désirée* held for investment purposes (*monnaie d'épargne*).[27] Without delving in detail into an extremely difficult and hotly disputed issue,[28] it is nevertheless necessary to clarify briefly the logic of this last model of saving and capital formation: how could Walras find a way of treating savings explicitly within his utility-maximization framework without leaving the realm of statics? Building on Jaffé's enlightening explanation, van Daal and Jolink summarize Walras's stratagem very aptly: 'instead of introducing magnitudes relating to future periods, and thus introducing dynamics into his equations system, Walras introduced in the fourth edition of the *Eléments* the notion of *present utility of the expectation of future additional income*' (1993, p. 64; original italics).[29] As an 'imaginary commodity' (and not a perpetuity[30]), (E) embodies future additional income to which agents are assumed to attach utility. (E) is treated like any other commodity, displays its own positive marginal utility and appears in the agents' budget equations. In other words, agents use their saving (E) to buy capital goods directly and not perpetuities: capital goods are thus indirectly linked to agents' utility. This device is nothing more than a formal version of the hypothesis barring the use of new capital goods during phase 2 (see above, Section 1). Likewise, (E'), is the demand for money saving in phase 1 in order to buy in phase 2 a predetermined quantity of new capital goods that will not be put to use before phase 3. Jaffé summarizes in the following fashion the introduction of (E) in the agents' utility function:

> What the individual is purchasing when he buys [a unit of (E)] is betterment. And in Walras's static system, betterment is a commodity which can be bought and sold like any other commodity and for which an individual is presumed to have a desire or utility function. The price of a unit of betterment (the reciprocal of the rate of capitalisation) is thus determined in the same [static] way as all other prices. (1942, p. 146)

As earlier, and for the sake of simplicity, money (U) is different from the *numéraire* good (A). The *service d'approvisionnement* of money is measured in units of money: one unit of money (U) renders one unit of money service. Accordingly, the price in *numéraire* of the *service d'approvisionnement* of money, $p_{u'}$, is the quantity of *numéraire* that has to be paid for the use, or the availability of one unit of money during phase 2. Of course, the price of money p_u should not be confused with the price of the *service d'approvisionnement* of money. Just as for any other circulating capital, the relationship between the price of (U) and its *service d'approvisionnement* is expressed as $p_{u'} = p_u i$.[31]

At the start of his demonstration, Walras assumes an agent with a certain initial endowment of goods and money q_u at the outset of phase 1. His excess demands for the goods (A),(B),...(E) are represented by $d_a, d_b, ..., d_e$ and his excess supplies of productive services are defined as $o_t, o_p, o_k, ...$. Given the respective prices of these goods and services, the agent's budget equation is then

$$o_t p_t + o_p p_p + o_k p_k + ... + o_{a'} p_{a'} + o_{b'} p_{b'} + ... + q_m p_{m'} + ... + o_u p_{u'}$$
$$= d_a + d_b p_b + d_c p_c + d_d p_d + ... + d_e p_e \tag{4.1}$$

in which the left-hand side is the income and the right-hand side gives the expenditure of this particular agent. Clearly, and already at this early stage, equation (4.1) includes a term $o_u p_{u'}$: the agent is ready to offer a quantity o_o of money as circulating capital, that is, to lend such an amount to the entrepreneurs, and, consequently to keep for him – or herself the availability of an *amount of money* equal to $q_u - o_u$. o_o is simply the difference between the initial and optimum values of nominal money holdings. How, then, are the optimal quantities offered and demanded in equation (4.1) determined? Walras refers the reader to the 'equations of maximum satisfaction' determined in earlier chapters on the theory of exchange, production and capital formation:

$$\varphi_{a'}(q_{a'} - o_{a'}) = p_{a'} \varphi_a(d_a),$$
$$\varphi_{b'}(q_{b'} - o_{b'}) = p_{b'} \varphi_b(d_b), \tag{4.2}$$
$$............................$$

Together with equation (4.1), Walras can then write the equation of the quantities effectively offered (in terms of *numéraire*):

$$o_{a'} = f_{a'}(p_t, p_p, p_k \cdots p_b, p_c, p_d \cdots p_{a'}, p_{b'} \cdots p_{m'} \cdots p_{u'}, p_e),$$
$$o_{b'} = f_{b'}(p_t, p_p, p_k \cdots p_b, p_c, p_d \cdots p_{a'}, p_{b'} \cdots p_{m'} \cdots p_{u'}, p_e), \tag{4.3}$$

Again, $p_{u'}$, the price of the *service d'approvisionnement* of money, is present among the arguments of all the agent's supply functions. Walras turns finally to the penultimate variable: o_u. His treatment of money is perfectly symmetrical to that of all other goods:

Finally, as regards money, let $r = \varphi_\alpha(q), r = \varphi_\beta(q), \ldots, r = \varphi_\varepsilon(q)$ be our individual's utility or want equations for the *service d'approvisionnement* of products $(A'),(B'),\ldots$ and perpetual net income (E') not *in kind* but *in money*. The quantities $\alpha, \beta, \ldots \varepsilon$, positive or negative, of these services which he desires at the prices $p_{a'}, p_{b'}, \ldots$ will be determined at one and the same time by the equation of exchange [budget equation] and by the following equations of maximum satisfaction:

$$\varphi_\alpha(\alpha) = p_{a'}\cdot\varphi_a(d_a),$$
$$\varphi_\beta(\beta) = p_{b'}\cdot\varphi_a(d_a),$$
$$\ldots\ldots\ldots\ldots\ldots\ldots \tag{4.4}$$
$$\varphi_\varepsilon(\alpha) = p_{a'}\cdot\varphi_a(d_a).$$

from which we obtain first, the quantities desired of the services $(A'),(B'),\ldots,(E')$ [in the form of money]

$$\alpha = f_\alpha(p_t, p_p, p_k \cdots p_b, p_c, p_d \cdots p_{a'}, p_{b'} \cdots p_{m'} \cdots p_{u'}, p_e),$$
$$\beta = f_\beta(p_t, p_p, p_k \cdots p_b, p_c, p_d \cdots p_{a'}, p_{b'} \cdots p_{m'} \cdots p_{u'}, p_e),$$
$$\ldots\ldots\ldots\ldots\ldots\ldots\ldots\ldots\ldots\ldots\ldots\ldots\ldots\ldots\ldots\ldots\ldots\ldots\ldots \tag{4.5}$$
$$\varepsilon = f_\varepsilon(p_t, p_p, p_k \cdots p_b, p_c, p_d \cdots p_{a'}, p_{b'} \cdots p_{m'} \cdots p_{u'}, p_e),$$

secondly, the value of these quantities expressed in terms of *numéraire*

$$\alpha p_{a'} + \beta p_{b'} + \ldots + \varepsilon p_{a'},$$

and finally the quantity of money effectively offered [by the agent]

$$o_u = q_u - \frac{\alpha p_{a'} + \beta p_{b'} + \ldots + \varepsilon p_{a'}}{p_{u'}}. \tag{4.6}$$

In a similar manner we could derive the quantities effectively offered by the other parties [agents] and, consequently, the total [aggregate] effective offer of money

$$O_u = Q_u - \frac{d_a p_{a'} + d_\beta p_{b'} + \ldots + d_\iota p_{a'}}{p_{u'}}.$$ (4.7)

The value of all or part of the final products and perpetual net income which individuals wish to purchase, and which they desire to keep in their possession in the form of cash or money savings [transactions or investment purposes] constitutes their *encaisse désirée*. (1954, pp. 320–21; original italics).

Clearly, in the last two equations defining the agents' individual or aggregate *encaisses désirées*, the first terms of the numerator of the fraction on the right-hand side of the equality sign express the demand for transaction purposes and the last term the demand for saving (or investment) purposes.

Walras's passion for symmetry calls naturally for a mathematical expression of the demand for money exerted by the entrepreneurs, that is, an explanation of the reason why entrepreneurs are ready to demand the difference between the overall supply of money Q_u and the aggregate *encaisses désirées* kept by consumers. As seen above (Section 1), in Walras's framework, entrepreneurs are supposed to need money in the production processes just as they need any other factors of production. In other words, if the *encaisses désirées* have to be included in the consumer's utility function, symmetrically the entrepreneur's demand for money has to be an argument of his or her production function. The total quantities demanded of the *services d'approvisionnment* of $(A'),(B'),\ldots,(M),\ldots,(K),\ldots$ not in kind but *in the form of money* are defined by Walras as $\delta_a, \delta_\beta, \ldots, \delta_\mu, \ldots, \delta_\kappa$. These quantities are determined by the following equations:

$$\alpha_{a'}(D_a + D_{a'}) + \beta_{a'}(D_b + D_{b'}) + \ldots + \mu_{a'}D_m + \ldots + \kappa_{a'}D_k + \ldots = \delta_\alpha,$$

$$\alpha_{b'}(D_a + D_{a'}) + \beta_{b'}(D_b + D_{b'}) + \ldots + \mu_{b'}D_m + \ldots + \kappa_{b'}D_k + \ldots = \delta_\beta,$$

$$\ldots\ldots\ldots\ldots\ldots\ldots\ldots\ldots\ldots\ldots\ldots\ldots\ldots\ldots\ldots\ldots\ldots$$

(4.8)

$$\alpha_m(D_a + D_{a'}) + \beta_m(D_b + D_{b'}) + \ldots + \mu_m D_m + \ldots + \kappa_m D_k + \ldots = \delta_\mu,$$

$$\ldots\ldots\ldots\ldots\ldots\ldots\ldots\ldots\ldots\ldots\ldots\ldots\ldots\ldots\ldots\ldots\ldots$$

$$\alpha_k(D_a + D_{a'}) + \beta_k(D_b + D_{b'}) + \ldots + \mu_k D_m + \ldots + \kappa_k D_k + \ldots = \delta_k.$$

in which $\alpha_{a'}$ is the quantity of (A') in the form of money necessary for the production of one unit of (A), $\beta_{a'}$ is, in turn, the quantity of (A') in the form of money necessary for the production of one unit of (B'), and so on Walras eventually writes down the equations defining, in terms of *numéraire*, the total quantities of money entrepreneurs need for the production of one unit of $(A),(B),\ldots(M),\ldots(K),\ldots$:

$$a_u = \alpha_{a'} p_{a'} + \alpha_{b'} p_{b'} + \ldots + \alpha_m p_{m'} + \ldots + \alpha_k p_k + \ldots,$$

$$b_u = \beta_{a'} p_{a'} + \beta_{b'} p_{b'} + \ldots + \beta_m p_{m'} + \ldots + \beta_k p_k + \ldots,$$

$$\ldots\ldots\ldots\ldots\ldots\ldots\ldots\ldots\ldots\ldots\ldots\ldots\ldots\ldots\ldots$$

$$m_u = \mu_{a'} p_{a'} + \mu_{b'} p_{b'} + \ldots + \mu_m p_{m'} + \ldots + \mu_k p_k + \ldots, \qquad (4.9)$$

$$\ldots\ldots\ldots\ldots\ldots\ldots\ldots\ldots\ldots\ldots\ldots\ldots\ldots\ldots\ldots$$

$$k_u = \kappa_{a'} p_{a'} + \kappa_{b'} p_{b'} + \ldots + \kappa_m p_{m'} + \ldots + \kappa_k p_k + \ldots,$$

$$\ldots\ldots\ldots\ldots\ldots\ldots\ldots\ldots\ldots\ldots\ldots\ldots\ldots\ldots\ldots$$

This set of equations simply reflects in a complicated way that $a_u, b_u, \ldots m_u \ldots k_u \ldots$ and so on are the values in *numéraire* of the cash reserves which producers of $(A), (B), \ldots (M), \ldots (K), \ldots$ and so on wish to hold in the form of money per unit of output.

The total amount demanded of the service of money by entrepreneurs for productive purposes in terms of *numéraire* can eventually be expressed as

$$a_u(D_a + D_{a'}) + b_u(D_b + D_{b'}) + \ldots + m_u D_m + \ldots + k_u D_k + \ldots =$$
$$\delta_a p_{a'} + \delta_\beta p_{b'} + \ldots + \delta_\mu p_{m'} + \ldots + \delta_\kappa p_k + \ldots \qquad (4.10)$$

and the total quantity of money demanded by entrepreneurs is defined as

$$\frac{\delta_a p_{a'} + \delta_\beta p_{b'} + \ldots + \delta_\mu p_{m'} + \ldots + \delta_\kappa p_k + \ldots}{p_{u'}} = O_u, \qquad (4.11)$$

this equation 'expressing [also] the equality between the demand [by entrepreneurs] and offer [by consumers] of the service of money (U)' (1954, p. 323).[32]

Finally, the equilibrium in the market for the service of money can be expressed by equating the total demand by entrepreneurs and the quantity kept by consumers to the exogenously given supply Q_u. Simultaneously, such a procedure provides Walras with a direct link back to his quantity equation:

$$Q_u = \frac{d_a p_{a'} + d_\beta p_{b'} + \ldots + d_\varepsilon p_{a'}}{p_{u'}}$$
$$+ \frac{\delta_a p_{a'} + \delta_\beta p_{b'} + \ldots + \delta_\mu p_{m'} + \ldots + \delta_\kappa p_k + \ldots}{p_{u'}} = \frac{H_\alpha}{p_{u'}} \qquad (4.12)$$

where H_α, the sum of the two numerators of the central term is Walras's old 1874 friend, this time, however, expressing the *encaisses désirées*, that is, the total value in *numéraire* of all the money services consumers and entrepreneurs need for transaction and saving/investment purposes. Walras's efforts seem at last to have succeeded in subsuming the quantity theory to marginal utility and maximization under constraint.

Walras concludes this crucial Lesson 29 by demonstrating that the introduction of money in his model has not affected the equilibrium between the number of equations and variables.[33] All in all, the existence theorem of his monetized general equilibrium seems to be mathematically determinate.

This important demonstration calls for three intermediate remarks.

First and foremost, whatever may be said about Walras's procedure to incorporate money into utility and production functions, like any other of the $(n-1)$ goods, money is, after all, an argument of his equilibrium equations. In particular, equations (4.1) and (4.3) leave no doubt about the dependence of the agents' supply and demand functions on the price of the *service d'approvisionnement* of money $p_{u'}$. The supply and demand for money, as well as the price of its *service d'approvisionnement* are firmly anchored to *real* variables: however, indirectly and weakly, the ds and δs actually depend on $p_{u'}$; alternatively, H_α is not independent from $p_{u'}$. In short, there is no dichotomy between the real and monetary sectors. In this respect, and keeping in mind their purely static interpretation of Walras's model (1993, p. 159), Van Daal and Jolink rightly remark: 'What Walras ... did from the fourth edition of the *Eléments* onwards was [to] devise a comprehensive economic theory in which the dichotomy between the real and monetary sector *does not exist at all*' (1993, p. 105; italics in original).

Similarly, forty years earlier, and as far as statics is concerned, Schumpeter had reached a similar conclusion:

[Walras's] theory of money ... is simply part of his general theory of economic equilibrium ... And, *so far as monetary statics is concerned*, all propositions developed about money and monetary processes are either contained in his system or may be derived from it by introducing additional assumptions. (1954, p. 1082; original italics)

The central problem raised by today's dominant (Patinkin's) reading of Walras's monetary theory is to assess, *when stepping outside the equilibrium (existence) conditions* outlined above to discuss the *tâtonnement* mechanism, whether Walras does, or does not, tend to dichotomize the real from the monetary market processes.[34] This discussion in Section 2.2 will, of course, revolve around the static or dynamic reading given to Walras's *tâtonnement*.

Second, and as already mentioned apropos the *Théorie de la monnaie*, Walras envisions the demand for money not as a single function but as being broken up into various components linked to the different quantities of goods each individual plans to purchase. Accordingly, the utility of the *service d'approvisionnement* of money is represented by a sequence of functions of these respective quantities. In this way, Walras clearly expresses utility as a function of the *real* (and not nominal) amount of money the agent wishes to hold.

Third, in equilibrium, the marginal utility of the *service d'approvisionnement* of the optimum quantity of fiat money (U), like that of the optimum quantities of any other commodity, is proportionate to its relative price; as shown in equations (4.1) to (4.3), the factor of proportionality is, of course, the marginal utility of the *numéraire* (A).

2.2 The Instantaneous *Tâtonnement* 'Mechanism' on the Money Market

Having reached this stage in his presentation, Walras is now in a position to crown his demonstration with a discussion of the *tâtonnement* through which an economy that fiat money (U) reaches the equilibrium solution of the system of market excess-demand equations just defined. This system includes, of course, the market excess demand for money.[35]

Lesson 30[36] is devoted entirely to the analysis of this ultimate in Walrasian pyrotechnic. Keeping in mind all that Walras has written about the phase of 'preliminary *tâtonnement* to define equilibrium prices *in principle*' on the once-and-for-all market, the very first sentence of this lesson may seem, to say the least, rather perplexing: 'Our next step is to pass from the theoretical solution which was formulated mathematically to the practical solution which is reached on the market' (1954, p. 325[37]).

Though in perfect symmetry with previous versions of the *tâtonnement* in exchange, production and capital formation,[38] this statement seems in contradiction with the very logic of the timeless phase of preliminary *tâtonnement sur bons* postulated *ab initio* in Lesson 29. This *tâtonnement* cannot be at the same time a purely theoretical anecdote *and* a practical dynamic process taking place on real markets in historical time. This crucial ambiguity has baffled and keeps baffling most commentators of Walras's *magnum opus*.[39] Be that as it may, the sympathetic reader must have also realized by now what the tenor of the present writer's argument is amounting to. Desperately struggling from one edition to the other to formally close his theoretical system, Walras could not bring himself, at the same time, to give up his cherished wish to contribute with his pure theory to the solution of the 'question sociale'. However abstract, in Walras's overall scheme, general equilibrium is clearly more than a thought experiment, more than an exercise in pure logic. In his own words, it 'is indeed the abstract expression and rational explanation of facts of the real world' (1954, p. 46).[40] Constantly torn between the internal and external coherence of his model, Walras never managed to solve this ambiguity satisfactorily.[41] Again, Jaffé has a unique way of expressing this central dilemma:

The changes in the structure and organisation of the *Eléments* from the first to the last edition bear witness to a long and difficult struggle to achieve formal unification of his comprehensive system, while still keeping his vestigial non theoretical interests before him and yet within proper bounds. The 'purification' of his theory was progressive over the years, but never complete, so that his definitive version reads like a palimpsest with earlier inscriptions imperfectly rubbed out. (1981, p. 367)

Even if the structure of Walras's last monetary model reflects unequivocally the predominance of formal unification over external coherence, the reference to the *tâtonnement* as the practical solution reached on the market cannot be bypassed. Last remnant of an earlier mode of thought, and despite the clear-cut threefold time structure of Walras's monetary model, many commentators have been tempted to use it to support a 'realistic' interpretation of the monetary *tâtonnement*. Patinkin's reading of Lesson 30 is among the best examples at hand (1965, pp. 558–69).[42] Carefully avoiding any reference to the very notion of 'preliminary tâtonnement towards the establishment of equilibrium *in principle*' and to the static framework it implies, Patinkin centres the whole of his critical comments on Walras's inability to offer an accurate dynamic analysis (including a real-balance effect) of a *tâtonnement process* on the money market:

At a higher degree of criticism, [Walras's] theory of money is not fully integrated with his theory of production and capital formation. This manifests itself in his failure to follow the basic pattern of this earlier theory in presenting a detailed and precise description of the *tâtonnement* in the money market. ... At no point does Walras even advert to the real-balance effect in the commodity market in his analysis of the determination of the absolute price level. (1965, p. 571)

Perfect illustration of the good old Whiggish tradition in the history of economic thought, Patinkin criticizes Walras for not dealing in 1900 with a problem that began to be relevant only much later.[43] In other words, Walras cannot be castigated for leaving unsolved a theoretical problem he was clearly not addressing. The spirit, if not every letter, of Walras's demonstration is here to prove it: monetary dynamics are best left to the realm of applied economics and, more specifically, to the forced savings mechanism, not to pure economics. Walras is, however, undoubtedly responsible for such a confusion. The 'detailed and precise description' of 'earlier' *tâtonnements* which, according to Patinkin or Walker (1994a, pp. 251–2), Walras should have emulated in his monetary theory, come in fact straight from earlier editions of the *Eléments* in which the time structure is completely different. In fact, while, in the first three editions, disequilibrium behaviour and transactions are grudgingly tolerated (though eliminated through *ad hoc* assumptions), the *tâtonnement sur bons* excludes them formally from the fourth. Accordingly, while attempts at a 'detailed and precise[44] description of the *tâtonnement*' appear in Walras's earlier models, *by definition*, the timeless *tâtonnement in principle* conducted in phase 1 to reconcile *ex ante* the agents' intentions cannot be the subject of an empirical description. In the fourth edition, the explicit elimination of all 'trading out of equilibrium' (and hence of historical time) by way of the *tâtonnement sur bons* rigorously implies the identity between 'existence' and 'process', between the roots of the equation system and the solution reached through an iterative timeless mechanism conducted in principle within a 'hypothetical régime of perfectly free competition'. At long last, Walras's confusion between a durationless equilibrating mechanism taking place in 'logical time' and an intuitive process of price formation in historical time is solved. However, some earlier inscriptions on Walras's palimpsest are imperfectly rubbed out and somewhat inconsistent with the logic of his final model. Walker sums up this whole issue in a very lucid way:

> Since in [his 1900 model] Walras eliminated disequilibrium production and acquisition of consumer goods and new capital goods ..., none of the parameters of his system of equations of general equilibrium undergoes endogenously induced changes during the *tâtonnement* phase of behaviour. Walras believed that the equilibrium is therefore the one given by the solution to that system, and that this new version of *tâtonnement* in production converges to it for the same general reasons as the old one. (1987a, p. 859)

Before turning to Walras's demonstration, two further textual evidences should go some way towards solving the difficulties raised by this ambiguity about the significance of the static/dynamic nature of the *tâtonnement* in the 1900 monetary model. In the 'Note' appended to the 'Equations de la circulation' and reproduced in Lesson 29, Walras suggests, during his outline of the *tâtonnement sur bons*, a sentence nearly identical to that quoted above and used by Patinkin as a stepping-stone towards his 'realistic' interpretation of the *tâtonnement*: 'We shall describe[45] equilibrium in principle, as before, first theoretically and mathematically, and then practically as it manifests itself in the market' (1954, p. 318).

However, this pronouncement is immediately followed by two sentences that leave no doubt about the static, instantaneous and durationless character of Walras's price-adjustment rule:

> Our economy will **then** be ready to function, and we shall be in a position, if we so desire, to pass from the static to the *dynamic* point of view. In order to make this transition we need only suppose the data of the problem ... to vary as a function of *time*. (1954, p. 318; original italics, bold emphasis added)

Similarly, in the abbreviated version of the 'Equations de la circulation' translated by Pareto for the *Giornale degli Economisti*,[46] Walras reminds the reader in 'a last observation' contained in a brief paragraph 6 of the perfectly static nature of his four-tier *tâtonnement* mechanism:

> Le mécanisme de la circulation a été envisagé ici au point de vue *statique*, comme l'avaient été antérieurement ceux de l'*échange*, de la *production*, et de la *capitalisation*. Dans tous ces cas, on a supposé des entrepreneurs achetant à des propriétaires fonciers, travailleurs et capitalistes certaines quantités de services producteurs et leur vendant certaines quantités de produits, **les données du problème restant invariables pendant les tâtonnements** et l'équilibre ayant lieu quand le montant des services et celui des produits en numéraire étaient égaux. Cet équilibre une fois atteint, la société ... est prête à se mettre en mouvement; et l'on pourrait passer du point de vue statique au point de vue *dynamique*. Il suffirait, pour cela, de supposer les données du problème ... [47] variant en fonction du *temps*; alors l'équilibre fixe se transformerait en un équilibre *mobile* se rétablissant de lui-même au fur et à mesure qu'il serait troublé. (*OEC*, XI, p. 588; original italics, bold emphasis added; from the original manuscript)

In short, and once again, there is no practical real-market dynamic adjustment process without historical time; or, alternatively, without historical time, there is no sequence, no genuine monetary theory: only a static theoretical parable of a durationless *tâtonnement* conducted in 'logical' time, to which we now turn.

From all that has just been said, it is evident that Walras conducts his discussion of the monetary *tâtonnement* against the explicit backround and along the method of the detailed *tâtonnement* procedure presented in earlier chapters on exchange, production and capital formation. In his mind (and for once!) there is clearly no need to rehearse a logic he has already carefully thought about three times over.

Accordingly, in the first paragraph of Lesson 30, Walras shows how the additional equations linked to the introduction of money in his earlier models leaves them perfectly determined: the equality between the number of equations and variables is still holding. The monetary equation, however, remains to be solved.

Given the crucial importance of that analysis, and the various interpretations it has given, a lengthy quotation from the relevant lesson of the *Eléments* does not seem superfluous here:

> Only the offer equation [4.7] of (U) and equation [4.11] remain outside (this solution).[48] Consequently, if a price p'_u is cried at random and is held fixed during the process of *tâtonnement* in production and capital formation, we come to the last equation from which the equality between the price of the *numéraire* and unity is deduced at the same time as the equality between the

demand and offer of the *numéraire*, so that there remains only to solve the equation

$$Q_u - \frac{d_a p_{a'} + d_\beta p_{b'} + \ldots + d_\varepsilon p_{a'}}{p_{u'}}$$

$$= \frac{\delta_a p_{a'} + \delta_\beta p_{b'} + \ldots + \delta_\mu p_{m'} + \ldots + \delta_\kappa p_k + \ldots}{p_{u'}}.$$

If we set

$$d_a p_{a'} + d_\beta p_{b'} + \ldots = D_\alpha,$$

$$\delta_a p_{a'} + \delta_\beta p_{b'} + \ldots + \delta_\mu p_{m'} + \ldots + \delta_\kappa p_k + \ldots = \Delta_\alpha,$$

$$d_\varepsilon p_{a'} = E_\varepsilon,$$

and

$$D_\alpha + \Delta_\alpha + E_\alpha = H_\alpha,$$

then the equation at the close of the preceding paragraph becomes

$$Q_u = \frac{H_\alpha}{p_{u'}}.$$

The three terms $D_a/p_{u'}$, $\Delta_a/p_{u'}$ and $E_a/p_{u'}$ represent respectively *cash* in the hands of consumers, *cash* in the hands of producers and *money savings*. But since there cannot be one $p_{u'}$ for savings and another for cash in circulation, nor one $p_{u'}$ for cash circulating in business transactions and another for cash circulating in current [private] transactions, one price common to both the service of money in circulation and the service of money in savings results from the single equation of monetary circulation given above. Hence, if perchance,

$$Q_u p_{u'}' = H_\alpha,$$

the question would be completely settled. Generally, however, we find that

$$Q_u p_{u'}' \neq H_\alpha,$$

and the problem is to determine how equality between the demand and offer of money is reached by *tâtonnement* through adjustment in $p_{u'}$.

On referring back to the various terms that enter into the composition of H_α, we perceive that they are not absolutely independent of $p_{u'}$, since $p_{u'}$ figures in the term $o_u p_{u'}$ of the equation of exchange which, together with the equations of maximum satisfaction, enables us to deduce the quantities $\alpha, \beta, \ldots, \varepsilon$ for any one party to the exchange and, consequently, the aggregate quantities $d_\alpha, d_\beta, \ldots, d_\varepsilon$ for all parties together. We must admit, however, that the dependence of these items on $p_{u'}$ is very indirect and very weak. That being the case, the equation of monetary circulation, when money is not a commodity, comes very close, in reality, to falling outside the system of equations of [general] economic equilibrium. If we first suppose [general] economic equilibrium to be established, then the equations of monetary circulation would be solved almost without any *tâtonnement*, simply by raising or lowering $p_{u'}$ according as $Q_u \rightleftharpoons H_a / p'_{u'}$ at a price $p'_{u'}$ which had been cried at random. If, however, this increase or decrease in $p_{u'}$ were to change H_a ever so slightly, it would only be necessary to continue the general process of adjustment by *tâtonnement* in order to be sure of reaching equilibrium. This is what actually takes place in the money market.

Thus: *The price of the service of money is established through its rise or fall according as the* desired cash balance *is greater or less than the quantity of money.*

There is, then, an equilibrium price $p_{u'}$; and, if i is the equilibrium rate of net income, the unit quantity of money will be worth $p_u = p_{u'} / i$. Then also $p_{u'} / i = p_u / 1$; so that, if there is an *aggio*, it is the same for the price of money as for the price of its service; so that is to say, setting $H_a = H_a i$, we have

$$Q_u = \frac{H_a}{p_u}.\text{''}$$

(1954, pp. 325–7; original italics, bold emphasis added)

This passage contains all that Walras ever wrote on the *tâtonnement* on the money market. A careful study of the letter and of the spirit of this passage is thus absolutely central for an exact understanding not only of Walras's monetary theory but also for a correct intelligence of his general equilibrium model as a whole. As Patinkin noticed in 1956, Walras's 'usual detailed and extended examination of the workings of the *tâtonnements* is [seems?] significantly absent' from this passage (1965, p. 562). This economy in Walras's demonstration does not imply, however, that this 'meagre description ... shows no recognition of the vital necessity ... for the existence of a mutual interdependence between this [monetary] *tâtonnement* and that taking place in the other markets of the economy' (1965, p. 571).[49] To support an interpretation such as this, three important comments are now called for.

First, as a tired and sick man racing with time to tackle the most difficult of issues,[50] Walras himself is well aware of the parsimony of his demonstration. Commenting on his 'Equations de la circulation', Walras writes to Hermann Laurent:

Mon mémoire ... est un peu succinct. Je l'ai publié dès-à-présent avec l'intention d'en développer quelques points.[51] Cependant, à la condition de se reporter à la résolution des *Equations* antérieures *de la Capitalisation*, on y peut bien saisir l'enchaînement des ... équations. (1965, III, p. 81; original italics)

The reader is thus clearly referred to the previous discussions of the *tâtonnement* and to the specific mechanism through which, in 'logical' time, discrepancies between the supply and the demand for any good generate self-eliminating variations in prices. At this stage of his reading, any sympathetic interpreter of the *Eléments* would be aware of Walras's market interdependence device used in his study of the convergence of the *tâtonnement*. A *tâtonnement* on one price that brings it to equilibrium would generally, because of the interdependence of the system, disturb the equilibrium on other markets. *Tâtonnements* on all the other markets will thus have to be re-started again; and this procedure of successive approximations conducted until the whole system ultimately converges to its equilibrium vector of prices.[52] Walras probably saw no necessity for making a special case for money subsumed as it is for any of the other $(n-1)$ goods to this static iterative *tâtonnement* procedure: why make a special case of the real-balance effect while there are $(n-1)$ 'real-good' effects? To paraphrase Walras's own terminology used in the case of the exchange of several commodities, the direct pressure of excess demand in a given market undoubtedly pushed its price towards its equilibrium level while the variations in other prices

> exerted indirect influences, some in the direction of equality and some in the opposite direction ... so that up to a certain point they cancelled each other out. Hence the new system of prices ... is closer to equilibrium than the old system of prices ... and it is only necessary to continue this process along the same lines for the system to move closer and closer to equilibrium. (1954, p. 172)

Once again, Walras could not literally suppose that markets come into equilibrium in some definite order. Rather, the procedure is a convenient way of showing how the market system in fact could solve the system of equilibrium equations.

Second, in the lengthy previous quotation from Lesson 30 (see pp. 187–8), there is admittedly no such sophisticated discussion of this specific mechanism by which the equilibrium level of $p_{u'}$ (and hence of p_u) is reached through *tâtonnement* on the money market. There is, however, clearly room for it: 'The various terms that enter into the composition of H_a, ... are not absolutely independent of $p_{u'}$ [even if] the dependence of these items on $p_{u'}$ is very indirect and very weak'. As mentioned earlier, Walras's equilibrium equations leave no doubt about the dependence of the agents' supply and demand functions on the price of the *service d'approvisionnement* of money $p_{u'}$: however 'indirectly and weakly', the ds and $δs$ of these equations actually depend on $p_{u'}$; or, alternatively, H_a is not independent from $p_{u'}$. In fact, Walras's strategy is clearly aimed at showing that *if*[53] all other equilibrium equations of the system were holding, then the solution of the monetary equation could be obtained by a *tâtonnement* on $p_{u'}$ only. Walras in fact attempts to list with great care all the conditions that would be necessary for the *d*s and *δ*s as well as H_a not to depend on the price of the *service d'approvisionnement* of money. To defend this indefensible assertion, Walras tries to eliminate rather clumsily from his model these functional relationships by adding 'qualitative' considerations to minimize their influence:

> Indeed, in the case of money which is not a commodity ... whenever the quantity [Q_u] changes, the changes in the q_u's will entail a change in the $q_u p_{u'}$'s, and consequently in the $\alpha, \beta, ..., \varepsilon$'s, the $d_a, d_\beta, ..., d_\varepsilon$'s and all the items of utility. Though this is perfectly true, we must nevertheless note in the general case that:
> (1) the $q_u p_{u'}$'s constitute only a fraction of the income of the parties to the exchange and changes in the $q_u p_{u'}$ are spread over all expenditures on reserve stocks, consumption goods, and savings;
> (2) to the extent that the changes in the q_u's are not uniformly proportional [that is, that there is a distribution effect[54]], if the $q_u p_{u'}$'s, the $(q_u - o_u)p_{u'}$'s and the $o_u p_{u'}$'s increase or decrease for some parties, they will decrease or increase for other parties, so that the $d_a, d_\beta, ..., d_\varepsilon$'s and the $\delta_a, \delta_\beta, ..., \delta_\mu, ..., \delta_\kappa, ...$'s will **not be appreciably affected**; and
> (3) since the $d_a, d_\beta, ..., d_\varepsilon$'s and the $\delta_a, \delta_\beta, ..., \delta_\mu, ..., \delta_\kappa, ...$'s on the one hand, and the [marginal utilities of the services $(A'),(B')...(M)...(K)...$] on the other, vary in opposite directions, it follows that, **if the quantities change but little**, their products, that is, the rectangular utilities [total utilities] will change still less with changes in the quantity of money. We may, therefore, enunciate with what amounts **to almost rigorous exactness** that: *The rareté* [marginal utility] *or value of the service of money is directly proportional to its utility and inversely proportional to its quantity.* (1954, pp. 328–9; original italics, bold emphasis added)

From the words and expressions in bold characters, one clearly gets the impression that, in perfect contradiction with the structure of his equilibrium model, Walras is happiest when 'the dependence of these items of $p_{u'}$ is very indirect and very weak' (1954, p. 326). Money being after all an argument of all equilibrium equations, why is Walras trying to convince his readers that a *tâtonnement* on the money market could be carried out without *appreciably* reacting back on and disturbing the equilibria initially achieved in the other markets? Or, more precisely, that this retroaction, although theoretically present, can be empirically safely neglected or worse, *has to be discarded* if the familiar conclusions of the quantity theory are to be upheld. Again, and even if admittedly Walras offers not a single hint at some sort of price-adjustment mechanism in terms of real-balance effect, and tries to minimize any functional dependence on $p_{u'}$, the overall structure of the Walrasian model makes it hard to believe that, for Walras, money prices are indeterminate. Why, then, is Walras, the most careful and painstaking of all theorists, displaying a schizophrenic fracture between his watertight theoretical model and a less than thorough use of its logical conclusions in his *tâtonnement* mechanism? Why is Walras giving up theoretical rigour for 'almost rigorous exactness'? The logical structure of his timeless model doubtlessly provides the beginning of an answer.

Third, and last but not least, since Walras is avowedly using in his 1900 theory of money and circulation a purely static 'instantaneous' version of his *tâtonnement*, one can hardly blame him for failing to analyse the behaviour of a price-adjustment *process* on real markets. Even if there is clearly room for a real-balance-like effect in his general equilibrium model, Walras sees no need to fill this particular theoretical slot, which is irrelevant to the timeless logic of his last monetary model. This is precisely the argument he invokes at the beginning of paragraph 281 when substituting commodity money (A) for fiat money (U):[55]

> The [quantity theory] is not absolutely rigorous. It is so however, at least with respect to [variations in] quantity [of money] under the following conditions: (1) if we adopt the static point of view, as we have been doing, in the establishment of equilibrium *ab ovo* under the supposition that consumers, whether landowners, workers or capitalists, possess fixed and circulating capital goods which they lend to entrepreneurs engaged in production; and (2) if we let the quantity of money in the hands of capitalists vary proportionately. In that case, since the $o_u p_{u'}$ terms in the [individual] equations of exchange remain constant under the assumption that the value [of money] varies inversely with the quantity, economic equilibrium will not be disturbed under this assumption. (1954, p. 331)

Everything eventually falls neatly into place. Walras has to bring in additional conditions that eliminate *ex definitione* any dynamic adjustment mechanism (including , of course, the real-balance effect) to save the validity of 'the rigorous quantity theory' of money. On the threshold of interesting and new discoveries in the field of monetary dynamics, both the then dominant comparative static tradition of the quantity theory[56] and, above all, his wish to close his static general equilibrium system, force him to eradicate from his model any dynamic implication.

Again, the differences between the pseudo-dynamic nature of earlier *tâtonnement* mechanisms and the static nature of this 1900 procedure in the money market are perhaps the most revealing indications that Walras had at last realized that to save the internal consistency of his general equilibrium model, he had to give up all pretence to realism and thus to dynamic analysis. After all, for what other reason would Walras, the epitome of the fastidious theorist, have discarded from the 1900 edition the detailed discussions conducted in the second edition on the dynamic adjustment process on the money market together with the three lessons on applied monetary theory? Why would he had added *ad hoc* hypotheses to his monetary model to eliminate disturbing functional relationships between real and monetary sectors? Why did he never try to reconcile his brilliant analysis of the dynamic forced saving *process* with his pure theory of money?

The remainder of Lesson 30 contains a straightforward extension of this model to a commodity (*A*) which is both *numéraire* and money. With a rather acrobatic footnote[57] explaining why the price of money can replace the price of the *service d'approvisionnement*, the end paragraph 283 reproduces verbatim from the second and third editions the three-curve geometric demonstration of the determination of the price of commodity money when it is no longer *numéraire* (see Chapter 1 above): Walras is thus back to his own traditional 1872 formulation of the quantity equation with the illusion of having subsumed it to the litmus test of the general equilibrium model: 'the value of money is directly proportional to its utility and inversely proportional to its quantity' (1954, p. 328).

2.3 The Static Properties of Aupetit's Monetary Model

Aupetit's *Essai sur la théorie générale de la monnaie* (1901) and the correspondence to which this doctoral dissertation gave rise between Walras and its author represent the ultimate step in the evolution of Walras's monetary theory. This episode breathes some welcome fresh air into the presentation of his monetary theory.[58] For the first time one of Walras's ablest young disciples has taken the trouble to rework critically the master's painstaking theoretical efforts. If nothing really new emerges from a book seldom quoted and practically never read,[59] this episode provides a welcome clarification about the final limits put by Walras to his monetary theory *circa* 1901.

Despite questionable efforts to devise a dubious cardinal measure of utility, Aupetit is a 'great economist' (Zylberberg, 1994, p. 78). Though with no particular mathematical training,[60] he is responsible for introducing singlehandedly into Continental economic theory the Lagrangian multipliers method.[61] His contribution to monetary theory *stricto sensu* is modest. However, the strictly static characteristics of general equilibrium theory, including monetary theory, are spelled out more clearly than in the *Eléments*.

In his interesting methodological introduction,[62] Aupetit adopts part and parcel Edgeworth's position[63] about the strictly static nature of Walras's equilibrium equations:

Il est très exact, comme l'a observé Edgeworth, que [l'analyse mathématique] ne nous a permis de résoudre jusqu'ici que des problèmes statiques. Les équations de Jevons on de M. Walras définissent certains états d'équilibre sans nous renseigner sur la voie par laquelle ils sont atteints. (1901, p. 31)

Similarly, a few pages later, Aupetit can write without Walras annotating his copy or reacting in any way:

> L'étude des mouvements d'un système économique est une étude beaucoup trop complexe pour qu'elle puisse être dès maintenant tentée. Tous ceux qui ont abordé l'étude rationnelle des phénomènes économiques [including, of course, Walras], se sont bornés à définir et à déterminer certaines positions d'équilibre d'un pareil système. ... Le problème fondamental de la statique [existence] ne se confond pas rigoureusement avec celui que résout la pratique économique. ... Si les équations qui l'expriment [the equilibrium], ne nous renseignent pas sur la voie par laquelle le point d'équilibre est réellement atteint [*tâtonnement*], elles fixent exactement la position de ce point. ... L'erreur d'adaptation la plus grave que présentent nos formules, c'est qu'elles ne se rapportent qu'à une série d'états statiques artificiels, sans nous renseigner sur le mouvement véritable des systèmes économiques. (1901, pp. 49–50 and 79)⁽ ⁹

Who could wish for a better separation between existence and stability theorems? Who could wish for a clearer distinction between *tâtonnement* as a purely theoretical static anecdote and *tâtonnement* as a practical dynamic process taking place *réellement* on actual markets in historical time?

The three strictly monetary chapters of the theoretical part of Aupetit's dissertation are organized around a threefold distinction between *numéraire* (Chapter 2), transaction money (Chapter 3) and money savings (Chapter 4). The gist of Aupetit's analysis does not really differ from Walras's: terminology, notations, ordering and results are practically identical. Again, the only notable differences are linked with the author's comments on Walras's framework and time structure. More than once, Aupetit perceives that, for the sake of the discussion, Walras's three-phase model can be treated as a succession of temporary equilibria ('in principle' first and '*ab ovo*' second). The link established by money between phase 1 and phase 2 is, however, a purely formal device:

> Pour construire la théorie de la circulation, nous avons du décomposer cette circulation en une série d'états statiques, distincts et successifs. Dans la réalité, les opérations se poursuivent d'une manière continue sans comporter des divisions aussi nettes. La véritable théorie de la circulation serait une théorie dynamique, dans laquelle interviendrait la considération de la vitesse, soit des échanges eux-mêmes et de la production, soit de la circulaion monétaire. Cette théorie est encore à faire ... (1901, pp. 127–8)

Similarly, when assessing the conclusions of Walras's quantity equation, Aupetit writes:

> Il ne s'agit que d'une étude statique, s'appliquant seulement à des situations d'équilibre bien définis et différents, sans avoir égard aux phénomènes de

transition, les plus importants à la vérité. La vie économique réelle n'est qu'une perpétuelle transition entre des états d'équilibre fugitifs et insaisissables [Walras's phase 3]. L'étude dynamique de ces mouvements a été objet de travaux nombreux et approfondis, mais elle ne comporte pas encore la précision de l'analyse mathématique. (1901, p. 114)

Again, Walras's distinction between a timeless inclusion of money into equilibrium equations and a parallel, but uncoordinated, forced saving process on actual markets is to the forefront.

The correspondence between master and pupil linked to Aupetit's dissertation amounts to four letters only.[65] In his letter acknowledging the receipt of the volume, Walras is obviously delighted at discovering that a 'disciple encore ignoré' had made extensive and 'remarkable' use of his latest piece of theoretical work (1965, III, pp. 151–2). In the more substantial letter sent two months later, Walras registers only two points of dispute not directly linked to monetary theory.[66] The only comment indirectly linked to money sees, paradoxically, Walras encouraging Aupetit to avoid treading on dynamic grounds and to stick to the study of purely static theory. At no point does the master reprimand his disciple for doing so. Hence, in the realm of pure monetary theory, the internal consistency of abstract theory has finally taken the lead over any pretence of realism.

2.4 Concluding Methodological Remarks: Formal Development and Interpretative Contents

To wind up this Chapter by simply summarizing the various stages Walras's monetary theory went through during three decades would not add much to the already detailed account given in previous chapters. However, two methodological considerations on the logic of this evolution seem more appropriate to tie up the threads of these central chapters on Walras's monetary theory.

On the one hand, the initial inconsistency between money and the theory of exchange is fatal to the whole Walrasian edifice: the superiority of *monetary* exchanges is not demonstrated; it is simply assumed (Chapter 1, Section 1). Even under the highly restrictive and static conditions reached after three decades of uninterrupted research (Chapter 4, Sections 1 and 2), Walras's attempt to bypass his initial cash-in-advance justification for the transaction role of money by inserting money into the utility function, is a failure. The idea that money has a special role as a means of payment is not well approximated by simply putting money into the utility function: monetary phenomena are clearly optional add-on elements rather than an integral component of his purely static general equilibrium theory: money has no part to play in the instantaneous, durationless *tâtonnement*/bargaining mechanism. Hence, from the very first chapters of the earliest 1874 formalization of general equilibrium, money can have no genuine part to play in its core logic. Since this analytical issue has only recently (and eventually) been brought to light and without constricting in any way its critical theoretical importance, we shall not go over it again here.

On the other hand, during the long march leading to the solution of the 'fourth big [monetary] problem' in pure economics and even when finally reluctantly adopting a clumsy version of the money-in-the-utility-function solution, Walras constantly wavered between the internal consistency of a virtual mechanistic timeless simulation of the process that would operate on 'real (even if idealized) markets and the interpretative contents of such an iterative mechanism. Even if Walras eventually gave a clear priority to the internal consistency of his monetary model, the pretence of realism[67] is still constantly lurking beneath the apparently smoothed surface of his static timeless general equilibrium.

From the outset of his scientific career, Walras has always drawn a clear-cut distinction between the 'ideal types' of pure economics and the 'real types' of applied and social economics.[68] By definition, real types cannot be put on the same level as ideal types. Though ideal types are inferred from real types, Walras does not accumulate details in order to build up realistic hypotheses: for him, ideal types are purely abstract phenomena. Furthermore, this rationalistic approach also excludes any confrontation of the results of pure economics with reality for validation. Ideal types can only become real types again with the addition of all their local characteristics. In particular, real-world facts cannot help 'closing' a theoretical demonstration: nowhere should 'reality' be called on to help the understanding of equilibrium equations or the working of an analytical adjustment process. 'Natural facts' of pure economics are clearly opposed to 'humanitarian facts', which are dealt with by applied and social economics. Commenting on what he sees precisely as such a methodological weakness in Cournot's system, Walras explicitly declares that 'pure theory does not expect any confirmation from reality'.[69] In opposition to most modern economic theorists who consider that the realism of a model is judged on its ability to reflect essential characteristics of the reality,[70] Walras adopts a firmly rationalistic 'anti-realistic' epistemology: his pure economics is entirely built by abstracting the unessential characteristics of economic phenomena. Hence, his general equilibrium model is 'in essence, the theory of the determination [not definition!] of prices under a hypothetical régime of perfect competition' (1954, p. 40), that is, an *ideal simulation* of the *process* that would operate on real competitive markets. Why, then, these constant appeals to the so-called selfsameness view? Why should the competitive market solution 'solved *empirically* on the market by the mechanism of free competition' be identical to the solution formulated mathematically? What is 'empirical' in a solution reached instantaneously through a virtual *tâtonnement* conducted in 'logical' time on a hypothetical durationless competitive market, the epitome of Walras's ideal types?

This delicate problem of epistemological unification between the construction of an imaginary system capable of functioning according to laws akin to those of physics while remaining subject to real-world constraints has led to furious interpretative dispute and polemics. As repeatedly shown, Walras's view about the meaning of *tâtonnement* evolved over time from a pseudo-realistic theory of the behaviour of real markets in some definite order to a mere algorithm[71] for the calculation of equilibrium prices. Trapped from his very first edition in a general equilibrium model that is congruent only with a purely static approach, Walras fell victim of his relentless search for an internal coherence from which any claim of describing a price formation process is excluded. As a virtual process in logical time, the *tâtonnement* mechanism is at the centre of this maelstrom; and the part not played by money in this mechanism is the very eye of this cyclone.

Clearly, the lineage from Adam Smith's 'invisible hand' to Walras's general equilibrium theory is straightforward if not as neat as most theorists[72] and some historians of thought wish it to be. Walras himself is very clear about his attempt to formalize Adam Smith's intuition and to demonstrate theoretically the viability of a decentralized economy. Recalling in 1898 a climacteric discussion held in 1860, Walras sums up in a few sentences not only the links between the invisible hand and his central theoretical speculation but also the reason why mathematics are needed to solve this issue.

> [My discussant] admettait bien que la libre concurrence fût un moyen de déterminer des quantités fabriquées des produits et des prix de ces produits; mais il n'admettait pas, ou du moins il n'acceptait pas comme démontré par les économistes ni par moi, que ces quantités et ces prix fussent les seuls ni les meilleurs possibles ... . Je m'en allai en disant: 'Evidemment! il faudrait *prouver que la libre concurrence procure le maximum d'utilité*'. J'étais ramené à l'économique mathématique. (1898, p. 466; *OEC*, X, pp. 419; original italics)

However, if mathematical economics is clearly indispensable in defining the conditions of existence of a vector of equilibrium prices, they do provide only the first half of the explanation of the central puzzle raised by Smith. As a matter of fact, and as Menger was keen to remark, what is the point of defining mathematically static equilibrium conditions if nothing is said on possible dynamic price formation *processes*? Without a link between 'existence' and 'process', without a way to coordinate a reasonably realistic *tâtonnement* process (not mechanism) with the equilibrium prices to which it should lead, the invisible hand enigma remains uncracked. Since, without sequences, there is no monetary theory, the painstaking discussion of Walras's monetary theory conducted throughout Chapters 1 to 4 has clearly shown Walras torn between the two rival versions of *tâtonnement*, between the selfsameness (practical) view and the timeless algorithm for the calculation of equilibrium prices. Even if he eventually yielded to the latter in order to uphold both the internal consistency and the mathematical coherence of his model, Walras could not completely reject the former for fear of undermining the bridge between pure, applied and social economics. As Jaffé thoughtfully sums it up:

> Léon Walras, without renouncing his interest in the empirical relevance of his theory, nevertheless retreated, in the end, from his realistic conception of the *tâtonnement* and left us with a formal portrayal of the process, which, as [he] finally admitted, was neither empirical nor dynamical. (1981, p. 262)

To put it yet in another way, these constant tensions between 'theory' and 'reality', between ideal and real types, between 'static' and 'dynamic', between a logical and a historical process, are simply the expression of the yawning gap which divides what Walras's model can actually demonstrate from what Walras would have wished it to rationalize. Short of having satisfactorily solved this central issue, Walras was bound to face appalling intellectual difficulties when trying to confront (certainly not to verify) the results of pure economics with the working of actual economies. Even if a century later this problem has not been properly solved,[73] Walras's oscillations are the best proof that the founding father of general equilibrium had already glimpsed at this central analytical difficulty which most modern general equilibrium theorists are reluctant to face. As the most notable and lucid exception, Hahn put down with extreme clarity what was only confusedly and reluctantly perceived by Walras: 'General equilibrium is strong on equilibrium and very weak on how it comes about' (1973a, p. 140).

Hence, the perfectly rational strategy adopted by Walras and epitomized by the hypothetical and abstract characteristics progressively brought to monetary theory. From the earliest edition, but more clearly from 1889 onwards, torn between the internal coherence of his model and the paucity of its interpretative results, Walras beyond doubt gave the preference to the former at the expense of the latter. Heuristically ineffective, this attempt to marry a relatively weak analytical model (to which Walras, however, gave pride of place) with even weaker interpretative results goes a long way towards explaining the low ebb reached at the hands of both economists and mathematicians by general theory in the first decade of this century.

However, and in opposition to Ingrao and Israel's contention, the evolution of Walras's monetary theory shows beyond doubt that 'the indissoluble bonds joining the theory's economic and hence empirical foundations and the mathematical problems' did not wait for the 1930s to be progressively loosened (1990, p. 172). Walras's gradual attempt to solve the mathematical problems raised by the introduction of money already shows a growing indifference to the theory's specific economic subject matter. Pareto's total lack of interest for Walras's efforts to make room for money in general equilibrium is probably the best early indicator that intrinsically this model cannot provide any interpretative result. In 1866, and with great prescience, Cournot – the actual founding father of mathematical economics – had already perfectly understood this methodological limitation of pure economics:

> Aussi nos modestes prétentions étaient-elles non d'accroître de beaucoup le domaine de la science proprement dite, mais plutôt de montrer (ce qui a bien son utilité) tout ce qui nous manque pour donner la solution vraiment scientifique de questions que la polémique quotidienne tranche hardiment. (1877, p. 168)[74]

NOTES

1. Collard (1966), Cirillo (1986), De Caro (1985, 1988), Denizet (1977), Falise (1971), Hall (1982, 1983), Howitt (1973), Jaccoud (1994), James and Lecoq (1961), Kuenne (1954, 1959, 1961, 1963), L'Huillier and Guggenheim (1971), McKenzie (1987), Ménard (1990), Montesano (1986, 1991), Morishima (1974), Negishi (1977, 1989), Ostroy (1987, 1992), Patinkin (1965), Schumpeter (1954), Walker (1987a, 1991, 1994a, 1994b).
2. Moreover, and thanks to Jaffé's translation, this last monetary model is the only one to be available in English.
3. Patinkin (1965), Morishima (1977) and Witteloostjuin and Maks (1990) are good examples of such an approach.
4. In particular the theorists linked to the so-called post Keynesian neoclassical synthesis.
5. Despite Walras's deteriorating state of health, it should be obvious that the present writer does not share Walker's view about Walras's declining intellectual abilities after 1889 (see, among numerous examples, Walker, 1994b, pp. 134–5). Quite the contrary. Whatever opinion one might entertain about this last monetary model (and the subsequent literature to which it gave rise), one cannot fail to be impressed by the stubbornness and creativity shown by Walras in finally closing his model after thirty years of incessant toil and labour. In a supreme and excruciatingly painful intellectual push, Walras plugged the last remaining gap in his equation system. The exhausted hedgehog had finally come home.
6. In the fourth edition, Lessons 29 and 30 took the place of this Lesson 33.
7. '(Viz. the quantities possessed of capital goods, the utilities of consumers' goods and services, and the utility of additions to net incomes)' (1954, p. 378). As shown below, the *encaisses désirées* are clearly included in the two former variables.
8. As a matter of fact, Walras's article will form Lessons 29 and 30 of the fourth edition of the *Eléments* (paras 272–83). The editor's notes to the 'Equations de la circulation'

carefully record 136 alterations between the original version and the final text of the *Eléments*: most of them are of a purely stylistic nature (*OEC*, XI, pp. 706–14). Quotations in this section are taken from Jaffé's translation and are from the original 1899 article.

9.   In particular, fixed coefficients of production between fixed and circulating capital which allow the assumption of equilibrium on these markets.

10   As Walras does in paragraphs 273–4 of the *Eléments* (1954, pp. 316–19).

11. Walras had used exactly the same technique for 'out-of-equilibrium' exchanges in his theory of exchange. See above, pp. 30–36.

12. On the exact working of this timeless *tâtonnement sur bons*, see Jaffé's interesting footnote (1954, p. 528, n. 6) and Walker's excellent summary (1987a, p. 859).

13. See, in particular, the new paragraph 207 where 'the equilibrium in production will be first established *in principle*' (1954, p. 242) and the new paragraph 251 where 'the equilibrium in capital formation will be first established *in principle*' (1954, p. 282; italics added). See also paragraph 257 (1954, pp. 292–3).

14. This implies, of course, a strictly cash-on-delivery technology.

15. Curiously, while admitting this fact, Patinkin carries on his dissection of Walras's monetary theory 'as if' Walras had explained the economic meaning of such a utility function (1965, p. 551).

16. See, for example, Patinkin (1965, p. 549); Bridel (1987, pp. 28–9); or Laidler (1991, pp. 60–64).

17. As in previous editions, credit is either absent from the discussion or considered as raising no particular problem.

18. Walras's system knows of no credit or banking systems: payments are made in cash at the time of delivery (see, for example, Kuenne, 1963, p. 316).

19. On the same page, Negishi thoughtfully adds: 'Money can play its essential role only in a non-Walrasian world where transactions take place out of equilibrium'. For a similar opinion about Walras's pure transaction demand for money, see Montesano (1986, p. 938 and 1991, pp. 368–73).

20. See also the discussion in Chapter 1 above, on the difficulties linked to the use of money as a medium of exchange in Walras's pure theory of exchange.

21. See Marget (1935, pp. 160–1); Kuenne (1963, pp. 291–3).

22. Clearly incompatible with a cash-balance approach, this circularity charge ('money as such has no utility except what is derived from its exchange value, that is to say from the utility of things which it can buy'); Keynes (1923, p. 61) was later supported by writers such as Wicksell (1901–06, pp. 20 and 130), Fisher (1911, p. 32), Divisia (1928, pp. 423–33), Helfferich (1927, pp. 526–7), Mises (1912, pp. 114–23) and Fossati (1957, pp. 223–4). More on this confusion later, in particular with the case of Pareto's disciples.

23. Arguing that money, as a capital good, should not be included in the utility function, Morishima (1974, pp. 160–2 and 1977, pp. 137–41) and Hall (1982, pp. 253–4 and 1983, pp. 251–3) suggest an analysis of Walras's money demand in terms of a *semi-indirect* utility function.

24. Hicks was clearly inspired by Walras when he devised this term for his own model (see, for example, 1939, p. 136). See also Robertson (1926, Chap. 5).

25. In modern literature, the spot economy is called temporary equilibrium.

26. To use van Daal and Jolink's apposite wording (1993, p. 94).

27   In the previous editions and in the 1899 'Equations', and in sharp contrast with the fourth edition, the incorporation of savings into the general equilibrium model is still based on *empirical* savings functions of i and not on its reciprocal p_e (see *OEC*, VIII, pp. 358–60 and XI, p. 567). Walras explicitly acknowledges on the same pages that this procedure entitled him to avoid the distinction between *present* and *future* utility. Up until 1900, Walras considered that a proper explanation of savings and capital formation would require a dynamic system of equations through historical time.

28. For an introduction to Walras's devilishly difficult demonstration, see, in particular, Jaffé (1942, 1953 and 1980) as well as the editor's footnotes to the relevant lessons of his translation, van Daal and Jolink (1993), Mouchot (1994) and Patinkin (1965, pp. 551–4).

29. As seen above, these expectations are formed under the hypothesis of perfect certainty.
30. For Jaffé's introduction of this notion of 'imaginary commodity', see his editor's note in 1954, p. 274. For the problems linked to (E) as a perpetuity see Patinkin (1965, p. 554, n. 42) and Jaffé (1980, p. 359).
31 This conceptual distinction between 'two prices' for money is crucial even if, in what follows, (U) has no utility as such and that *numéraire* and money are two different things. Furthermore, within the time period considered by Walras, the quantity of money (U) being given, only the price of the service of money is of analytical interest. Furthermore, Walras assumes that, at the outset of his analysis, the total stock of money Q_u is held by consumers only; entrepreneurs will borrow from them on the money market for the duration of phase 2. Finally, the price of money p_u can also be viewed as the reciprocal of the absolute price level. The price of money comes into play as soon as Walras considers (A) as being both *numéraire and* money.
32 From (4.7) and (4.11), one can easily derive the market excess-supply equation for money as $(Q_u - \delta_{u}p_{a'} + \delta_{\beta}p_{b'} + ... + \delta_{\mu}p_{m'} + \delta_{e}p_{k'} + ...)/p_{u'} = 0$.
33. In so doing, Walras states explicitly in another way the equilibrium conditions for circulating capital goods in which the price of money and the price of its *service d'approvisionnement* are again shown to be only special cases: $1 = p_{a'}/i$, $p_{b} = p_{b'}/i$, $p_{m} = p_{m'}/i$, $p_{u} = p_{u'}/i$ (1954, p. 323).
34. See also Kuenne (1963, pp. 329ff).
35. See above note 26.
36. Which corresponds to paragraphs 6 to 10 of the original 'Equations' (*OEC*, XI, pp. 572–81).
37. See also p. 318 for a similar statement.
38. See, for example, 1954 (pp. 106, 162–3, 170, 184–5, 241–2, 282, 294, 427).
39. From Edgeworth down to Lucas, interpretations have been torn between outright rejections and unconditional acceptance of *tâtonnement* as a 'realistic', though 'stylized', representation of real market forces (or at least of some aspects of price *formation*).
40. This most intriguing methodological question is discussed in the concluding section 2.4, below.
41. And for that matter, Walras is the first in line of a tradition that has been of the essence of neoclassical economic theory ever since.
42. But see also Walker (1994b).
43. In many ways, and with the benefit of hindsight, Patinkin might have learnt from Walras's reluctance to dynamize the *tâtonnement* in the money market. The same year that Patinkin published the second edition of his famous *Money, Interest and Prices*, Hahn showed that 'the assertion that the [real-balance effect] ensures the existence of an equilibrium is unproved' (1965, p. 201). And, ever since, the best theorists have been unsuccessfully trying to crack this toughest of all theoretical enigma – an attempt that, according to Hahn, might well be 'in some intrinsic sense ... impossible' (1982a, p. 747).
44. In fact, they were not at all as 'detailed and precise' as Patinkin wishes them to be.
45. Actually, 'establish' would be a better translation of *établir* than Jaffé's 'describe'.
46. 'Sulle equazioni della circulazione', *Giornale degli Economisti*, 19, 1899, pp. 110–16.
47. In both cases, the fixed data of the problem are 'the quantities possessed, the utility or want curves, the coefficients of production, etc.'(1954, p. 318).
48. Jaffé's brackets.
49. In other words, that the lack of a genuine analysis of the real-balance effect leaves money prices indeterminate.
50. 'Le quatrième grand problème de l'économique' (Walras. 1965, III, p. 80).
51. As mentioned earlier, Walras left this text pratically unchanged.
52. As Pareto soon noticed (1896, I, p. 61, note 2), such a simplistic procedure is hardly applicable without serious amendments. This question about the uniqueness of equilibrium prices (only properly solved by Wald in 1936 and 'popularized' by Samuelson in 1941) is, however, irrelevant to the present discussion.

53. But it is clearly a very big 'if'!
54. See above, Chapter 1, Section 2.
55. It is obviously even more difficult to neglect the interdependence between 'real' and 'money' markets when money is (1) commodity money displaying a utility of its own and (2) the *numéraire*. The substitution mechanism between (A) as money-metal and (A) as metal in non-monetary use is the best illustration of this direct interdependance between money and a 'real' market. In the margin of his own copy of Aupetit's dissertation, Walras goes as far as to write: 'Si le numéraire est monnaie, la loi [that is, quantity theory] est approximativement exacte (à un moment donné)' (1901, p. 92).
56. For a brilliant synthesis of this dominant neoclassical doctrine, see Patinkin's chapter 8 (1965, pp. 162–95).
57. 'For the sake of typographical simplicity' (1954, p. 334, footnote 1).
58. Aupetit quotes Walras on the third edition of the *Eléments* although he also refers to the 1899 'Equations de la circulation'. The marginal annotations in Walras's own copy of Aupetit's book kept in Lausanne are mainly devoted to an update of Aupetit's references. By courtesy of Walras, Aupetit got hold of the fourth edition in May 1901 well after the publication of his dissertation. In fact, the correspondence between the two men starts on the initiative of Aupetit, who sent Walras an inscribed copy of his volume during the same month of May 1901.
59. The literature on Aupetit is small and mainly descriptive. See Patinkin (1965, pp. 535, 565–6 footnote 76 and 571), Bousquet (1957, pp. v–viii) and Zylberberg (1990 and 1994, pp. 76–9); for an early 'Paretian' appraisal, see Boninsegni (1902, pp. 106–7).
60. In a letter to Walras, Hermann Laurent finds him even 'pas très fort en mathématique' (Walras, 1965, III, p. 207).
61. Aupetit (1901, pp. 42ff and 57ff). In 1877, Walras had been advised by his mathematics colleague Amstein that such a technique would greatly simplify his argument. Walras never came round to using it in the *Eléments*. For a detailed account of this episode, see Jaffé (1977, p. 83) and Walras (1965, I, pp. 516–20). See also Creedy (1986, pp. 371–6) for a discussion of Edgeworth's 1877 first ever application of Lagrange's technique.
62. Displaying an interesting mixture of Walrasian and Paretian arguments (1901, pp. 1–36).
63. See Edgeworth's 1891 article which, ten years earlier, had provoked Walras's wrath and Bridel (1996, pp. 252–9).
64. An early anticipation of Hahn's 1973 dictum: 'General equilibrium is strong on equilibrium and very weak on how it comes about' (1973a, p. 140).
65. The remainder of this correspondence extending over a decade is mainly devoted to Aupetit's failed attempt to obtain his *aggrégation*, Walras's efforts to recruit Aupetit for a course of lectures at the *Ecoles des hautes études sociales* in Paris and to visits made by Aupetit at his *maître*.
66. Aupetit's idea of average and absolute measures of cardinal utility through time (see the note kept with the draft letter and reproduced by Jaffé (Walras, 1965, III, pp. 156–7).
67. The so-called selfsameness view expressed time and again by Walras (see pp. 34–5) As far as the 'monetary *tâtonnement*' is concerned: 'Our next step is to pass from the theoretical solution which was formulated mathematically *to the practical solution which is reached in the market*' (1954, p. 325; italics added); Walras is even clearer when mentioning the 'exchange *tâtonnement*': 'There remains only to show – and this is the essential point – that the problem of exchange for which we have just given a theoretical solution is *the selfsame problem that is solved empirically on the market by the mechanism of free competition*' (1954, pp. 162–3; italics added).
68. See Lendjel (1996).
69. Walras's marginal note in his own copy of Cournot (1863, p. 17).
70. Prestigious modern representative of such a 'realistic' epistemology, Lucas even speaks of the model as 'an explicit set of instructions for building a parallel or analogue system – a mechanical imitation economy' (1981, p. 697).
71. Later identified as the Gauss–Seidel method of solving simultaneous equations (see, for example, Arrow and Hahn, 1971, pp. 305–6).

72. See, again, Arrow and Hahn: 'There is by now a long and fairly imposing line of economists from Adam Smith to the present who have sought to show that a decentralized economy motivated by self-interest and guided by price signals would be compatible with a coherent disposition of economic resources that could be regarded, in a well-defined sense, as superior to a large class of possible alternative dispositions. Moreover, the price signals would operate in a way to establish this degree of coherence. It is important to understand how surprising this claim must be to anyone not exposed to this tradition. The immediate "common sense" answer to the question "What will an economy motivated by individual greed and controlled by a very large number of different agents look like?" is probably: There will be chaos. That quite a different answer has long been claimed true and has indeed permeated the economic thinking of a large number of people who are in no way economists is itself sufficient grounds for investigating it seriously. The proposition having been put forward and very seriously entertained, it is important to know not only whether it *is* true, but also whether it *could* be true. A good deal of what follows is concerned with this last question...

    Other questions, of course remain. But the point is this: It is not sufficient to assert that, while it is possible to invent a world in which the claims made on behalf of the "invisible hand" are true, these claims fail in the actual world. It must be shown just how the features of the world regarded as essential in any description of it also make it impossible to substantiate the claims. In attempting to answer the question "Could it be true?", we learn a good deal about why it might not be true' (1971, pp. vi–vii; original italics).
73. According to Hahn, this question might even be insoluble (1982a, p. 747).
74. Once again what better early echo of Arrow and Hahn's pronouncement could one imagine: 'In attempting to answer the question "Could it be true?", we learn a good deal about why it might not be true' (1971, p. vii).

5. The Fate of a Still-born Tradition: Pareto and After

Pareto tratta la moneta per accenni frammentarii, e quindi potrebbe dirsi che *evita* il problema stesso. (Del Vecchio, 1929, p. 135; original italics)

Walras's immediate followers ... did not develop his marginal utility theory of money any further. (Patinkin, 1965, p. 575)

In the field of pure theory, the links between Walras and Pareto are easy to draw. The sharp discontinuity between their respective monetary theories is thus all the more surprising. Moreover, and in opposition to Walras's path-breaking 1900 analysis, very little has been written on Pareto's monetary theory (mainly footnotes in articles devoted to Walras's monetary theory). The difficulty in appraising this apparent weakness has more to do with methodological issues linked to the status of pure theory than with monetary theory *stricto sensu*. Very clearly, and from the beginning, for Pareto, monetary theory does not belong to the 'first approximation' of pure theory. Section 1 offers an attempt to re-examine the status of money within Pareto's general equilibrium model, to explain the sharp discontinuity with Walras's *encaisse désirée* and to contrast Pareto's narrow monetary theory with that of Walras.

The concluding Section 2 offers an attempt at understanding the fate of Walras's monetary theory at the hands of his immediate non-Lausanne epigones. On the one hand, the pre-1914 contributions of Schumpeter (the theorist, not the historian of thought) and Schlesinger, display hardly any progress on Walras's attempt to find a solution to the integration of money into general equilibrium theory. On the other, the (modest) efforts invested into monetary theory by Boninsegni (Pareto's successor in the Lausanne chair) and a handful of Italian epigones during the same period confirm this sharp discontinuity. Worse, some of these contributions even mark a step backwards on the results reached around 1900: in particular, the infamous 'circularity argument' looms large over many of them. Monetary theory as a subset of 'marginal utility analysis [that is,] nothing else than a general theory of choice' (Hicks, 1935, p. 62) will not resume its course until the mid-1930s. During this decade of high theory, jumping on the bandwagon of the Wald–Schlesinger revival of interest for the generalization of Walras's existence theorem, Hicks and Samuelson eventually resumed work on the Walrasian monetary yard which had been deserted more than thirty years earlier.

1 PARETO, MONEY AND MONETARY THEORY

In Section 1.1, some factual and methodological elements linked to Pareto's overall intellectual development are suggested in order to explain if and why he 'was [allegedly] altogether blind to [Walras's work on money] and slid back rather than advanced in this particular field' (Schumpeter, 1954, p. 1082). Section 1.2 provides a reconstruction of Pareto's modest contribution to pure monetary theory despite empirical knowledge far exceeding Walras's rustic and old-fashioned understanding of banking and finance.

1.1 Money as a 'Second-order Approximation'

Given Pareto's highly original mind, it is not surprising to realize that the evolution of his attitude towards monetary theory is uniquely idiosyncratic. From the mid-1880s, Pareto very regularly contributed columns to numerous daily newspapers in Italy and in France. Even a cursory look at the topics discussed reveals his particular interest in fiscal and monetary matters.[1] The enormous empirical material collected during these years eventually found room in the chapters of the *Cours* devoted to applied monetary theory and banking (mainly in 1896, pp. 163–299 and 347–90). In these chapters, Pareto displays an astonishing mastery of the nuts and bolts of the everyday working of contemporary (and past) monetary and banking systems. The statistical material is abundant and up to date; as usual the historical illustrations are encyclopaedic; the bibliographical references are to the then best and most recent works in the Italian, French, English and German languages. In short, Pareto's money and banking chapters compare very favourably with the best standard European works of the day.

As is well known, of the *Cours'* 800 pages, fewer than seventy are devoted to a brilliant and terse presentation of the 'Principles of Pure Economics'. In a Walrasian fashion, from exchange to capital formation, the whole static 'analytical abstraction' (1896, p. 70) is conducted in terms of *numéraire*. Nowhere is money provided with a particular niche of its own: it is mentioned only once in connection with a scathing critique of economists using the trick of a constant marginal utility of money to facilitate their theoretical demonstrations (pp. 36–8[2]). Clearly, for Pareto, the theory of money is an appendix to pure economics not even worth mentioning in the course of the introductory chapter on principles: 'la théorie de la monnaie ... doit venir après celle de la théorie générale de l'équilibre économique' (1909, p. 209).

Since Pareto's contribution to general equilibrium theory can probably be regarded as the most consistent attempt at building a mechanics of the agent's economic behaviour, money and monetary theory can thus be seen as extraneous to the chief aim he set himself when writing his *Cours*: 'to give an outline of economic science considered as a natural science' (p. 2). Since,

> We do not and we never will understand any concrete phenomenon in all its particulars; we can only understand ideal phenomena as they get closer to concrete phenomena ... Similarly, pure economics shows us the general form of the phenomenon; applied economics provides a second approximation: but neither will ever be able to show us how to manage the economic life of every individual. (1896, pp. 16–17; see also *Oeuvres complètes*, henceforth *OC*, IX, p. 79 for a similar passage in his May 1893 inaugural lecture)

Accordingly, to link real-world phenomenon with the abstractions of pure theory, Pareto introduces the technique of *successive approximations* as *the* criterion for the construction of scientific theories. Different from Walras's, this method is another attempt to bridge the gap between pure and applied theory. As early as 1892, Pareto is already preoccupied with the bridging of this gap – a difficulty Walras had, in his mind, largely underestimated.[3] By the successive introduction of the perturbations left out of the ideal phenomenon dealt with in the first approximation of the principles of pure economics,[4] second- or third-order approximations help provide increasingly detailed representations of concrete phenomena. Hence, and even before taking up his chair at Lausanne, Pareto is fully aware of the dangers of separating from applied economics a pure theory based exclusively on the fictional *homo oeconomicus*. From the outset Pareto considered the study of economics as a partial aspect of a broader study of social sciences; furthermore, he always held that pure theory could analyse only the statics of the economic system but neither its dynamics nor its evolution.[5] The axiomatic of pure economics is only a (very) first approximation because economic facts cannot be isolated within a purely economic world; pure economics cannot be insulated from philosophy, history, politics[6] and of course sociology. Underestimated by Walras,[7] this gap is central to Pareto's intellectual evolution and heralds his highly original distinction between logical and non-logical actions, between actions in which emotion and feeling are, or are not, the predominant forces. For Pareto, money as a *social* phenomenon *par excellence* is clearly not part of the first-order class of approximations and has accordingly a very small part, if any, to play in pure economics.[8]

Furthermore, and Pareto never tired of repeating this argument, monetary theory belongs to a peculiar class of theories constantly oscillating between two extreme types:

> Les théories sont en rapport avec les autres faits du milieu où elles se produisent. Si on les étudie objectivement, sans aucun parti pris ... si en d'autres termes on fait la théorie des théories, on remarque tout d'abord qu'on

peut les partager en deux grandes classes. Dans l'une, les théories s'approchent indéfiniment d'une limite; on peut dire, en faisant usage du langage mathématique, qu'elles ont une asymptote .... Dans l'autre classe, les théories, au lieu de s'approcher indéfiniment d'une limite, d'avoir une asymptote, oscillent perpétuellement entre des points extrêmes. ... *Pour la théorie de la monnaie, on peut dire sommairement que les deux points entre lesquels elle oscille sont d'une part la théorie de la* monnaie-marchandise, *et de l'autre la théorie de la* monnaie-signe. La première correspond à un point de vue **exclusivement** économique, la seconde à un point de vue politique et social. Les phénomènes concrets pouvant être considérés sous ces deux points de vue, on comprend comment et pourquoi la théorie de la monnaie oscille entre ces extrêmes. (1919 as in *OC*, IX, p.175 and *OC*, XXI, pp. 152–3; bold emphasis added[9])

Rabidly opposed to fiat money (always rapidly turned for him into 'false money' through over-issue by reckless governments), Pareto always upheld a strictly money-good theory of money.[10] This approach goes a long way towards explaining his neglect, or lack of interest for monetary theory. On the one hand, if money is one of the n goods in the economy, whatever the relative size of fiat money as long as it is fully convertible, monetary theory belongs to economic theory; as such, and in terms of economic theory, money is no special case and his analysis no different from that of the other $(n-1)$ goods. On the other hand, the lack of full convertibility turning fiat money into false money makes money a topic for sociological or political analysis. His understanding of the various late nineteenth-century monetary systems discussed in the *Cours* leaves no doubt about Pareto's choice: money is the least suitable topic for an asymptotic-type of theory.[11]

Some other factual evidence should eventually help set the stage for understanding Pareto's lack of interest for pure monetary theory. Leaving aside the non-strictly scientific columns contributed to various newspapers and magazines, the bulk of Pareto's contributions on money is written between 1892 and 1897. After the *Cours*, and except for a few rather pedestrian pages in the *Manuel* (1909, pp. 450–58), Pareto never came back to monetary theory. Furthermore, while researching and writing his *Cours*, Pareto could only refer to the monetary theory Walras had reached in the second 1889 edition of his *Eléments*.[12] Even more intriguing is the fact that Pareto could not be unaware of Walras's seminal 1899 article on the 'Équations de la circulation': the Italian translation of this crucial paper, if not made by Pareto himself, was at least closely supervised by him on behalf of Walras.[13] Clearly, Walras's introduction of money into the utility/production functions by way of the *encaisse désirée* left no impression whatsoever on Pareto's mind or theory. If there is an explanation to Pareto's failure to advance Walras's pioneering monetary theory, it is probably to be found in the shift of intellectual interest experienced by Pareto at the turn of the century during the very years Walras was trying to promote his new approach to monetary theory. The little interest Pareto had ever displayed for monetary theory was probably lost in this process: never part of first-order approximations, money definitely had no substantial role to play in pure economics.

1.2 Monetary Theory and Non-logical Actions: 'Real' Versus 'False' Money

As the sole exception of the constant marginal utility of money mentioned earlier, the basics of Pareto's very modest contribution[14] to monetary theory are contained in the applied chapters of the *Cours* and in a highly condensed form in the *Manuel*.

Pareto starts his contribution with a questionable – although at the time standard – distinction between 'true' and 'false' money. The former is metallic currency; the latter unbacked paper money. Fiat money, as fully convertible paper money is a half-way house between these two extreme cases. Like Walras's 1874 graphical demonstration,[15] the marginal utility (or more properly for Pareto the ophelimity) of 'true' money is defined as the utility of money-commodity in its non-monetary uses:

> Si A est la monnaie, on doit avoir $\varphi_a = (1/p_b)\varphi_b = \ldots$; φ_a étant l'ophélimité de la *marchandise* qui sert de numéraire ou de monnaie; c'est une ophélimité d'un bien direct, résultant de l'emploi de A comme simple marchandise, *et non une ophélimité indirecte du numéraire ou de la monnaie*. (1896, p. 164, n. 1; italics added)

Although fully aware of the three traditional functions of money,[16] Pareto considers that money (unless metallic or fully convertible) has no utility of its own. The fear of the inflationary consequences of *monnaie signe* (endlessly developed page after page) is the only consideration offered by Pareto for dismissing any positive marginal utility for unbacked fiat money.[17] In 1889, Walras had already abandoned such a primitive framework with the prolegomenon of his *encaisse désirée*. Victim of his realistic bias against fiduciary money, and unlike Walras[18] or Wicksell,[19] Pareto refuses, even out of pure theoretical interest, to be drawn into an analytical discussion of a pure credit/fiat money economy. Again, money derives its positive value from its physical nature, not from any service it could provide. As a result, the price of (real) money is determined simultaneously and along the same purely static lines than the prices of all the other $(n - 1)$ goods.[20]

To quote a summary of Pareto's position suggested by one of his Italian disciples:

Si la monnaie devait servir uniquement d'intermédiaire des échanges, il suffirait qu'elle fût un *symbole* sans aucune utilité économique, à part celle que lui donnerait sa fonction; mais comme elle doit aussi *garantir* les échanges, il est nécessaire qu'elle ait une utilité propre indépendamment de sa fonction d'intermédiaire. De là dérivent toutes ces distinctions entre *vraie* et *fausse* monnaie. (Murray, 1920, p. 329; original italics)

In other words, the positive marginal utility of money stems from the twin functions of *medium of exchange* and *reserve of value*. However, for Pareto, the former function is a necessary but not a sufficient condition: to display a positive price, money has to be one of the *n physical* commodities endowed *per se* with a positive marginal utility independent of its role as a medium of exchange. In a nutshell, even if the positive marginal utility of a metallic currency is the result of both its monetary and non-monetary uses, money, as a pure medium of exchange, cannot display any utility. This asymmetry could not but bar Pareto from discussing Walras's fiat money which has no utility except that provided by its *service d'approvisionnement.*

If Pareto shares with Walras the same approach to the existence theorem, he is only moderately enthusiastic about devising a *tâtonnement*-like market analogue to the stability of his equation system.[21] In fact, and within his narrow treatment of real money, Pareto enlarges slightly his earlier discussion of 'the way market tentatively solves equilibrium equations' (1896, p. 184): a procedure he calls *marchandage.*[22]

This mechanism appears first to be in both exchange and production a *disequilibrium* process taking place in historical time: false quantities can be exchanged at false prices and, accordingly, equilibrium vectors of prices are path dependent, constantly redefined and, hence, never attained. However, and, for once, more explicitly than Walras, Pareto is crystal clear about the thought-experiment nature of his *marchandage* in production theory:

Mr Walras a fait voir que la concurrence des entrepreneurs et des échangeurs est un moyen de résoudre par tentatives [sur le marché] les équations de l'équilibre de la production. Cette idée, en général, paraît être très féconde pour la science économique.
    En réalité, il [the equilibrium] n'est jamais atteint; car, à mesure qu'on tâche de s'en rapprocher, il change continuellement, parce que les conditions techniques et économiques de la production changent. *L'état réel est donc celui de continuelles oscillations autour d'un point central d'équilibre, qui lui-même se déplace.* La théorie que nous exposons nous donne donc seulement un *état limite.* C'est une première approximation. (1896, pp. 45–7; italics added)[23]

What better statement of the purely mechanical analytical nature of the *tâtonnement /marchandage* could one wish for? How could this *état limite* reasonably be considered as a dynamic theory of the equilibrating behaviour of real competitive markets?[24]

Pareto sticks firmly to this approach when reworking this *marchandage* mechanism to make room for real money, considered along Walrasian lines as one of the capital goods:

> Le marché résout par tentatives les équations de l'équilibre. Nous n'avons qu'à reprendre le raisonnement [from capital formation] en comprenant la monnaie circulante parmi les capitaux. ... C'est ainsi que, par des tentatives répétées, on tâche de se rapprocher de *l'état limite* donné par [les équations de] l'équilibre économique. (1896, p. 184; original italics)

Hence, nowhere in the realm of pure theory is there any formal attempt to suggest a 'realistic' dynamic stability analysis involving money: even more clearly than Walras's *tâtonnement*, Pareto's *marchandage* including real money is only a highly symbolic allegory of a way the market could move a monetary economy towards a purely abstract *état limite* defined by general equilibrium equations. Briefly, and in Pareto's own vocabulary, the *marchandage* is a very first logical approximation to a real-world process replete with non-logical actions.

Pareto's modest endeavour to formulate monetary dynamics appears only very traditionally in terms of comparative statics within a very simple version of the quantity theory. His analysis is a long way from the rich intuitions on the working of the money market contained in the 1889 edition of the *Éléments*. For Pareto, the 'essence of the quantity theory' (1896, p. 177) rests on two necessary conditions:

- the necessity for nominal prices to be expressed in false money;
- that equilibrium positions, though nominally different, are independent from the path followed during the adjustment process initiated by a monetary shock.

The first condition is again the consequence of Pareto's narrow definition of money: since, in the short run, the quantity of real money cannot be arbitrarily changed, and even if he offers an exercise in comparative static with a doubling of the quantity of metallic money, for Pareto, the quantity theory is not directly relevant to the determination of the price of real money. How could the quantity and price of real money change without altering the entire vector of equilibrium prices? Furthermore, and given the influence of changes of real money on relative prices, the second condition is also incompatible with metallic money.[25] In a nutshell, the conclusions of the quantity theory are irrelevant to real metallic money.

For Pareto, the quantity theory of money is thus best used as a comparative static instrument applied to changes in false money only. In particular, such a rigorous framework is the only one within which a strict neutrality of money can be established: '[Pour] arriver à une nouvelle position d'équilibre stable, nominalement différente, mais au fond, identique à la position primitive, il faudrait ... que les deux états économiques fussent indépendants l'un de l'autre, et qu'on passât instantanément de l'un à l'autre' (1896, p. 190).

By contrast, when moving to monetary dynamics (1896, p. 186), Pareto offers interesting comments on the path dependency of monetary equilibria following a change in the (false) money supply. Far less impressive than Walras's forced saving analysis,[26] Pareto offers nevertheless some remarks on the changes of the *real* variables of the economy taking places in historical time during the adjustment *process* following a monetary shock. Like Walras's, these remarks owe more to mainstream classical forced saving analysis than to general equilibrium theory. In Pareto's own words: 'Quelles sont les forces qui rétablissent l'équilibre monétaire, quand il est troublé [because] ... si, d'une manière quelconque on dérange l'équilibre monétaire, immédiatement se développent des forces qui tendent à le rétablir' (1896, pp. 189 and 192).

Using the time-honoured case of a once-and-for-all increase (doubling) in the (false) money supply, in less than twenty pages, Pareto examines briefly in turn: inflation growth through lower interest rates, distributional effects between debtors and creditors, forced saving, government's systematic use of seigniorage and inflation to raise revenues, artificial (and temporary) increases in the stock of fixed capital, workers' money illusion resulting in price-wage lags and exchange-rate corrections via the specie-flow mechanism (1896, pp. 183–201). However, whatever disruptions changes in the (false) money supply may bring to the economy, 'en conclusion, on finit bien par revenir, au bout d'un certain temps à une position à peu près égale en réalité à celle dont on est parti' (1896, p. 191). What is eventually very surprising in Pareto's applied monetary theory is not so much that, in the real world, money is only approximately neutral but the unproved assertion that, if left to its own devices, an economic system submitted to a monetary shock is 'naturally' (though approximately) self-adjusting. In a very Friedmanite way, Pareto's careful theorizing seems to have been slightly overtaken by the ultra-liberal 'vision' displayed in the *Cours*.[27]

Pareto never came back to monetary theory proper. The change of emphasis in his research programme confirms that, for him, money is and has always been more influenced by non-logical than by logical actions and, thus, has no part to play in general equilibrium. Hence, in a different way from Walras, with his method of successive approximations, Pareto tries to solve the difficult relations between general equilibrium theory and the need to provide a descriptive representation of reality by escaping into sociology: a difficult decision indeed for a scientist who had devoted his life to the application to economic theory of the experimental method, the key criterion of which is based on empirical regularities.

As Pareto puts it in his speech delivered on the occasion of his jubilee in 1917:

> Arrivé à un certain point de mes recherches d'économie politique, je me trouvai en une impasse. Je voyais la réalité expérimentale [for example, money] et ne pouvais l'atteindre. Plusieurs obstacles m'arrêtaient: entre autres la mutuelle dépendance des phénomènes sociaux ... Il est hors de doute que fort souvent les conclusions des théories économiques ne sont pas vérifiées par l'expérience; et nous nous trouvons embarrassés pour les y faire correspondre. Comment lever cette difficulté? (*OC*, XX, p. 67)

Eliminating various solutions (among which, an outright rejection of economic theory), Pareto finally calls for a recourse to sociology to correct the deficiency and limits of pure economics: 'C'est poussé par le désir d'apporter un complément indispensable aux études de l'économie politique ... que j'ai été amené à composer mon *Traité de sociologie*' (*OC*, XX, p. 69).

In his *Manuale*, Pareto had already inaugurated this vision of pure theory in general and monetary theory in particular: 'Whoever wants to make a scientific study of the social facts has to take account of reality not of abstract principles and the like ... . In general, men act in a non-logical way, but they make believe that they are acting logically' (1906, pp. 35 and 37).

In conclusion, Pareto's lack of interest for monetary theory is not the result of some inability to pick up the pieces where Walras had left them. Quite the contrary. It is the well-reasoned conclusion that money does not belong to first-order approximations to real phenomena which make up pure general equilibrium theory. The extensive factual and institutional material gathered on money is Pareto's answer to the exclusion of money from pure theory. Eighty years later, with the now widely accepted analytical result that there is no room for money in general equilibrium, one can only appreciate Pareto's prescience, if not necessarily the primitive quantity theory of money he eventually had to fall back on. All in all, it does not seem to be far-fetched to consider Pareto as the first modern theorist to whom Hicks's famous dictum on monetary theory can be applied:

> [Pareto's] Monetary theory is less abstract than most economic theory; it cannot avoid a relation to reality, which in other economic theory is sometimes missing. It belongs to monetary history, in a way that economic theory does not always belong to economic history. (1967, p. 156)

2   DISCONTINUITY AND TEMPORARY NEMESIS: THE YEARS IN THE WILDERNESS

The development of the monetary theory in the tradition of the Lausanne School underwent a sharp discontinuity at the turn of the century. On the one hand, the correspondence with Aupetit in 1901 marks Walras's last foray in the field before his death in 1910. On the other, Pareto's lack of interest for monetary theory already present in the *Cours* grew stronger at about the same time.[28] In total contrast with what was happening at Cambridge, the two Lausanne theorists had no disciple available to carry on their monetary analysis. Unlike Marshall, Walras and Pareto had no Keynes or Pigou available to pick up their monetary argument where they had left it. Leaving outside the tenor of the present discussion, the three separate lines of monetary inquiry inaugurated independently and almost simultaneously by the Austrian School,[29] Marshall's pupils at Cambridge[30] and the Swedes (Wicksell[31] and Cassel[32]), few theorists specifically claimed the Lausanne monetary heritage before the Hicksian revival of the 1930s.

Accordingly, this section falls into two parts. Section 2.1 examines the contributions of Schumpeter (the theorist, not the historian of thought) and Schlesinger – the only two economists to have specifically claimed Walras as their (main) source of inspiration in the field of monetary theory. Section 2.2 attempts to assess the (modest) efforts invested in monetary theory by Boninsegni (Pareto's successor to the Lausanne chair) and a handful of Italian epigones during the same period. Neither sub-section reveal any substantial attempts to find a solution to the integration of money into general equilibrium theory. Worse, some of these contributions even mark a step backwards on the results reached around 1900: in particular, the infamous 'circularity argument' looms large over many of them. Jumping on the bandwagon of the 1930's Wald–Schlesinger[33] revival of interest for the generalization of Walras's existence theorem, Hicks and Samuelson will eventually resume work on the Walrasian monetary yard which had been deserted more than thirty years earlier.

2.1   The Austrian Connection: Schumpeter and Schlesinger

The few historians of thought who have studied post-Walrasian monetary theory have always displayed a good deal of hesitation about the respective importance of Schumpeter and Schlesinger. Marget frequently mentions Schumpeter but, surprisingly for such a punctilious scholar, and without being very specific on the originality of this contribution, briefly discusses Schlesinger's book only once (1931, pp. 594–5). Ellis adopts the same approach. Though mentioned twice, Schlesinger's theoretical chapter is referred to only in a footnote because of 'the difficulties of a mathematical treatment in a foreign tongue prevent a proper understanding of his argument' (1934, p. 175n; see also p. 190). With characteristic elegance, Schumpeter (the historian!) never refers to his own work in his *History* in which Schlesinger's monetary theory is briefly mentioned once in a very approving footnote, where Schlesinger's book is seen as a 'striking instance of the fact that in our field first-class performance is neither a necessary nor a sufficient condition for success' (1954, p. 1082). Finally, while practically silent on Schumpeter's monetary theory, Patinkin vigorously praises Schlesinger for his 'highly stimulating originality' (1965, p. 576).

Schumpeter's and Schlesinger's common admiration for Walras (though from different angles) is probably the ground for their mutual respect; hence, the confusion about their respective titles as heirs to the Walrasian monetary tradition. If clearly, and from the outset, Schlesinger's technical superiority is evident, his Walrasian understanding of the relation between money and general equilibrium has been filtered through Schumpeter's own vision.

Actually, the very first paragraph of Schlesinger's highly original chapter 3 on the 'Basic Principles of the Money Economy' is very revealing:

> The merit of having built a bridge between the theory of exchange and the theory of money belongs to Walras and Schumpeter. They showed that direct exchange is not enough to bring about equilibrium and that the market mechanism requires also indirect exchange, *i.e.* the acquisition of goods for the sole purpose of reselling them. (1959, p. 20)

If Walras's *Eléments* are specifically quoted in three different places,[34] and if, as will be shown below, Schlesinger's argument is largely inspired from Walras's 1900 monetary Section,[35] Schumpeter's early survey of static general equilibrium analysis is very probably the link between Walras and Schlesinger. In fact, Schumpeter's very first (and somewhat wordy) book *Das Wesen und der Hauptinhalt der theoretischen Nationalökonomie* (1908) is the key to the modest spread of Walrasian theory into the German-speaking word.[36] The fact that *Wesen* has never been translated into English goes some way towards explaining the relative neglect of this book and of Schumpeter's role in the early development of Lausanne monetary thought. As the first expression of Schumpeter's enthusiasm for Walras and his remarkable understanding of the master's monetary theory this volume calls for a brief, but long overdue, reassessment.

In the covering letter sent in 1908 to Walras with a copy of *Wesen*, Schumpeter (barely twenty-five at the time) displays a somewhat boyish but revealing devotion to the old Lausanne master:

Je ne vous connais pas et pourtant c'est un livre d'un disciple ... Une nouvelle époche [sic] pour l'économie scientifique est marquée par vos beaux mémoires ... Moi, je m'efforcerai toujours de travailler sur les bases indiquées par vous, de continuer votre oeuvre. ... Je ne demande pas mieux que d'être considéré comme votre disciple et de contribuer quelque chose à l'oeuvre inaugurée par vous. (Walras, 1965, III, p. 378).

Wesen's core theoretical chapters are Walrasian through and through. Characteristically entitled *Das Problem des statischen Gleichgewicht*, the eight chapters of this Part II rework Walras's static framework from exchange to capital and monetary theory. In the chapter on price theory, Schumpeter makes no mystery of his source of inspiration:

Alles, was wir wollen, ist, diese [Preis]theorie in ihrer Bedeutung zu zeigen, einige wenige Punkte zu berühren ... und den Leser einzuladen, sich mit der Literatur dieses Gegenstandes vertraut zu machen, ehe er über Wesen und Wert der theoretischen Ökonomie urteilt, ihn vor allem an den grossen Meister der exakten Theorie zu weisen, an Léon Walras. (1908, p. 261)[37]

Not surprisingly, and until money is introduced in the penultimate chapter on the 'Foundations of Monetary Theory' (*Grundlagen der Geldtheorie*), the entire analysis is conducted in terms of *numéraire* (p. 130).[38] In various places Schumpeter insists repeatedly on the crucial difference between *numéraire* and money as if he had just understood Walras's distinction (pp. 288–9, 292). More important, and explicitly for the first time outside Lausanne, monetary theory is considered as an integral part of price theory:

Nach unserer Auffassung ... bildet die Geldtheorie einen integrierenden Bestandteil des Systemes der reinen Ökonomie überhaupt, in dem Sinne, daß man sie nicht von den übrigen Teilen desselben trennen kann. ... Es ist einfach unmöglich, die Geldtheorie 'an sich' zu behandeln. (1908, pp. 279–80[39])

Unfortunately, apart from these two all-important methodological distinctions, Schumpeter's strictly theoretical discussion displays no originality and a good deal of repetition. The few pages devoted to the determination of the value of money (pp. 293–5) do not even summarize Walras's principle of *encaisse désirée*: Schumpeter simply restates a straightforward comparative static quantity theory.[40] No attempt whatsoever is made to build upon Walras's monetary foundations, which are not even referred to. In a 1915 book review of Schlesinger's *Theorie des Geld- und Kreditwirtschaft*, Schumpeter explicitly admits that this honour was reserved for Schlesinger (1915, p. 239).[41]

The third chapter of Schlesinger's brilliant monograph is unmistakably Walrasian. Using exactly the same ordering (and largely the same symbols) as those adopted by Walras in the *Eléments*, Schlesinger discusses successively the central question of the money demand theory in a 'pure paper currency' (1959, p. 33), a more pedestrian version based on Walras's commodity money and, eventually, the theory of the bimetallic standard. These are none other than the three logical steps taken in Lessons 29 to 31 of the 1900 edition.

From the viewpoint of post-Walrasian developments, Schlesinger's highly stimulating and original analysis of the payment procedure that generates a demand for money is clearly the pivotal conceptual development of Walras's monetary framework. However, as shown presently, great care has to be exercised to assess the extent of the compatibility between Walras's purely static framework in which there is no uncertainty about unsynchronized transactions and Schlesinger's final introduction of a probability distribution of such discrepancies between cash inflows and outflows. In other words, is Schlesinger's 'monetary' move into the logic of the continuous market compatible with Walras's overall theoretical framework? Are we not in fact witnessing the very first attempt to go beyond the very strict static limits of Walras's model?

On the very page on which Walras (and Schumpeter) are praised for building a bridge between price and monetary theories, Schlesinger makes it brutally clear that general equilibrium is built on a barter assumption, leaving no room for money. As a matter of fact, referring to Chapter 1 of his volume,[42] and sending the reader back to Walras's *tâtonnement* conducted in terms of *numéraire* (1914, p. 5), Schlesinger argues that in a purely static framework characterized by perfect foresight and perfect competition, the difficulties linked with indirect exchanges and double coincidence of wants inherent to a barter moneyless exchange economy are kept at bay:

> We used to get around this difficulty in our analysis of exchange relationships by assuming that market knowledge was perfect and that the market mechanism functioned without friction. In such circumstances, it seemed plausible that the paths of indirect exchange could be discovered without trouble and followed. (1959, p. 20)

However, for Schlesinger, 'this assumption does not correspond to reality, and one of the major consequences is the existence of money' (1959, p. 20). Moreover, in the following paragraph, using an approach directly inspired by Menger (for example, 1892c, p. 250) and anticipating Clower's cash-in-advance constraint, Schlesinger asserts ingenuously that 'for monetary theory, it is simply a datum that people are in the habit of exchanging goods not by barter but against money' (1959, p. 20): as in Walras's *Eléments*, the existence of a positive price for money is simply *assumed*. Cutting through a Gordian knot not yet untied eighty years later, he concludes that a 'money economy as such cannot be explained rationally, but must be understood as the outcome of an historical and psychological development' (1959, p. 20). Schlesinger's intentions are clear and very different from Walras's: even if the demand for money (and hence its price) under uncertainty can be discussed using utility analysis, the existence of money cannot be explained rationally and no niche can be provided for it within a general equilibrium framework. For Schlesinger, 'the core of the phenomenon of money' eventually amounts to a brilliant partial equilibrium discussion of the means-of-exchange function of money. The five successive models offered by Schlesinger provide more and more realistic specifications of the payment procedure that generates a demand for money; in a very Friedmanite way, nowhere does he venture to confront money with the 'real values of transactions as determined by the exchange economy [in] which value is independent of the value of money' (1959, p. 30). Within chapter 3, this dichotomy of the pricing process is reiterated in at least four different places (1959, pp. 26, 30, 34, 38); no mention is made of Walras's attempt to introduce money into utility functions; no explicit reference to the *encaisse désirée* is suggested. In fact, as Marget surmises (1931, p. 595) and Patinkin conjectures, Schlesinger 'deals with a problem that Walras neglected' (1965, p. 576, n. 19). While Walras tried to force money into a two-period static general equilibrium model in which in phase 1 the discrepancy between cash inflow and outflow during phase 2 is fully anticipated, Schlesinger concentrates on the ambitious – but different – problem of the demand for money as a precautionary stock in the presence of an uncertain future payment stream. In other words, Walras's paramount objective is to close his static general equilibrium model by adding money while keeping intact its internal coherence. For his part, Schlesinger is interested in building a dynamic money demand theory: by simply *assuming* the existence of money, he disconnects his demonstration from Walras's framework which he explicitly considers as a barter model.

A compressed exposition of the logic of Schlesinger's model should be enough to convince the reader that, although highly original, Schlesinger's money demand theory points to conclusions unable to fit within the narrow limits of Walras's static general equilibrium analysis.

Schlesinger proceeds by a series of five successively more complicated models, at each stage relaxing very strict initial assumptions. A careful examination of the first and last models are enough to get the tenor of the argument.

In model 1, four initial assumptions are laid down:

• as in Walras's original model, U is pure paper money having no other use and existing in a given quantity;

- the means-of-exchange function of money is its only function to be considered;
- there are no money substitutes;
- the receipts and disbursements of agents are evenly distributed over all the business days of the year 'but are concentrated at one single point of time within each day, so that one day's receipts can be used only for the following day's expenditures' (1959, p. 21).

Moreover, the value v, in terms of A, of the goods sold and bought by any agent 'is given by the equilibrium condition of the exchange economy' (1959, p. 21). Money is beyond doubt an *ad hoc* addition to a level of transactions exclusively determined by real variables. It allows a gap to be bridged between the receipts in t and the disbursements in $t + 1$; or, alternatively, the individual demand for money is equal to v (the aggregate demand for money being of course defined as $V = v' + v'' + \ldots + v^l$ and equal to the real volume of transactions).

p_u being the unit price of A in terms of U;

Q_u, the total money stock; and

q_u' the individual agent's cash holding;

$v'/p_u, v''/p_u, \ldots, v^l/p_u$ are the real 'amounts of means of circulation which economic units must have in hand at the end of each day for the expenditures of the next' (1959, p. 21).

Schlesinger's equilibrium conditions are laid down in the following equations:

$$\left.\begin{array}{l} q_u' = \dfrac{v'}{p_u} \\[4pt] \ldots\ldots\ldots \\[4pt] q_u^l = \dfrac{v^l}{p_u} \end{array}\right\} \tag{5.1}$$

where

$$q_u' + q_u'' + \ldots + q_u^l = Q_u. \tag{5.2}$$

The number of equations and unknowns being identical $(l + 1)$, this system admits one unique equilibrium solution for the price of money:

$$p_u = \frac{V}{Q_u}. \tag{5.3}$$

To this existence theorem, Schlesinger adds the demonstration of the stability of this equilibrium. To this end, he builds a complicated case with which he traces the conflicting influences on the value of money resulting from a single agent's decision to withdraw part of his cash holdings from circulation. This demonstration leads finally to straightforward quantity theory conclusions: 'it is proved that the value of money ... alters in inverse proportion with the quantity of money' (1959, p. 23).

The crucial part of Schlesinger's whole demonstration rests on his initial fourth assumption: one day's money receipts cannot be spent until the following day; it has, however, to be spent entirely during one single point during this second day: unity of time and space is assumed for all the business transacted. Exactly as in Walras's 1900 model, Schlesinger's first model defines away all possible discrepancy between cash inflows and outflows: there is no uncertainty about the payment procedure. While Walras used this analytical device to make a niche for money in his general equilibrium model, Schlesinger considers it only as a first step[43] in his bid to build a 'realistic' theory of money demand. As a result, and without questioning the consistency of this strategy with the logic of the Walrasian general equilibrium model outlined in his first chapter, Schlesinger progressively relaxes his initial assumptions throughout models 2 to 5.

In model 2, the assumption that one day's money receipts cannot be spent until the following day is dropped: receipts can be re-spent at once in the course of the day. Although the cash requirements are greatly diminished, the value of money is still inversely proportional to the existing quantity of money even if it is no longer proportional with the total value of transactions. Much more important to Schlesinger's argument is the introduction of probability theory to estimate the now possible discrepancies between 'expenditures which have, or may have, to be made in the course of the day in advance of receipts' (1959, p. 23). To paraphrase Schlesinger, and despite the introduction of a clearing system, the more one moves away from the initial static model, the smaller the unity of time and space for the business transacted, the higher the probability of discrepancies during the day between cash inflows and outflows, the larger the amount of cash requirements.

In model 3, Schlesinger drops the assumption that such discrepancies compensate each other in a time scale of hours within a single day: 'longer lasting ones have to be taken care of' (1959, p. 25). Again, real variables rule the roost:

> The year's purchases and sales, and their order, are independent of the value of money and are conditioned only by the economy's other data. Therefore, the real balances and the amount of monetary purchasing power required for the transactions can be determined without reference to p_u. (1959, p. 26)

With the help of two functions expressing, as functions of time, minimum debit and credit balances (calculated in terms of the initial day's cash holdings), Schlesinger offers a mathematical and graphical representation of the maximum cumulative discrepancies between payments whose magnitudes and future due-dates during the year are *fixed*.

Cash holdings are then determined by the maximum cumulative discrepancy between daily cash outflows and inflows generated during the one-year period by this given payment stream. In other words, and very much as in Walras's 1900 model, in order to avoid certain default, the agent clearly has *no choice*: he or she is *compelled* by this given payment stream to hold cash balances at the beginning of a period defined, however, by Schlesinger in historical, not analytical time.

In model 4, adjusting his 'assumptions yet more closely to reality', Schlesinger further relaxes his initial hypotheses. By introducing an *uncertain* payment stream, he not only breaks new ground in the money demand theory but also parts ways with Walras's purely static approach:

> Having started out with expenditures and receipts at predetermined hours, we had then moved on to the assumption that expenditures and receipts may be expected at any hour of the day. Now we shall consider the possibility that expenditures, or the dates at which they become due, may not be foreseeable at all, and that receipts may fail to come in. (1959, pp. 28–9)

Clearly, the introduction of uncertainty linked to the payment stream implies alternative choices (and utility analysis): the agent is faced with a tradeoff between holding (at a cost) a cash reserve against these uncertain payments and facing the costs of meeting them by the forced sale of assets (at the risk of a loss).[44] Hence, it is perfectly rational for the agent to hold money even if it is dominated by all the other income-yielding assets. Like Walras in his 1889 edition, Schlesinger considers explicitly the rate of interest as the cost of holding money:[45]

> If these frictions are considerable, it may well pay to forestall this risk by larger cash reserves ... The individual loss involved in not earning interest on these cash reserves can be regarded as *a risk premium*. (1959, p. 29; italics added).

Hence, the marginal utility of this insurance service is positive; the price of holding money is positive and measured by the rate of interest: real balances are one of the determinants of the agent's utility function. Defining the real value of cash balances by r_v, Schlesinger defines the marginal utility (price) of the insurance service provided by money as $f(r_v)$. The agent's optimum position is eventually defined as $i = f(r_v)$.[46]

Finally, in the fifth stage of his demonstration, Schlesinger writes down an excess-demand equation for real balances where C stands for credit transactions:

$$Q_u = F(V, C, p_u) + \Phi(i, V, C, p_u). \qquad (5.4)$$

The first half of the right-hand side of this equation expresses the demand for *real* balances generated by fixed payments and the second half the demand generated by uncertain payments. As Patinkin remarked in 1956, this equation displays 'a remarkable similarity between the preceding excess-demand equations and Keynes's $L_1(Y) + L_2(r) = M_0$' (1965, p. 577).[47] Clearly, and beyond doubt, and well before the industry that sprang up after the *General Theory*, Schlesinger inaugurates as early as 1914 the era of the macroeconomic demand function for money. During the same pre-war years, English (Marshall, Keynes or Pigou) and American (Fisher and Newcomb) economists were still content with standard formulations of the quantity theory in which the rate of interest was still conspicuously lacking.

However, and in so far as the central theme of this book is concerned, Schlesinger does not offer a single clue as to the coherence between his excess-demand equation and general equilibrium. Although highly stimulating, his analysis of the payment dynamic procedure that generates a demand for money is not compatible with Walras's purely static framework in which there is no uncertainty (even in terms of probability distributions) between unsynchronized cash inflows and outflows. In other words, Schlesinger offers no theoretical bridge between his move into the logic of the continuous market in terms of sequences and expectations linked to the demand for money and a static general equilibrium framework. Furthermore, and characteristically, not a word is offered on the crucial problem of finding room for such a dynamic notion of money demand as one of the determinants of the agent's utility function. Even if, more than twenty years earlier than Hicks, Schlesinger suggests a formalization of the demand for money as 'a choice at the margin' (Hicks, 1935, p. 64), his analysis suffers from the same lack of coordination. Short of being able to insert money into a fully specified general equilibrium theory, Schlesinger is among the first in a long line of economists[48] to use a procedure which carefully bypasses Walras's ambitious attempt to 'deduce rationally [the value of money] from the equations of exchange and maximum satisfaction' (1954, p. 38): Patinkin's so-called invalid dichotomy.[49] Although a reserve against contingencies discussed with the marginal-utility apparatus, money (and the theory of money) are, however, introduced *after* the equilibrium price relations are set for the purpose of determining absolute prices. As far as money is concerned, Walras refused to be dragged beyond the narrow limits of his static framework; Pareto excluded it *ex definitione* from general equilibrium theory; for his part, while proclaiming his objective of integrating monetary and price theory, Schlesinger completely fails to formally bridge this gap by including a stability analysis in his monetary theory.

2.2 The Twilight of a Tradition

As Ellis[50] and Marget[51] noticed long ago, until the 1930s, most leading marginalist theorists[52] paradoxically denied the applicability of marginal-utility analysis to money and fell victims of the so-called *circularity charge*. As a latter-day example, Keynes still claimed in the early 1920s that 'money as such has no utility except what is derived from its exchange-value, that is to say from the utility of the things which it can buy' (1923, p. 61). Hence, the positive marginal utility of money stems exclusively from the marginal utility of the goods against which money can be exchanged and not from the liquidity advantage of holding it. In other words, money *as such* has no positive value; money is not an argument of the agent's utility function.

During Pareto's lifetime, and under the influence of the Austrian School, Pantaleoni[53] and Del Vecchio[54] had already inaugurated an elaborate version of this circularity argument which was to dominate monetary theory, particularly in Italy, until the 1930s. Even Barone, with his sharp eye for analytical deficiencies, entirely missed the opportunity of avoiding this pitfall and improving on Walras's theory.[55] With the help of some straightforward mathematics, Divisia managed to give some credibility to a thesis that collapses as soon as one drops the basic assumption that 'utility of money' is another way of defining the utility of the commodities which money can buy.[56]

As discussed earlier, Pareto's central distinction between real (commodity) and false (paper) money led him to use the terms 'marginal utility of money' to denote only 'the utility of the commodity-money in its non-monetary uses' never, *à la* Walras, the utility of the *service d'approvisionnement* of money.[57] Boninsegni, Pareto's successor to the Lausanne chair, failed to escape from his master's real/false money dichotomy and slavishly repeated his exposition.[58] In his lectures 'according to the doctrine of the Lausanne School', Murray recycled the same story, insisting heavily on the zero-marginal utility of a means of exchange that would not at the same time be a physical good.[59]

These two lines of inquiry did not lead very far along the road towards the integration of money into general equilibrium theory. Deliberately keeping out of the discussion the equally modest developments taking place on separate tracks in Vienna, Stockholm or Cambridge, from 1914 to 1930 nothing of importance happened in this crucial field of research: Walras's intuition had simply been forgotten. With the advent of the so-called temporary equilibrium models, Myrdal in 1927, Hayek and Lindhal in 1929, Lundberg in 1930 and above all Hicks in 1935 and Samuelson in 1941 eventually resumed work on the Walrasian monetary confines which had been deserted thirty years earlier.

In a nutshell, between 1900 and the early 1930s, a complete nemesis fell on Walras's brilliant monetary intuition: the so-called Lausanne monetary tradition was purely and simply still-born. When the problem was squarely faced again, it was neither in Lausanne, nor even in Continental Europe but tentatively in the United Kingdom (with Hicks and Pigou) and principally in the United States (with Samuelson). Radically different from Walras's purely static model, this temporary equilibrium approach dominated the profession for more than thirty years. The way to the first attempt at an 'Integration of Monetary and Value Theory' along Walrasian lines was eventually opened by Patinkin in 1948 and the argument brought to fruition in 1956. In this framework, the demand for money is derived from a utility function that includes real-money balances as one of its argument and that rationalizes this inclusion as a representation of the 'liquidity service' of such balances in providing 'insurance' against the 'financial embarrassment' that might otherwise be caused by the assumed stochastic payment process.[60] It would take the profession another ten years to conclude with Hahn that, unfortunately, this temporary equilibrium avenue was nothing but a dead end: 'I conclude ... that the assertion that the Pigou effect [the real-balance effect] ensures the existence of a [Walrasian monetary] equilibrium is unproven' (1965, p. 201). Going back to the logic of the pure theory of exchange, twenty-five additional years later, Ostroy and Starr in 1990 eventually hammered the ultimate nail into the coffin of Walras's money-in-the-utility-function approach:

> The goal of the [Walras–Hicks–Patinkin] tradition was the integration of monetary and value theory but it was understood that this would be achieved by integrating monetary theory *into* the structure of existing value theory.
>
> [Unfortunately,] in an exchange economy, putting money, even real money balances, into the utility function is an unreliable choice-theoretic short cut for modelling the transactions role of money. (1990, p. 6)

Indeed, Ostroy and Starr send the reader back to the central static properties common to all general equilibrium models (from Walras to the Arrow–Debreu versions): their inability to let money play an *essential* role, that is, the inability of known general equilibrium models to display *sequential* trading which involves more than the time-indexing of commodities. At this point, the little fairy tale mentioned in Chapter 1, Section 1, is worth recalling. To determine the utility of real balances, a household must first have a general idea of the volume of transactions that these balances will have to perform; and this can be known only *after* the household has determined the outcome of the utility-maximization process. In the extreme case in which the composition of the household's initial endowment is the same as its optimum one, it will not plan to carry out any transactions, and, hence, the holding of money balances will not generate any utility. In short, the so-called Walras–Hicks–Patinkin tradition – and all the conclusions it implies (notably the neutrality of money) – is, to put it mildly, problematic. Ostroy and Starr have largely contributed to finally bringing it to rest. To quote from Ostroy's seminal contribution:

> By introducing money after he had completed his theory of exchange, Walras clearly made monetary phenomena an optional add-on rather than an integral component of the mechanism of exchange. Further it was an add-on that would have to be valued for its own sake rather than as a component enhancing the performance of the rest of the system. (1992, p. 784)

A century after Walras initiated this money-in-the-utility-function approach, a coordination between money and value theory is still wanting. As Walras wrote in the early 1874 edition of the *Eléments*:

> En somme, la [monnaie] constitue une simplification pratique et une complication théorique; c'est pourquoi, quand nous aurons bien défini son rôle, nous en ferons très souvent abstraction dans l'étude scientifique des phénomènes de la vie économique. (1874, pp. 175, same passage in *OEC*, VIII, p. 544)

One hundred and twenty years later, it is about time to jettison such a procedure and accept that money is not an add-on but an integral part of the mechanism of exchange; and that to abstract from this 'theoretical complication' hardly helps the 'scientific study of economic phenomena'. But, and to paraphrase again Hahn – within the logic of Walrasian general equilibrium models – 'it may be that in some intrinsic sense such a theory is impossible'.

NOTES

1   See *Oeuvres complètes*, henceforth *OC*, XX, pp. 73–7. Shortly after Pareto's death, Del Vecchio was already mentioning the relative neglect Pareto's applied work was suffering from (1924, p. 62).
2.   This question already raised by Walras is linked to the principle of *general* (and not partial) equilibrium in connection with the difficult link also established by Walras between utility and demand functions. Pareto had already discussed it extensively in 1892

(*OC*, XXVI, pp. 53–4) and in 1893 with caustic comments on the relevant chapters of Marshall's *Principles* (*OC*, XXVI, pp. 168–9 and 178–80). The question is eventually briefly mentioned again in the mathematical appendix to the *Manuel* (1909, p. 585).

3. Discussing the superiority of his own equilibrium equations over Auspitz and Lieben's, Walras was pleased to acknowledge Pareto's support as far as pure theory is concerned: 'vous avez clairement montré que mes formules sont supérieures à celles d'Auspitz et Lieben comme formules d'économie pure'. In his answer, and without minimizing the importance of applied economics, Pareto writes: 'Vous faites de la science pure, je tâche d'appliquer cette science pure. Voici la différence principale de nos points de vue'. A few days later, Walras displays his inability to understand this contention destined to be at the heart of Pareto's economic and sociological models: 'Je ne vois pas' says Walras 'qu'il y ait tant de difficultés à concilier les exigences de la théorie pure et celles de la théorie appliquée' (Walras, 1965, II, pp. 491–2).

4. In a letter from 1897, Pareto is very clear about this role of pure economics in his overall model: 'Vous n'ignorez pas, sans doute, que j'ai emprunté simplement à M. Walras la représentation, par des formules mathématiques, d'une *première approximation* du phénomène économique' (*OC*, XIX, p. 335; italics added).

5. See Bridel (1990, pp. 183–91).

6. Since 1886, Pareto had been fully aware of the gap between the pure theory of foreign trade and the necessity of considering a much broader range of political and sociological elements before launching an all-out war in favour of free trade (on this crucial turning point in Pareto's intellectual development, see Busino (1967, pp. 15–25) and Valade (1990, pp. 27–49).

7. Particularly within his *tâtonnement* mechanism!

8. On this point, see Del Vecchio (1924, p. 66).

9. For a similar argument, see *OC*, XXVI, p. 637 and *OC*, XXI, p. 110. In the same article, Pareto expresses doubts on Walras's proposed method (inspired by Cournot) of stabilizing the value of money. See also Pareto's earlier lectures notes (*OC*, XXIV, pp. 121–3).

10. Unlike Walras, Pareto is fully aware of the small part played by metallic money in the sum total of all market transactions. He provides his readers with lengthy explanations and international statistical comparisons about the ratio between metallic money, cheques and 'compensations' to illustrate his case. Full convertibility in gold/silver of all fiat money is for him the only way to avoid 'real' money turning into 'false' money (1896, pp. 164–5). Needless to add, for Pareto, 'perfectly free trade' (that is, perfect competition) is the only economic system which ensures the existence of 'real' money.

11. If perfectly understandable for a theorist who has experienced during most of his adult life the convulsions of the late nineteenth-century Italian monetary regime, this dichotomy does not explain satisfactorily Pareto's lack of interest – even in the realm of pure theory – for a *rationale* behind the demand for money. As a matter of fact, and as discussed below in Section 1.2, nowhere does Pareto discuss marginal utility in connection with cash balances as such.

12. Testimony of the rapidly deteriorating relationship between the two men and of Pareto's growing irritation with the developments of Walras's work, up until his death in 1923, in the realm of monetary theory, Pareto never referred to the fourth or even to the third edition of the *Eléments*.

13. See above, Chapter 4, Section 2, p. 133 for the references given to the correspondence between Walras and Pareto on this translation.

14. Marget goes as far as to write the word contribution between inverted commas and to contend that it 'may safely be disregarded' because of 'Pareto's complete lack of sympathy with, or understanding of, Walras's analytical contributions to the field of monetary theory' (1935, pp. 154 and 147, n. 6). Comparing in an earlier article Pareto's monetary theory with that of Walras, Marget asserts that 'Pareto, from first to last seems to have been completely blind to ... the implications of the [monetary] analysis of his great predecessor ... The consequence of this really extraordinary procedure ... was that

it set an unfortunate model for those members of the "School of Lausanne" who seem to have derived their inspiration from Pareto, rather than from Walras directly' (Marget, 1931, pp. 596–7). Kuenne considers it as 'neither very extensive nor original' and suffering 'from a non-typical lack of clarity' (1963, p. 294, n. 8 and 304). In his posthumously published *Wesen des Geldes*, Schumpeter considers that in the realm of monetary theory 'Vilfredo Pareto hat auf diesem Gebiet völlig versagt' (1970, p. 80). Patinkin maintains that Pareto 'almost completely ignored ... monetary theory' (1965, p. 571).

15. Quoted approvingly in 1892 by Pareto in a column written for the French daily *Le Monde économique* (*OC*, IX, pp. 28–9).

16. The *monnaie de circulation* helps make arbitrages between goods (medium of exchange); the *monnaie d'épargne* 'sert aussi à transformer les biens présents en biens futurs' (1896, p. 172) (store of value): this is Pareto's only mention of uncertainty linked with money as an instrument of intertemporal allocation of resources; the *numéraire* used in pure theory is, of course, the common means of measurement. This double distinction is naturally taken over directly from Walras's *Eléments*.

17. This position is rather odd for someone who kept claiming to be a 'nominalist among nominalists' (*OC*, XXVI, p. 448).

18. See above, pp. 28, 71 and 73–74.

19. See 1898, p. 68 for Wicksell's 'pure credit economy'.

20. With the introduction of 'false money', Pareto illustrates easily that without the introduction of a variable R_m standing for the amount of false money, the equilibrium equation system would remain *undetermined* (1896, p. 176, n. 2): 'Avec la vraie monnaie, il n'y a qu'une position d'équilibre stable; avec la fausse monnaie, il y en a une infinité' (1896, p. 177). Obviously, the limitation of the amount of false money is, for Pareto, one of the conditions of general equilibrium. This piece of analysis can be found in the works of some of his Italian disciples, especially Murray (1920, pp. 340–2), Boninsegni (1930, pp. 150–1) and Bresciani-Turoni (1931, p. 401) where it is even attributed to Walras.

21. To argue, like Patinkin, that 'Pareto, perhaps more than the others [successors], realized the power and the beauty of [Walras's *tâtonnement*] theory' (1965, p. 535) seems somehow far-fetched.

22. In fact none other than Walras's good old *tâtonnement*: 'Mr Walras a fait voir que le marchandage qui s'établit avec la libre concurrence est le moyen de résoudre par tentatives les équations de l'échange. Mr Edgeworth a objecté que ce n'était là qu'*un* moyen. Il a raison; mais le moyen indiqué par Mr Walras est bien celui qui représente la partie principale du phénomène économique' (1896, pp. 24–5). Pareto clearly takes Edgeworth's side in the famous debate around the so-called 'realism' of the *tâtonnement* (see Bridel, 1996, pp. 252–60). Moreover, in a very revealing passage, Pareto draws a comparison between 'this very fruitful idea for economic science' and Smith's distinction between market prices oscillating in the short run around a long-run centre of gravity expressed by normal prices (1896, p. 46). For the first time in the literature, an explicit parallel is drawn between the Smithian invisible hand and Walras's *tâtonnement*.

23. This approach seems very similar to Walras's parallel between the once-and-for-all market as a first approximation to the permanent market.

24. When dealing with capital formation, Pareto adopts the same strategy: 'Le marchandage produit les phénomènes décrits, auxquels s'ajoutent ceux qui dépendent de la production des capitaux. Les échangeurs vont sur le marché et y portent certaines quantités de produits et de services. L'équilibre s'établit pour l'échange. Alors les entrepreneurs qui fabriquent des produits et ceux qui fabriquent des capitaux, augmentent ou restreignent leur production, en se rapprochant de l'égalité du coût de production au prix de vente. Cela dérange l'équilibre de l'échange; il se rétablit. De nouveau, la production s'adapte à ce nouvel équilibre de l'échange, et ainsi de suite, jusqu'à ce que l'équilibre soit atteint. *Dans le cas de la libre concurrence, une première idée du phénomène économique nous est* [ainsi] *donnée ... nous devrons, comme seconde approximation,*

tenir compte des circonstances que nous avons maintenant négligées dans l'étude du phénomène économique (1896, pp. 61–2; italics added). In a mathematical footnote to this text at the bottom of page 61, Pareto speculates about the stability (convergence) of his *marchandage* mechanism: do 'these successive approximations approach closer and closer to the solution of the [market excess-demand] equations'? Contrary to Patinkin's opinion (1965, pp. 535–6, n. 14), Pareto's answer seems perfectly in line with the idealized description of his *marchandage* suggested in the main text. Since the successive approximations of this *marchandage* are not the result of the 'normal operations of market forces' (to use Patinkin's terminology) but reflect a purely analytical iterative exercise, 'provided a sufficiently close value is taken' as Pareto adds, there is no reason why the *marchandage* mechanism should not foster the same solution as the 'general theory of equations'.

25. With a few additional remarks on the velocity of circulation, Pareto briefly repeats this demonstration in the *Manuel* (1909, pp. 368–71). More sceptical than in the *Cours*, Pareto admits that even with false money, the quantity theory of money is only 'approximately and roughly true' (1909, p. 369).

26. An analysis, incidentally, never mentioned by Pareto.

27. In the preface to the *Manuale* (1906, p. VII) as well as in the *Traité de sociologie* (1919, II, p. 1414), Pareto himself makes some highly ironical comments on 'the author of the *Cours*' and his 'synthèse incomplète ayant pour but de revenir de l'analyse scientifique à la doctrine concrète'. Contemporary economists could profitably ponder again Pareto's dire warning against this incomplete synthesis!

28 Immediately after the *Cours*, Pareto devoted most of his time to pure economics and, above all, to his massive two-volume *Systèmes socialistes* (1902–03).

29. The Menger (1892a)–Wieser (1889)–Mises (1912)–Hayek (1929) connection.

30. See Bridel (1987, pp. 52–137) and Laidler (1991, pp. 49–84).

31. The connection between Walras's monetary theory and Wicksell's is difficult to establish with accuracy. Even if fully aware of Walras's *Eléments*, for obvious chronological reasons, Wicksell wrote *Interest and Prices* (1898) totally unaware of Walras's 1900 version of his monetary theory. Although denying the relevance of marginal utility analysis for monetary theory, he developed in *Interest and Prices* and in his *Lectures* (1901–6) a cash-balance approach based implicitly on the services provided by money holdings as such. Nowhere in his post-1900 writings does Wicksell either mention Walras's fourth edition, or make a specific attempt at formally integrating money into his general equilibrium framework. In his intellectual biography, Uhr considers that Wicksell 'did not take up [Walras's] positions for extended discussion' (1960, p. 205).

32. See Patinkin's excellent Appendix H (1965, pp. 611–21) on Cassel's confused and confusing treatment of money leading to a clear-cut version of the dichotomy between money and relative prices (see, for example, Cassel, 1924, pp. 420–3).

33. On the amazing piece of intellectual history linking the mathematician Karl Menger (son of the economist Carl Menger) with Abraham Wald as Schlesinger's mathematical tutor and their famous joint 1934–5 articles giving the first proofs of existence for models of general equilibrium including the treatment of free goods, see Weintraub (1985, pp. 62–73).

34. Schlesinger (1914, pp. 5, 81 and 103), where mentions are made of the 1900 fourth edition.

35. In particular, the similarities are unmistakable in the algebraic symbols used by Schlesinger as well as in their definitions.

36. In his obituary to Schumpeter, Morgenstern mentions the excitement of the younger generation of Austrian economists upon discovering Wesen: 'This book ... has, for many years, been one of the greatest rarities of the book trade. The work was read avidly in Vienna even long after the First World War, and its youthful freshness and vigor appealed to the young students. I myself remember what sort of revelation it was to me when I first laid hands on it and ... resolved to read everything Schumpeter had written

and would ever write' (1951, p. 199). In passing, one might also mention the total lack of influence of either Walras's or Pareto's contributions in the debate on the nature of money which raged among German economists during the first quarter of this century (and this despite the part played in it by Bortkiewicz). For an old, but only, survey of this dispute, see Bilimovic (1931).

37. In the copy of *Wesen* presented and inscribed to Walras by Schumpeter (and kept with Walras's library at the *Centre d'études interdisciplinaires Walras–Pareto* at Lausanne), the old master has carefully ticked all the passages where his name or theory are mentioned.

38. Schumpeter had clearly digested Walras's crucial (and at the time still novel) distinction between *numéraire* and money: 'Die Theorie des Geldes als Wertmaßstab und die Theorie des Geldes als Tauschmittel sind völlig verschiedene Dinge' (1908, p. 289). In his marginal notes, Walras translates these two crucial words as *numéraire* and *monnaie*. See also Schumpeter (1970, p. 214, n. 9).

39. Throughout his scientific career, Schumpeter kept repeating on various occasions this crucial assertion. See, for examples, 1915, p. 239: 'Das letzte Jahrzehnt von Schöpferkraft, das dem einsamen Forscher von Lausanne beschieden war, war der Geldtheorie gewidmet'; 1917–18, p. 150: 'Walras was the first to penetrate more deeply, and only since then has monetary theory begun to be part of the general economic theory'; and 1970, p. 80: 'Léon Walras [machte] die Theorie des Geldes zu einem Bestandteil der allgemeinen Theorie des wirtschaftlichen Gleigewichts'.

40. The distributional effects are only briefly mentioned in connection with a short discussion of a forced saving mechanism.

41. Even if Aupetit and Del Vecchio are also mentioned as members of the Walrasian school of monetary economics. Clearly (and very rightly), Schumpeter considers their respective contributions as less original than Schlesinger's.

42. Entitled *Grundzüge der Tauschwirtschaft*; literally, Foundations of Exchange Economy.

43. The 'simplest form of the problem of the value of money' (1959, p. 21).

44. Schlesinger is not absolutely coherent in the use of the rate of interest as the criteria allowing the distinction between fixed and uncertain payment streams. He even suggests that a fixed payment stream could be altered by agents investing or disinvesting cash balances: 'It is fairly usual in times of large surplus receipts to invest spare cash ... with the intention of selling out again when large disbursements are due and to earn interest in the meantime' (1959, p. 27). However, this argument disappears from the first term of the right-hand side of equation (5.4) below, expressing the demand for real balances determined by fixed payments.

45. See above, p. 138 where it is shown that this tentative use of the rate of interest as the cost of holding the *encaisses désirées* was subsequently dropped by Walras in the 1900 fourth edition. Unlike Schlesinger, Walras had clearly understood the limits of his static general equilibrium model.

46. Patinkin noted long ago that this optimum condition is not properly defined. As a matter of fact, the rate of interest does not 'have the dimensions of utility. ... Instead of "i", Schlesinger should have written "the marginal utility of i dollars" worth of expenditure' (1965, p. 577).

47. Equation (5.4) should even be preferred to Keynes's in so far as by including p, Schlesinger excludes the money illusion hypothesis present in the *General Theory* (1936, p. 199).

48. For a long – though not exhaustive – list, see Patinkin (1965, p. 625).

49. Recall Schlesinger's assertion according to which 'the year's purchases and sales, and their order, are independent of the value of money and are conditioned only by the economy's other data' (1959, p. 26). See above, pp. 165–6.

50. Ellis (1934, pp. 67, 153, 157, 160, 189, 199).

51. Marget (1931, pp. 592, n. 53; 1938, pp. 442, 445, n. 86 and 450–8; 1942, pp. 84–6, 92–3). Marget notices in the same passages the contradictory tendency of many writers to exclude the use of marginal-utility analysis to money while, at the same time, adopting a

cash-balance approach which implies, by definition, a choice at the margin and, hence, an analysis of utilities. As the most surprising example, see Wicksell (1898, p. 29).

52. Patinkin includes in this list Wicksell, Mises, Helfferich and even his beloved Fisher (1965, pp. 573–4). Wieser should be considered as the founding father of this tradition. In 1889, he was already arguing in terms that were later taken over by Mises (1912, p. 97) and perpetuated in Vienna until Hayek: 'The exchange-value of money is the anticipated use-value of the things that can be obtained with it' (1889, p. 47).

53. 'Money is only endowed with an indirect utility consisting in its power of obtaining ... some direct utility' (1898, p. 221).

54. 'Non esiste un bisogno di approvvigionamento di moneta diverso e distinto dal bisogno dei beni, i quali saranno acquistati con la moneta. ... la teoria matematica dell'equilibrio monetario costituisce un tentativo di integrare la teoria quantitativa, corretto per il punto da cui procede, l'utilità della moneta, e per il procedimento generale; ma viziato dall'assunzione di un fatto irreale, come base di tutta la costruzione: il servigio della moneta come un altro servigio, oltre quelli resi agli individui concreti dagli altri beni su cui svolgono la loro attività economica' (1909, pp. 270–72; 1983, p. 153–5); see also 1917, p. 128: 'non esiste una utilità propria della moneta indipendente da quella a lei riferita dalle merci'.

55. Barone (1936, pp. 193–5).

56. Divisia (1928, pp. 423–33).

57. See Sensini's rather ineffectual defence of Pareto's 'real money' argument against Divisia's attack in terms of the circularity charge (1929, pp. 117–18). Like most Paretians, Sensini considered money as only one of the n physical goods endowed as such with a positive exchange value independent of its medium-of-exchange function.

58. Boninsegni (1930, pp. 129–30).

59. Murray (1920, pp. 329–31

60. Patinkin (1965, Chapter 5).

Bibliography

Allais, M. (1943). *A la recherche d'une discipline économique*, Paris, Saint-Cloud, Chez l'auteur (Privately printed).

Allais, M. (1945). *Economie pure et rendement social*, Paris, Sirey.

Allais, M. (1947). *Economie et intérêt*, Paris, Imprimerie nationale, 2 vols.

Anderson, B.M. (1917). *The Value of Money*, New York, Macmillan.

Antonelli, E. (1914). *Principes d'économie pure*, Paris, Marcel Rivière.

Antonelli, E. (1939). *L'économie pure du capitalisme*, Paris, Rivière.

Arrow, K. and Hahn, F.H. (1971). *General Competitive Equilibrium*, Amsterdam, North-Holland.

Arrow, K. and Intriligator, M.D. (1982). *Handbook of Mathematical Economics*, Amsterdam, North-Holland, 2 vols.

Aupetit, A. (1901). *Essai sur la théorie générale de la monnaie*, Paris, Guillaumin.

Bagehot, W. (1873). *Lombard Street*, London, Macmillan, 1888.

Barone, E. (1920). *Moneta e Risparmio*, Rome, Armani.

Barone, E. (1936). *Le Opere Economiche*, Bologna, N. Zanichelli, vol. 2.

Baumol, W.J. (1952b). 'The Transactions Demand for Cash: An Inventory Theoretic Approach', *Quarterly Journal of Economics*, **66**, pp. 545–56.

Baumol, W.J. and Becker, G.S. (1952). 'The Classical Monetary Theory: The Outcome of the Discussion', *Economica*, **19**, pp. 355–76.

Baumol, W.J. and Goldfeld, S.M. (1968). *Precursors in Mathematical Economics: An Anthology*, London, London School of Economics.

Bentham, J. (1804). *Manual of Political Economy, Economic Writings*, vol. I, London, Allen and Unwin, 1952, pp. 219–78.

Bertrand, J. (1883). 'Joint Review of A.A. Cournot, *Recherches sur les principes mathématiques de la théorie de la richesse* and L. Walras, *Théorie mathématique de la richesse sociale*', *Journal des savants*, September, pp. 499–508.

Bilimovic, A. (1931). 'Kritische und positive Bemerkungen zur Geldwerttheorie', *Zeitschrift für Nationalökonomie*, **2**, pp. 353–75 and 695–732.

Billoret, J.L. (1988). 'La période, le marché permanent et l'encaisse désirée dans l'oeuvre de Walras', *Cahiers de l'Association Charles Gide*, **2**, pp. 11–32.

Blaug, M. (1968). *Economic Theory in Retrospect* (2nd edn), London, Heinemann (1st edn 1962).

Blaug, M. (1984). 'Review of *William Jaffé's Essays on Walras* edited by D.A. Walker', *Economica*, **51**, pp. 480–81.

Bliss, C.J. (1975). *Capital Theory and the Distribution of Income*, Amsterdam, North-Holland.

Boccardo, G. (1878). *Raccolta delle più pregiate opere moderne italiane e straniere di economia politica*, Torino, UTET, vol. 2.

Böhm-Bawerk, E. von (1886). 'Grundzüge der Theorie des wirthschaftlichen Güterwerthes', *Jahrbücher für Nationalökonomie und Statistik*, **13**, pp. 477–541.

Bompaire, F. (1931). *Du principe de la liberté économique dans l'oeuvre de Cournot et dans celle de l'école de Lausanne (Walras, Pareto)*, Paris, Librairie du Recueil Sirey.

Boninsegni, P. (1902). 'I Fondamenti dell'Economia Pura', review of A. Aupetit's *Essai sur la théorie générale de la monnaie*, *Giornale degli Economisti*, **XII**, pp. 106–33.

Boninsegni, P. (1910). *Précis d'économie politique*, Lausanne, Rouge.

Boninsegni, P. (1930). *Manuel élémentaire d'économie politique*, Lausanne, Rouge.

Bonnet, V. (1859). *Questions économiques et financières: à propos des crises*, Paris, Guillaumin.

Bonnet, V. (1865). *Le crédit et les finances*, Paris, Guillaumin.

Bonnet, V. (1866). *L'enquête sur le crédit et la crise de 1863–64*, Paris, Guillaumin.

Bonnet, V. (1870). *Etudes sur la monnaie*, Paris, Guillaumin.

Bortkiewicz, L. von (1906). 'Die geldtheoretischen und währungstheoretischen Konsequenzen des "Nominalismus"', *Jahrbuch für Gesetzgebung, Verwaltung und Volkswirtschaft in Deutschen Reich*, **30**, pp. 1–34.

Bortkiewicz, L. von (1920). 'Der subjektive Geldwert', *Jahrbuch für Gesetzgebung, Verwaltung und Volkswirtschaft in Deutschen Reich*, **44**, pp. 153–90.

Bortkiewicz, L. von (1921). 'Neue Schriften über die Natur und die Zukunft des Geldes', *Schmollers Jahrbuch*, **44**, pp. 621–47 and 957–1000.

Boson, M. (1951), *Léon Walras, fondateur de la politique économique scientifique*, Lausanne, Rouge.

Bousquet, G.-H. (1957). 'Avertissement', in A. Aupetit, *Essai sur la théorie générale de la monnaie* (abridged re-edition), Paris, Rivière, pp. v–viii.

Bouvier, E. (1901a). 'La méthode mathématique en économie politique', *Revue d'économie politique*, **15**, pp. 817–50 and 1029–86.

Bouvier, E. (1901b). *La méthode mathématique en économie politique*, Paris, Librairie de la Société du Recueil général.

Boven, P. (1912). *Les applications mathématiques à l'économie politique*, Lausanne, Pache-Varidel.

Bowen, F. (1856). *Principles of Political Economy*, Boston, Houghton Mifflin.

Bresciani-Turoni, C. (1931). *The Economics of Inflation*, London, Allen and Unwin, 1937.

Bridel, P. (1987). *Cambridge Monetary Thought*, London, Macmillan.

Bridel, P. (1990). 'Equilibre, statique comparée et analyse dynamique chez Vilfredo Pareto', *Revue européenne des sciences sociales*, **XXVIII**, pp. 183–91.

Bridel, P. (1991). 'La contribution de Walras à la théorie du monopole de l'émission de monnaie', in *Hommage à un Européen* (Mélanges en l'honneur de Henri Rieben), Lausanne, Centre de recherches européennes, pp. 303–15.

Bridel, P. (1992a). 'The Lausanne Lectures in Pure Economics. From Walras to Pareto', *Revue européenne des sciences sociales*, **XXX**, pp. 145–69.

Bridel, P. (1992b). 'Gibson Paradox', in *The New Palgrave Dictionary of Money and Finance*, London, Macmillan, vol. 2, pp. 239–40.

Bridel, P. (1994). '"Dépréciation de la monnaie" et épargne forcée. Une contribution négligée de Walras à la théorie monétaire des cycles', *Economies et sociétés*, **28**, pp. 89–114.

Bridel, P. (1996). *Le chêne et l'architecte: un siècle de comptes rendus bibliographiques des* Eléments d'économie politique pure *de Léon Walras*, Paris–Genève, Droz.

Busino, G. (1967). *La sociologie de Vilfredo Pareto*, Genève, Droz.

Busino, G. (1987). 'Pareto Vilfredo', in *The New Palgrave. A Dictionary of Economics*, London, Macmillan, vol. III, pp. 799–804.
Cantillon, R. (1755). *Essai sur la nature du commerce en général*, Paris, INED, 1952.
Cassel, G. (1924). *The Theory of Social Economy*, New York, Harcourt & Brace.
Cirillo, R. (1979). *The Economics of Vilfredo Pareto*, London, Frank Cass.
Cirillo, R. (1986). 'Léon Walras' Theory of Money', *American Journal of Economics and Sociology*, 45, pp. 215–21.
Clower, R.W. (1967). 'Foundations of Monetary Theory', in Clower (ed.) (1969), pp. 202–25.
Clower, R.W. (ed.) (1969). *Monetary Theory*, London, Penguin Education.
Clower, R.W. (1984). *Money and Market* (ed. by D.A. Walker), Cambridge, Cambridge University Press.
Clower, R.W. and Howitt, P. (1995a). 'Les fondements de l'économie', in A. d'Autume and J. Cartelier (eds), *L'économie devient-elle une science dure?* Paris, Economica, pp. 18–37.
Clower, R.W. and Howitt, P. (1995b). 'La monnaie, les marchés et Coase', in A. d'Autume and J. Cartelier (eds), *L'économie devient-elle une science dure?* Paris, Economica, pp. 199–215.
Collard, D. (1966). 'Walras, Patinkin and the Money *Tâtonnement*', *Economic Journal*, 76, pp. 665–8.
Collard, D. (1973). 'Léon Walras and the Cambridge Caricature', *Economic Journal*, 83, pp. 465–76.
Conant, C. (1906). *The Principles of Money and Banking*, London, Harper, 2 vols.
Cournot, A.A. (1838). *Recherches sur les principes mathématiques de la théorie des richesses*, Paris, Hachette.
Cournot, A.A. (1863). *Principes de la théorie des richesses*, Paris, Hachette.
Cournot, A.A. (1877). *Revue sommaire des doctrines économiques*, Paris, Hachette.
Cournot, A.A. (1927). *Researches into the Mathematical Principles of the Theory of Wealth* (trans. by N.T. Bacon), New York, Macmillan.
Creedy, J. (1986). *Edgeworth and the Development of Neoclassical Economics*, Oxford, Blackwell.
Currie, M. and Steedman, I. (1990). *Wrestling with Time: Problems in Economic Theory*, Manchester, Manchester University Press.
Debreu, G. (1959). *Theory of Value: An Axiomatic Analysis of Economic Equilibrium*, New Haven, Yale University Press.
De Caro, G. (1985). 'Léon Walras dalla teoria monetaria alla Teoria generale della produzione di merci', in L. Walras, *L'economia monetaria*, Roma, Enciclopedia Italiana, vol 1, pp. 5–200.
De Caro, G. (1988). 'Le monde atemporel de Léon Walras', *Economies et sociétés*, 22, pp. 105–32.
Del Vecchio, G. (1909). 'I principii della teoria economica della moneta', *Giornale degli economisti*, 39, pp. 255–72 and 507–53.
Del Vecchio, G. (1917). 'Questioni fondamentali sul valore della moneta', *Giornale degli economisti*, 55, pp. 117–74.
Del Vecchio, G. (1924). 'Le teorie della circolazione negli scritti del Pareto', *Giornale degli economisti*, 64, pp. 62–8.
Del Vecchio, G. (1929). 'La moneta nella teoria dell'equilibrio economico', *Giornale degli economisti*, 69, pp. 135–6.

Del Vecchio, G. (1933). 'La teoria della moneta secondo W. Launhardt', in *Economic Essays in Honour of Gustav Cassel*, London, Macmillan, pp. 665–71.

Del Vecchio, G. (1983). *Antologia di Scritti di Gustavo Del Vecchio nel Centenario della Nascita* (ed. by F. Caffè), Milano, F. Angeli.

Denizet, J. (1977). 'L'équilibre général et la monnaie', *Economie appliquée*, 30, pp. 565–83.

De Vroey, M. (1990). 'The Base Camp Paradox. A Reflection on the Place of Tâtonnement in General Equilibrium Theory', *Economics and Philosophy*, 6, pp. 235–53.

De Vroey, M. (1995). 'Tâtonnement as a Social Contract. A Reflection on the Institutional Dimension of General Equilibrium Economy', Unpublished Working Paper, Université Catholique de Louvain, Département des Sciences économiques.

Divisia, F. (1928), *Économique rationnelle*, Paris, Doin.

Dockès, P. (1996). *La société n'est pas un pique-nique. Léon Walras et l'économie sociale*, Paris, Economica.

Donzelli, F. (1986). *Il concetto di equilibrio nella teoria economica neoclassica*, Roma, La Nuova Italia Scientifica.

Donzelli, F. (1989). *'The Concept of Equilibrium in Neoclassical Economic Theory. An Inquiry into the Evolution of General Competitive Analysis from Walras to the "Neo-Walrasian" Research Programme'*, unpublished PhD dissertation, University of Cambridge.

Dumez, H. (1985). *L'économiste, la science et le pouvoir: le cas de Walras*, Paris, PUF.

Dupuit, J. (1844). 'De la mesure de l'utilité des travaux publics', *Annales des ponts et chaussées*, 8, as in J. Dupuit, *De l'utilité et de sa mesure* (ed. by M. de Bernardi), Paris, Giard, 1934, pp. 29–65

Edgeworth, F.Y. (1881). *Mathematical Psychics*, London. Kegan Paul.

Edgeworth, F.Y. (1887). 'Report of the Committee ... appointed for the purpose of investigating the best methods of ascertaining and measuring Variations in the Value of the Monetary Standard. (Drawn by the Secretary [F.Y.E. Edgeworth])', in the *Report of the 57th Meeting of the British Association of the Advancement of Science held at Manchester in August and September 1887*, London, Murray, 1888, pp. 247–54 followed by 'A Memorandum by the Secretary', pp. 254–301.

Edgeworth, F.Y. (1889). 'Application of Mathematics to Political Economy', as in Edgeworth (1925), vol. II, pp. 273–312.

Edgeworth, F.Y. (1891). 'La théorie mathématique de l'offre et de la demande et le coût de la production', *Revue d'économie politique*, 5, pp. 10–28.

Edgeworth, F.Y. (1925). *Papers Relating to Political Economy*, London, Macmillan, vol. II.

Ellis, H.S. (1934). *German Monetary Theory: 1905–1933*, Cambridge, Mass., Harvard University Press.

Falise, M. (1971). 'Portée contemporaine des encaisses désirées', *Revue d'économie politique*, 81, pp. 410–34.

Feenstra, R.C. (1986). 'Functional Equivalence between Liquidity Costs and the Utility of Money', *Journal of Monetary Economics*, 17, pp. 271–91.

Fisher, I. (1897). *A Brief Introduction to the Infinitesimal Calculus, Designed Especially to Aid in Reading Mathematical Economics and Statistics*, London–New York, Macmillan.

Fisher, I. (1911). *The Purchasing Power of Money*, New York, Macmillan, 1931.

Floss, L. (1957). 'Some Notes on Léon Walras' Theory of Capitalization and Credit', *Metroeconomica*, **9**, pp. 52–69.

Fossati, E. (1957). *The Theory of General Static Equilibrium* (trans. by G.L.S. Shackle), Oxford, Basil Blackwell.

Friedman, B.M. and Hahn, F.H. (eds) (1990). *Handbook of Monetary Economics*, Amsterdam, North-Holland, 2 vols.

Friedman, M. (1949). 'The Marshallian Demand Curve', *Journal of Political Economy*, **57**, pp. 463–95.

Friedman, M. (1953). *Essays in Positive Economics*, Chicago, University of Chicago Press.

Friedman, M. (1955). 'Léon Walras and his Economic System', *American Economic Review*, **45**, pp. 900–909.

Friedman, M. (1957). *A Theory of the Consumption Function*, Princeton, NBER.

Friedman, M. (1969). *The Optimum Quantity of Money and Other Essays*, Chicago, Chicago University Press.

Gide, C. and Rist, C. (1913). *Histoire des doctrines économiques depuis les Physiocrates jusqu'à nos jours*, Paris, Sirey.

Goodwin, R.M. (1951). 'Iteration, Automatic Computers and Economic Dynamics', *Metroeconomica*, **III**, pp. 1–7.

Gossen, H.H. (1854). *Entwickelung der Gesetze des menschlichen Verkehrs und der daraus fliessenden Regeln für menschliches Handlen*, Braunschweig, Vieweg.

Guggenheim, Th. (1978). *Les théories monétaires préclassiques*, Genève, Droz.

Hadley, A.T. (1896). *Economics*, New York, Putnam.

Hahn, F.H. (1965). 'On some problems of proving the existence of an equilibrium in a monetary economy', in Clower (ed.) (1969), pp. 191–201.

Hahn, F.H. (1973a). 'The Winter of our Discontent', *Economica*, **40**, as in Hahn (1984), pp. 134–44.

Hahn, F.H. (1973b). 'On the Foundations of Monetary Theory', in Hahn (1984), pp. 158–74.

Hahn, F.H. (1982a). 'Stability', in Arrow and Intriligator (1982), vol. 1, pp. 745–93.

Hahn, F.H. (1982b). *Money and Inflation*, Oxford, Blackwell.

Hahn, F.H. (1984). *Equilibrium and Macroeconomics*, Oxford, Basil Blackwell.

Hahn, F.H. and Solow, R. (1995). *A Critical Essay on Modern Macroeconomic Theory*, Cambridge, Mass., MIT Press.

Hall, S.G. (1982). 'Money and the Economics of Léon Walras', *Scottish Journal of Political Economy*, **29**, pp. 246–55.

Hall, S.G. (1983). 'Money and the Walrasian Utility Function', *Oxford Economic Papers*, **35**, pp. 247–53.

Harrod, R.F. (1956). 'Walras: A Re-appraisal', *Economic Journal*, **66**, pp. 307–16.

Hayek, F.A. (1929). *Geldtheorie und Konjonkturtheorie*, Vienna, Hoelder-Pichler-Tempsky.

Hayek, F.A. (1931). *Prices and Production*, London, Routledge and Kegan Paul.

Hayek, F.A. (1932). 'A Note on the Development of the Doctrine of "Forced Saving"', *Quarterly Journal of Economics*, **47**, pp. 123–33.

Hayek, F.A. (1935). *Prices and Production*, London, Routledge & Kegan Paul (2nd edn).

Hayek, F.A. (1939). *Profits, Interest and Investment*, London, Routledge.

Hayek, F.A. (1941). *The Pure Theory of Capital*, London, Routledge & Kegan Paul.

Hegeland, H. (1951). *The Quantity Theory of Money*, Göteberg, Gumperts.

Helfferich, K. (1927). *Money*, London, Benn.

Hicks, J.R. (1933). 'Gleichgewicht und Konjonktur', *Zeitschrift für Nationalökonomie*, **4**, pp. 441–55.

Hicks, J.R. (1934a). 'Léon Walras', *Econometrica*, **2**, as in *Classics and Moderns – Collected Essays on Economic Theory*, Oxford, Basil Blackwell, vol. III, pp. 85–95.

Hicks, J.R. (with R.G.D. Allen) (1934b). 'A Reconsideration of the Theory of Value', *Economica*, **1**, as in *Wealth and Welfare – Collected Essays on Economic Theory*, Oxford, Basil Blackwell, vol. I, pp. 3–55.

Hicks, J.R. (1935). 'A Suggestion for Simplifying the Theory of Money', in Hicks (1967), pp. 61–82.

Hicks, J.R. (1939). *Value and Capital*, Oxford, Clarendon Press.

Hicks, J.R. (1966). 'The Two Triads. Lecture I', in Hicks (1967), pp. 1–16.

Hicks, J.R. (1967). *Critical Essays in Monetary Theory*, Oxford, Basil Blackwell.

Hildebrand, R. (1883). *Die Theorie des Geldes*, Jena, no publisher.

Hirsch, W. (1928). *Grenznutzentheorie und Geldwerttheorie*, Jena, Diehl.

Hoffmann, F. (1907). *Kritische Dogmengeschichte der Geldwerttheorien*, Leipzig, Hirschfeld.

Hornbostel, H. (1930). *La vitesse de circulation de la monnaie*, Paris, Dunod.

Howey, R.S. (1989). *The Rise of the Marginal Utility School, 1870–1889*, New York, Columbia University Press.

Howitt, P.W. (1973). 'Walras and Monetary Theory', *Western Economic Journal*, **11**, pp. 487–99.

Hume, D. (1752). 'Of Money', as in *Writings in Economics* (ed. by E. Rotwein), London, Nelson, 1955.

Ingrao, B. and Israel, G. (1985). 'General Economic Equilibrium Theory. A History of Ineffectual Paradigmatic Shifts', *Fundamenta Scientiae*, **6**, pp. 1–45 and 89–125.

Ingrao, B. and Israel, G. (1990). *The Invisible Hand. Economic Equilibrium in the History of Science*, London, MIT Press.

Isnard, A.N. (1781). *Traité des Richesses*, Lausanne, Mourer, 2 vols.

Jaccoud, G. (1994). 'Stabilité monétaire et régulation étatique dans l'analyse de Léon Walras', *Revue économique*, **45**, pp. 257–88.

Jaffé, W. (1942). 'Léon Walras' theory of Capital Accumulation', in O. Lange (1942), as in Jaffé (1983), pp. 139–50.

Jaffé, W. (1951). 'Walrasiana: the *Eléments* and its Critics', *Econometrica*, **19**, pp. 327–28.

Jaffé, W. (1953). 'Walras's Theory of Capital Formation in the Framework of his General Equilibrium Theory', *Economie Appliquée*, **6**, as in Jaffé (1983), pp. 151–75.

Jaffé, W. (1964). 'New Light on An Old Quarrel: Barone's Unpublished Review of Wicksteed's "Essay on the Co-ordination of the Laws of Distribution" and Related Papers', *Revue européenne des sciences sociales*, **3**, as in Jaffé (1983), pp. 176–212.

Jaffé, W. (1965). *Correspondence and Related Papers of Léon Walras*, Amsterdam, North-Holland, 3 vols.

Jaffé, W. (1967). 'Walras's Theory of *Tâtonnement*: a Critique of Recent Interpretations', *Journal of Political Economy*, **75**, as in Jaffé (1983), pp. 221–43.

Jaffé, W. (1972). 'Léon Walras's role in the "Marginal Revolution"', *History of Political Economy*, **4**, as in Jaffé (1983), pp. 288–310.

Jaffé, W. (1976). 'Menger, Jevons and Walras De-homogenized', *Economic Inquiry*, **14**, as in Jaffé (1983), pp. 311–25.

Jaffé, W. (1977). 'The Walras–Poincaré Correspondence on the Cardinal Measurability of Utility', *Canadian Journal of Economics*, **10**, as in Jaffé (1983), pp. 213–20.

Jaffé, W. (1980). 'Walras's Economics as Others see it', *Journal of Economic Literature*, **18**, as in Jaffé (1983), pp. 343–70.

Jaffé, W. (1981). 'Another Look at Léon Walras's theory of *Tâtonnement*', *History of Political Economy*, **13**, as in Jaffé (1983), pp. 244–66.

Jaffé, W. (1983). William Jaffé's *Essays on Walras* (ed. by D. Walker), London, Cambridge University Press.

James, E. and Lecoq, J. (1961). 'La pensée monétaire de Leon Walras', *Economie appliquée*, **14**, pp. 603–31.

Jevons. W.S. (1863). 'Notice of a General Mathematical Theory of Political Economy', Annex to 'Report of the Thirty-Second Meeting of the British Association for the Advancement of Science, Held at Cambridge in October 1862', *Notices and Abstracts of Miscellaneous Communications to the Sections*, London, Murray, pp. 158–9.

Jevons, W.S. (1866). 'Brief Account of a General Mathematical Theory of Political Economy', *Journal of the Statistical Society of London*, **29**, pp. 286–87.

Jevons, W.S. (1871). *The Theory of Political Economy*, London, Macmillan.

Jevons, W.S. (1875). *Money and the Mechanism of Exchange*, London, King.

Jevons, W.S. (1879). *The Theory of Political Economy*, London, Macmillan (2nd edn).

Jevons, W.S. (1972–81). *Papers and Correspondence* (ed. by R.D.C. Black), London, Macmillan, 7 vols.

Jolink, A. (1991). '*Liberté, Egalité, Rareté*, The Evolutionary Economics of Léon Walras', unpublished PhD dissertation, Erasmus Universiteit Rotterdam.

Jolink, A. (1994). 'Les "marées économiques": Léon Walras et la conjoncture', *Economies et sociétés*, **28**, pp. 183–95.

Jolink, A. (1996). *The Evolutionist Economics of Léon Walras*, London, Routledge.

Kemmerer, E.W. (1907). *Money and Credit Instruments in their Relation to General Prices*, New York, Holt.

Keynes, J.M. (1923). *A Tract on Monetary Reform, The Collected Writings of John Maynard Keynes*, vol. IV, London, Macmillan, 1971.

Keynes, J.M. (1930). *A Treatise on Money, The Applied Theory of Money*, vol. II, *The Collected Writings of John Maynard Keynes*, vol. VI, London, Macmillan, 1971.

Keynes, J.M. (1936). *The General Theory of Employment, Interest and Money, The Collected Writings of John Maynard Keynes*, vol. VII, London, Macmillan, 1973.

Keynes, J. M. (1973). *The General Theory and After – Part I Preparation, The Collected Writings of John Maynard Keynes*, vol. XIII, London, Macmillan.

Klotz, G. (1994). 'Achylle-Nicolas Isnard, précurseur de Léon Walras?', *Economies et sociétés*, **28**, pp. 29–52.

Kompas, (1992). *Studies in the History of Long-run Equilibrium*, Manchester, Manchester University Press.

Kuenne, R.E. (1954). 'Walras, Leontief, and the Interdependance of Economic Activities', *Quarterly Journal of Economics*, **68**, pp. 323–54.

Kuenne, R.E. (1956). 'The Architectonics of Léon Walras', *Kyklos*, **4**, pp. 241–49.

Kuenne, R.E. (1959). 'Patinkin on Neo-classical Monetary Theory', *Southern Economic Journal*, **26**, pp. 119–24.

Kuenne, R.E. (1961). 'The Walrasian Theory of Money: An Interpretation and Reconstruction', *Metroeconomica*, **13**, pp. 94–105.

Kuenne, R.E. (1963). *The Theory of General Economic Equilibrium*, Princeton, Princeton University Press.

Laidler, D. (1991). *The Golden Age of the Quantity Theory*, Princeton, Princeton University Press.

Lange, O. (1938a). *On the Economic Theory of Socialism*, Minneapolis, University of Minnesota Press.

Lange, O. (1938b). 'The Rate of Interest and the Optimum Propensity to Consume', *Economica*, **5,** as in *Readings in Business Cycle Theory* (ed. by G. Haberler), Philadelphia, Blakiston, pp. 169–92.

Lange, O. (1942). 'Say's Law: A Restatement and Criticism' in O. Lange et al. (eds), *Studies in Mathematical Economics and Econometrics*, Chicago, University of Chicago Press, pp. 4–82.

Launhardt, W. (1885a). *Mathematische Begründung der Volkswirtschaftslehre*, Leipzig, Engelmann.

Launhardt, W. (1885b). *Das Wesen des Geldes*, Leipzig, Engelmann.

Lendjel, E. (1996). 'Le biais réaliste dans l'interprétation de Walker du tâtonnement walrasien', *Economies et sociétés*, **30**, forthcoming.

Lerner, A. (1938). 'Alternative Formulations of the Theory of Interest', *Economic Journal*, **48**, as in A. Lerner, *Essays in Economic Analysis*, London, Macmillan, 1953, pp. 277–304.

Levasseur, P.E. (1858). *La question de l'or*, Paris, Guillaumin.

Lexis, W. (1886). 'Neuere Schriften über Edelmettale, Geld und Preise', *Jahrbücher für Nationalökonomie und Statistik*, **13**, pp. 96–121.

Lexis, W. (1906). 'Ein neue Geldtheorie', *Archiv für Sozialwissenschaft und Sozialpolitik*, **5**, pp. 127–146.

L'Huillier, J. and Guggenheim, T. (1971). 'Note sur la théorie monétaire de Walras', *Revue d'économie politique*, **81**, pp. 435–42.

Loria, A. (1880). *La Rendita fondiaria e la sua elisione naturale*, Milan, Hoepli.

Lucas, R.E. (1981). *Studies in Business-cycle Theory*, Cambridge, Mass., MIT Press.

Magnan de Bornier, J. (1992). 'The "Cournot–Bertrand Debate": A Historical Perspective', *History of Political Economy*, **24**, pp. 623–56.

Marget, A. (1931). 'Léon Walras and the "Cash Balance Approach" to the Problem of the Value of Money', *Journal of Political Economy*, **39**, pp. 569–600.

Marget, A. (1935). 'The Monetary Aspects of the Walrasian System', *Journal of Political Economy*, **43**, pp. 145–86.

Marget, A. (1938–42). *The Theory of Prices*, New York, Kelley Reprint, 1966, 2 vols.

Marshall, A. (1872). 'Mr Jevons' Theory of Political Economy', *Academy*, as in *Memorials of Alfred Marshall* (ed. by A.C. Pigou), London, Macmillan, 1925.

Marshall, A. (1890). *Principles of Economics* (ed. by C.W. Guillebaud), London, Macmillan, 1961, 2 vols.

Marshall, A. (1923). *Money, Credit and Commerce*, London, Macmillan.
Marshall, A. (1975). *The Early Economic Writings of Alfred Marshall 1867–1890* (ed. by J.K. Whitaker), London, Macmillan, 2 vols.
McKenzie, L.W. (1987). 'General Equilibrium' in *The New Palgrave. A Dictionary of Economics*, London, Macmillan, vol. II, pp. 498–512.
Ménard, C. (1979). 'Equilibre, déséquilibre, temps: un peu d'histoire', *Economie Appliquée*, **32**, pp. 229–52.
Ménard, C. (1980). 'Three Forms of Resistance to Statistics: Say, Cournot, Walras', *History of Political Economy*, **12**, pp. 524–41.
Ménard, C. (1990). 'The Lausanne Tradition: Walras and Pareto' in Klaus Hennings and Warren J. Samuels (eds), *Neo-Classical Economic Theory 1870 to 1930*, London, Kluwer Academic Publishers, pp. 95–136.
Menger, C. (1892a). 'Geld' in *Handwörterbuch der Staatswissenschaten* (2nd ed.), Jena, vol. IV, pp. 60–106.
Menger, C. (1892b). 'La monnaie mesure de la valeur', *Revue d'économie politique*, **6**, pp. 159–75.
Menger, C. (1892c). 'On the Origin of Money', *Economic Journal*, **2**, pp. 239–55.
Milgate, M. (1982). *Capital and Employment*, London, Academic Press.
Mill, J.S. (1844). *Essays on Some Unsettled Questions of Political Economy*, London, Longmans, Green, Reader & Dyer, 1874 (2nd edn).
Mill, J.S. (1848). *Principles of Political Economy* (Ashley ed.), London, Longmans, Green and Co, 1909.
Mises, L. von (1912). *The Theory of Money and Credit*, New Haven, Yale University Press, 1953 (trans. by H.E. Batson).
Mises, L. von (1917). 'Zur Klassifikation der Geldtheorien', *Archiv für Sozialwissenschaft und Sozialpolitik*, **36**, vol, pp. 332–347.
Montesano, A. (1986). 'Una riformulazione della teoria monetaria di Walras', *Rivista internazionale di Scienze economiche e commerciali*, **33**, pp. 901–38.
Montesano, A. (1991). 'A Revision of Walras' Theories of Capitalization and Money' in *Festschrift in Honour of Lazaros Th. Homanidis*, Piraeus, University of Piraeus, pp. 366–94.
Moret, J. (1915). *L'emploi des mathématiques en économie politique*, Paris, Giard & Brière.
Morgenstern, O. (1951). 'Joseph A. Schumpeter, 1883–1950', *Economic Journal*, **61**, pp. 197–202.
Morgenstern, O. (1968). 'Schlesinger, Karl' in *International Encyclopedia of the Social Sciences*, New York, Macmillan, vol. 14, pp. 51–52.
Morishima, M. (1974). 'Léon Walras and Money', in M. Parkin and A.R. Nobay (eds), *Current Economic Problems*, London, Cambridge University Press, pp. 153–85.
Morishima, M. (1977). *Walras' Economics. A Pure Theory of Capital and Money*, London, Cambridge University Press.
Morishima, M. (1980). 'W. Jaffé and Léon Walras: A Comment', *Journal of Economic Literature*, **18**, pp. 550–58.
Mouchot, C. (1994). 'L'impossible "théorème de l'utilité maxima des capitaux neufs"', *Economies et sociétés*, **28**, pp. 197–219.
Murray, R.A. (1920). *Leçons d'économie politique suivant la doctrine de l'Ecole de Lausanne*, Paris, Payot (trans. by P. Boven).
Negishi, T. (1977). 'Money in the Walrasian General Equilibrium Theory', *Economie Appliquée*, **20**, pp. 599–615.
Negishi, T. (1989). *History of Economic Theory*, Amsterdam, North Holland.

Newcomb, S. (1885). *Principles of Political Economy*, New York, Harper.
Newman, P. (1965). *The Theory of Exchange*, Englewood Cliffs, NJ, Prentice-Hall.
Nicholson, J.S. (1888). *A Treatise on Money*, London, Black, 1895.
Niehans, J. (1987). 'Launhardt, Carl Friederich Wilhelm', in *The New Palgrave Dictionary of Economics*, London, Macmillan, vol. 3, pp. 140–42.
Nogaro, B. (1906). 'Contribution à une théorie réaliste de la monnaie', *Revue d'économie politique*, **20**, pp. 681–724.
Nogaro, B. (1947). 'Théorie quantitative et théorie de la monnaie chez Léon Walras', in *La valeur logique des théories économiques*, Paris, PUF, pp. 99–110.
Osorio, A. (1913). *Théorie mathématique de l'échange*, Paris, Giard & Brière.
Ostroy, J.M. (1987). 'Money and General Equilibrium', in *The New Palgrave Dictionary of Economics*, London, Macmillan, vol. 3, pp. 515–8.
Ostroy, J.M. (1992). 'Money and General Equilibrium Theory', in *The New Palgrave Dictionary of Money and Finance*, London, Macmillan, vol. II, pp. 783–6.
Ostroy, J.M. and Starr, J.M. (1990). 'The Transactions Role of Money', in Friedman and Hahn (eds) (1990), vol. I, pp. 3–62.
Oulès, F. (1950). *L'école de Lausanne; textes choisis de L. Walras et V. Pareto*, Paris, Dalloz.
Pantaleoni, M. (1898). *Pure Economics*, London, Macmillan.
Pareto, V. (1892–3). 'Considerazioni sui principii fundamentali dell'economia politica pura', *Giornale degli economisti*, **IV–VII**, as in *Oeuvres complètes* (1964–1989), vol. XXVI, pp. 59–237.
Pareto, V. (1896–97). *Cours d'économie politique*, 2 vols, as in *Oeuvres complètes* (1964–1989), vols. I–II.
Pareto, V. (1902–1903). *Les systèmes socialistes*, 2 vols, as in *Oeuvres complètes* (1964–1989), vol. V.
Pareto, V. (1906). *Manuale di Economia politica*, Milano, Società Editrice Libraria.
Pareto, V. (1909). *Manuel d'économie politique*, as in *Oeuvres complètes* (1964–1989), vol. VII.
Pareto, V. (1911). 'Economie mathématique', as in *Oeuvres complètes* (1964–1989), vol. VIII, pp. 319–68.
Pareto, V. (1919). *Traité de sociologie générale*, 2 vols, as in *Oeuvres complètes* (1964–1989), vol. XII.
Pareto, V. (1964–89) *Oeuvres complètes* (ed. by G. Busino), 30 vols, Genève, Droz.
Patinkin, D. (1965). *Money, Interest and Prices*, New York, Harper and Row (1st edn, 1956).
Patinkin, D. (1989). 'Introduction to Second Edition, Abridged' in D. Patinkin, *Money, Interest and Prices* (second edn, abridged), London, MIT Press, pp. xv–lxv.
Pietri-Tonelli, A. de (1921). *Traité d'économie rationnelle*, Paris, Giard, 1927.
Pigou, A.C. (1917). 'The Exchange Value of Legal-Tender Money', *Quarterly Journal of Economics*, **32**, as in Pigou (1923), pp. 175–99.
Pigou, A.C. (1923). *Essays in Applied Economics*, London, Macmillan.
Pirou, G. (1934). *Les théories de l'équilibre économique – L. Walras and V. Pareto*, Paris, Domat-Montchrestien.

Poincaré, H. (1900). 'Les relations entre la physique expérimentale et la physique mathématique', *Revue générale des sciences pures et appliquées*, **11**, pp. 1163–75.

Potier, J.-P. (1995). 'Léon Walras et "l'école lombarde-vénitienne" à travers sa correspondance (1874–1886)', in *Mélanges en l'honneur de Henri Bartoli*, Paris, Publications de la Sorbonne, pp. 47–61.

Ricardo, D. (1815). *The Works and Correspondence of David Ricardo* (ed. by P. Sraffa), vol. I, *Principles of Political Economy* and vol. IV, *Pamphlets and Papers 1815–1823*, London, Cambridge University Press, 1951.

Rist, C. (1938). *Histoire des doctrines relatives au crédit et à la monnaie depuis John Law jusqu'à nos jours*, Paris, Sirey.

Robertson, D.H. (1926). *Banking Policy and the Price Level*, London, King.

Robertson, D.H. (1933). 'Saving and Hoarding', *Economic Journal*, **43**, as in *Essays in Monetary Theory*, London, Staples, 1940, pp. 65–82.

Roscher, W. (1854). *System der Volkswirtschaft*, Stuttgart, Gotta'schen Buchhandlung.

Samuelson, P.A. (1941). *Foundations of Economic Analysis*, New York, Atheneum.

Sanger, C.P. (1899). 'Walras M.E.L.', in R.H.I. Palgrave (ed.), *Dictionary of Political Economy*, London, Macmillan, vol. III, pp. 653–5.

Schlesinger, K. (1914). *Theorie des Geld- und Kreditwirtschaft*, Munich, Duncker & Humblot.

Schlesinger, K. (1959). 'Basic Principles of the Money Economy', *International Economic Papers*, **9**, pp. 20–38 (transl. of Chapter 3 of Schlesinger (1914)).

Schumpeter, J.A. (1908). *Das Wesen und der Hauptinhalt der theoretischen Nationalökonomie*, Munich and Leipzig, Duncker & Humblot.

Schumpeter, J.A. (1910). 'Marie Esprit Léon Walras', *Zeitschrift für Volkswirtschaft, Sozialpolitik und Verwaltung*, **19**, pp. 397–402.

Schumpeter, J.A. (1912). *The Theory of Economic Development: An Inquiry into Profits, Capital, Credit, Interest, and the Business Cycle*, Cambridge, Mass., Harvard University Press, 1934.

Schumpeter, J.A. (1915). 'Review of "Karl Schlesinger: Theorie der Geld und Kreditwirtschaft"', *Archiv für Sozialwissenschaft*, **41**, pp. 239–42.

Schumpeter, J.A. (1917–18). 'Money and the Social Product', *Archiv für Sozialwissenschaft und Sozialpolitik*, **44**, as in *International Economic Papers*, **6**, 1956, pp. 148–211.

Schumpeter, J.A. (1954). *History of Economic Analysis*, London, Oxford University Press.

Schumpeter, J.A. (1970). *Das Wesen des Geldes*, Göttingen, Vandenhoeck & Ruprecht.

Sen, A.K. (1981). *Poverty and Famines: An Essay on Entitlement and Deprivation*, Oxford, Clarendon Press.

Sensini, G. (1929). 'Vilfredo Pareto e la teoria della moneta', *Giornale economico*, **7**, pp. 117–18.

Shubik, M. (1987). 'Bertrand, Joseph', in *The New Palgrave. A Dictionary of Economics*, London, Macmillan, vol. I, p. 234.

Smith, A. (1776). *An Inquiry into the Nature and Causes of the Wealth of Nations* (R.H. Campbell and A.S. Skinner, eds), 1976, Oxford, Clarendon Press, 2 vols.

Solow, R.M. (1956a). 'A Contribution to the Theory of Economic Growth', *Quarterly Journal of Economics*, **70**, pp. 65–94.

Solow, R.M. (1956b). 'Review of *Elements of Pure Economics*', *Econometrica*, **24**, pp. 87–9.

Starr, R.M. (ed.) (1989). *General Equilibrium Models of Monetary Economies*, London, Academic Press.

Steiner, P. (1994). 'Pareto contre Walras: le problème de l'économie sociale', *Economies et sociétés*, **28**, pp. 53–73.

Stigler, G.J. (1941). *Production and Distribution Theories 1870 to 1895*, New York, Macmillan.

Tarascio, V.J. (1969). 'The Monetary and Employment Theories of Vilfredo Pareto', *History of Political Economy*, **1**, pp. 101–22.

Theocharis, R.D. (1983). *Early Developments in Mathematical Economics*, London, Porcupine Press (2nd ed.).

Thornton, W. (1802). *An Inquiry into the Nature and Effects of the Paper Credit of Great-Britain* (ed. by F.A. Hayek), New York, Kelley Reprint, 1965.

Tobin, J. (1985). 'Theoretical Issues in Macroeconomics', in G.R. Feiwel (ed.), *Issues in Contemporary Macroeconomics and Distribution*, London, Macmillan, pp. 103–33.

Tsiang, S.C. (1989). *Finance Constraints and the Theory of Money* (ed. by M. Kohn), London, Academic Press.

Uhr, C. (1960). *Economic Doctrines of Knut Wicksell*, Berkeley and Los Angeles, University of California Press.

Université de Lausanne (1909). *Jubilé Walras*, Lausanne, Imprimerie Réunies.

Valade, B. (1990). *Pareto: la naissance d'une autre sociologie*, Paris, PUF.

Valéry, P. (1919). *Introduction à la méthode de Léonard de Vinci*, Paris, NRF.

Van Daal, J. (1994). 'De la nature de la monnaie dans les modèles d'équilibre de Léon Walras', *Economies et sociétés*, **28**, pp. 115–32.

Van Daal, J. and Jolink, A. (1993). *The Equilibrium Economics of Léon Walras*, London, Routledge.

Viner, J. (1937). *Studies in the Theory of International Trade*, London, Allen & Unwin.

Wagner, V.F. (1937). *Geschichte der Kredittheorien*, Vienna, Julius Springer.

Wald, A. (1936). 'Über einige Gleichungssysteme der mathematischen Ökonomie', *Zeitschrift für Nationalökonomie*, **7**, pp. 637–70 (trans. by O. Eckstein as 'On Some Systems of Equations in Mathematical Economics', *Econometrica*, **19**, 1951, pp. 368–403).

Walker, D. (1972). 'Competitive Tâtonnement Exchange Markets', *Kyklos*, **25**, pp. 345–63.

Walker, D. (1983). 'Introduction', in Jaffé (1983), pp. 1–14.

Walker, D. (1987a). 'Walras, Léon', in *The New Palgrave. A Dictionary of Economics*, London, Macmillan, vol. IV, pp. 852–63.

Walker D. (1987b). 'Walras's Theories of Tatonnement', *Journal of Political Economy*, **95**, pp. 758–74.

Walker, D. (1987c). 'Bibliography of the Writings of Léon Walras', *History of Political Economy*, **19**, pp. 667–702.

Walker, D. (1989). 'A Primer on Walrasian Theories of Economic Behavior', *History of Economics Society Bulletin*, **11**, pp. 1–23.

Walker, D. (1990). 'Disequilibrium and Equilibrium in Walras's Model of Oral Pledges Markets', *Revue économique*, **41**, pp. 961–78.

Walker, D. (1991). 'The Markets for Circulating Capital and Money in Walras's Last Monetary Model', *Economie Appliquée*, **44**, pp. 107–29.

Walker, D. (1994a). 'The Adjustment Processes in Walras's Consumer Commodities Model in the Mature Phase of his Thought', *Revue économique*, **45**, pp. 1357–76.

Walker, D. (1994b). 'Le modèle du marché de la monnaie de Walras durant la phase de maturité de sa pensée théorique', *Economies et sociétés*, **28**, pp. 133–57.

Walker, D. (1996). *Walras's Market Models*, Cambridge, Cambridge University Press.

Walker, F.A. (1877). *Money*, London, Macmillan.

Walras, A. (1831). *De la nature de la richesse et de l'origine de la valeur*, Paris, Johanneau.

Walras, A. (1849). *Théorie de la richesse sociale*, Paris, Guillaumin.

Walras, A. (1990). *Richesse, Liberté et Société, Auguste et Léon Walras – Oeuvres économiques complètes*, vol. I, Paris, Economica.

Walras, L. (1860). *L'économie politique et la justice. Examen critique et réfutation des doctrines économiques de M. P.-J. Proudhon*, précédés d'une Introduction à l'étude de la question sociale, Paris, Guillaumin.

Walras, L (1869). 'Application des mathématiques à l'économie politique (2ᵉ tentative 1869–70)', as in *Théorie mathématique de la richesse sociale (et autres écrits mathématiques et d'économie pure), Auguste et Léon Walras – Oeuvres Économiques complètes*, vol. XI, pp. 341–59.

Walras, L. (1871). 'Des billets de banque en Suisse', *Bibliothèque universelle et Revue suisse*, **76**, pp. 321–42.

Walras, L. (1872). 'Système des phénomènes économiques. Leçons publiques faites à l'Hôtel de Ville de Genève (1872)', as in *Théorie mathématique de la richesse sociale (et autres écrits mathématiques et d'économie pure), Auguste et Léon Walras – Oeuvres économiques complètes*, vol. XI, pp. 413–73.

Walras, L. (1874–77). *Eléments d'économie politique pure*, Lausanne, Corbaz.

Walras, L. (1875). 'La loi fédérale sur l'émission et le remboursement des billets de banque', as in *Mélanges d'économie politique et sociale, Auguste et Léon Walras – Oeuvres économiques complètes*, vol. VII, pp. 203–18.

Walras, L. (1879).'De l'émission des billets de banques', *Gazette de Lausanne*, 2 and 3 December.

Walras, L. (1880). 'Théorie mathématique du billet de banque', *Bulletin de la Société vaudoise des Sciences naturelles*, **16**, pp. 553–92.

Walras, L. (1883). 'Théorie mathématique du billet de banque', reprinted with some changes in *Théorie mathématique de la richesse sociale*, Lausanne, Corbaz, pp. 145–75.

Walras, L. (1885). 'Un économiste inconnu, Hermann-Henri Gossen', *Journal des Economistes*, **30**, as in *Auguste et Léon Walras – Oeuvres économiques complètes, Etudes d'économie sociale*, vol. IX, Paris, Economica, pp. 311–30.

Walras, L. (1886). *Théorie de la monnaie*, Lausanne, Corbaz, as in *Auguste et Léon Walras – Oeuvres économiques complètes*, vol. X, Paris, Economica, pp. 63–145.

Walras, L. (1889). *Eléments d'économie politique pure*, Lausanne, Corbaz (2nd edn.).

Walras, L. (1892). 'The Geometrical Theory of the Determination of Prices', *Annals of the American Academy of Political and Social Science*, **III**, pp. 45–64 (trans. under the supervision of I. Fisher).

Walras, L. (1896). *Eléments d'économie politique pure*, Lausanne, Corbaz (3rd edn.).

Walras, L. (1898). *Etudes d'économie politique appliquée, Auguste et Léon Walras – Oeuvres économiques complètes*, vol. X, Paris, Economica.

Walras, L. (1900). *Eléments d'économie politique pure*, Lausanne, Corbaz (4th edn.).

Walras, L. (1926). *Eléments d'économie politique pure*, Lausanne, Rouge ('définitive' edn.).

Walras, L. (1938). *Abrégé des éléments d'économie politique pure*, Lausanne, Rouge.

Walras, L. (1954). *Elements of Pure Economics or the Theory of Social Wealth* (trans. by W. Jaffé), London, G. Allen & Unwin.

Walras, L. (1965). *Correspondence of Léon Walras and Related Papers* (ed. by W. Jaffé), Amsterdam, North Holland, 3 vols.

Walras, L. (1987). *Mélanges d'économie politique et sociale, Auguste et Léon Walras – Oeuvres économiques complètes*, vol. VII, Paris, Economica.

Walras, L. (1988). *Eléments d'économie politique pure, Auguste et Léon Walras – Oeuvres économiques complètes*, vol. VIII, Paris, Economica.

Walras, L. (1990). *Les Associations populaires coopératives, Auguste et Léon Walras – Oeuvres économiques complètes*, vol. VI, Paris, Economica.

Walras, L. (1993). *Théorie mathématique de la richesse sociale (et autres écrits mathématiques et d'économie pure), Auguste et Léon Walras – Oeuvres économiques complètes*, vol. XI, Paris, Economica.

Weinberger, O. (1930). *Mathematische Volkswirtschaftslehre*, Leipzig, Teubner.

Weintraub, E.R. (1985). *General Equilibrium Analysis; Studies in Appraisal*, London, Cambridge University Press.

Weintraub, R. (1991). *Stabilizing Dynamics*, Cambridge, Cambridge University Press.

Weiss, F.X. (1910). 'Die moderne Tendenz in der Lehre vom Geldwert', *Zeitschrift für Volkswirtschaft, Sozialpolitik und Verwaltung*, **19**, pp. 502–60.

Wessels, T. (1925). *Die Geldtheorie Léon Walras'*, Köln, Welzel.

Wicksell, K. (1898). *Interest and Prices*, London, Macmillan, 1936.

Wicksell, K. (1899). 'Review of Walras's *Eléments d'économie politique appliquée*', *Jahrbücher für Nationalökonomie und Statistik*, III, 18, pp. 825–30.

Wicksell, K. (1901–06). *Lectures on Political Economy*, London, Routledge & Kegan Paul, 2 vols, 1934–35.

Wicksell, K. (1919). 'Review of G. Cassel's *Theoretische Sozialökonomie*', *Ekonomisk Tidskrift*, **9**, as in Wicksell (1905–06), vol. I, pp. 219–57.

Wicksell, K. (1958). *Selected Papers on Economic Theory*, London, Allen & Unwin.

Wicksteed, P.H. (1894). *The Co-ordination of the Laws of Distribution*, London, Macmillan.

Wieser, F. von (1889). *Natural Value*, London, Macmillan, 1893 (trans. by C.A. Malloch).

Wieser, F. von (1904). 'Der Geldwert und seine geschichtlichen Veränderungen', *Zeitschrift für Volkswirtschaft, Sozialpolitik und Verwaltung*, **13**, pp. 43–64.

Wieser, F. von (1909). 'Der Geldwert und seine Veränderungen', *Schriften des Vereins für Sozialpolitik*, **132**, pp. 497–540.

Wilson, J. (1847). *Capital, Currency and Banking*, London, The Economist.

Winiarsky, L. (1967). *Essai sur la mécanique sociale*, Genève, Droz.

Witteloostjuin, A. van and Maks, J.A.H. (1990). 'Walras on temporary equilibrium and dynamics', *History of Political Economy*, 22, pp. 223–37.

Zawadzki, W. (1914). *Les mathématiques appliquées à l'économie politique*, Paris, Librairie des sciences politiques et sociales.

Zylberberg, A. (1990). *L'économie mathématique en France, 1870–1914*, Paris, Economica.

Zylberberg, A. (1994). 'Les premiers disciples français de Léon Walras', *Economies et sociétés*, 28, pp. 75–85.

Index

Actions (logical and non-logical),
  152, 154–8
'Adam Smith puzzle', viii, 34,
  106, 143
American Economic Association,
  100, 109
Amstein, H. 148
Approximations (Paretian first and
  second-order), 150–4, 156–8,
  171
Arrow, K. xiii, 148, 149, 169
Auctioneer, 32–3
Aupetit, A. 123, 139–41, 148,
  159, 174
Auspitz, R. 171
Austrian School, 159–68

Bagehot, W. 43, 97
Banknote, theory of, 48–78
Baranzini, R. vii
Barone, E. 168, 175
Baumol, W.J. 5
Bentham, J. 56
Bertrand, J. 33, 45
Bilimovic, A. 174
Billoret, J.L. 45
Blaug, M., vii, 121–22
Boccardo, G. 78
Bodin, J. 43
Böhm-Bawerk, E. von, 68
Boninsegni, P. xii, 148, 150,
  159, 168, 172, 175
Bonnet, V. 43, 76
Bortkiewicz, L. von, 174
Bousquet, G. 148
Boven, P. 4
Bresciani-Turoni, C. 172
Bridel, P. 43, 64, 76–7, 146, 148,
  171–3
Busino, G. 171

Cambridge School, 21, 83, 107,
  119, 159, 168
Cantillon, R. 44, 56, 77
Capital,
  circulating, 36–40, 52–4, 59–
    70, 95, 146
  deepening/shallowing, 68
  fixed, 48, 59–70, 95, 146
  goods vs money capital vs
    numéraire capital, 95–99, 121
  increase of, 54–75
  quantity of, 56–60, 66–8
  rate of return of, 67, 93, 95, 97
  theory of capital formation, xi,
    1, 29–40, 45, 52, 59, 77, 89,
    91, 110, 114–17, 172
Cash balances, 8, 21, 65, 79, 83–
  7, 90, 93, 99, 107, 119, 123,
  146, 166, 171, 175
'Cash-in-advance constraint', viii,
  7, 42, 83, 141, 162
Cassel, G. 41, 45, 173
Cernuschi, H. 43–4, 78
Chevalier, M. 43
Cheysson, E. 78, 87
'Circulation à desservir', x, 15,
  38–9, 59, 77, 83, 90, 106–7,
  110
Cirillo, R. 76, 145
Clark, J.B. 108
Clower, R.W., xiii, 7, 41, 162
Clower constraint *see* 'Cash-in-
  advance constraint'
Coefficient of circulation, 16–20,
  38, 43
Collard, D. 145
Competition, (hypothetical
  regime of perfect), 85, 122,
  142
Competitive equilibrium, 80, 83,
  142
Conant, C. 78
Concertina effect, 78

Consumers cash holdings, 29,
114, 117–22, 127–30, 134
Convertibility, 58, 88
Copernic, 43, 59
Cournot, A.A. 3, 41, 45, 142,
145, 148
Credit and banking, theory of, 48–
54, 75, 88, 146
Creedy, J. 148
Crises, theory of, 48–54, 76, 78,
81, 106
liquidation, 57, 68–70
Cumulative process, 50, 57, 73–
4, 77
Cycles, 40–54

Debreu, G. 169
De Caro, G. 145
Decision-taking under certainty,
112–22
Del Pezzo, P. 78, 106
Del Vecchio, G. 105, 150, 168,
170–71, 174
Denizet, J. 47, 145
Dichotomy between relative and
nominal prices, 21-5, 94, 103,
108, 129, 163, 167
Distribution effect, 24, 61, 63–8,
174
Divisia, F. 146, 168, 175
Donzelli, F. 35
Dupuit, J. 11

Edgeworth, F.Y. 43, 105, 108,
139, 147–8, 172
Eléments,
first edition, 1–2, 12, 15–16,
29, 38, 40–41, 73, 77, 84, 110
second edition, 25, 64, 79–80,
89–92, 99, 107–8, 153
third edition, 64, 78–80, 92,
100, 107–8, 171
fourth edition, 25, 34, 40, 44–
5, 64, 92, 106, 108, 110, 129,
145–6, 148, 171, 173–4
time structure of, x-xi, 2, 27,

29–40, 45–6, 86, 94, 108,
112–22, 131, 140
various editions, x, xi, 130–31,
144
Ellis, H.S. 159, 168, 174
'Encaisses désirées', x, xi, xii, 13,
59, 79, 83, 89–99, 100–10,
124–30, 145, 153, 161, 174
Equation de la circulation, 99–
105, 112–22, 132, 146, 148,
153
Equilibrium,
ab ovo, 117–22, 138
effectively established, 121
in principle, 115–17, 121, 123,
129–32, 146
short/long run, 37, 47–48
temporary, 45, 75, 103, 120–
21, 146, 165, 169–70
Excess demand functions, 4, 41,
44, 63, 167
Exchange,
between commodities, xii, 7
direct vs. indirect exchange, 6,
162
monetary vs. barter exchanges,
6–11, 42
technology of, vii, 91, 118–19
theory of, ix, x, 1, 2-3, 6–11,
42, 89, 91, 110, 114–17, 125,
141, 146, 151, 62, 170
Existence of general equilibrium,
viii
for a monetary economy, xi,
85, 94, 99, 104–5, 123, 129,
140, 143, 157, 164
Expectations, viii, 44

Falise, M. 145
Fiduciary money, 28–9, 50, 54,
75, 107
Fisher, I. x, 15, 20, 43–4, 83,
100, 109, 146, 167
Forced saving, 28, 47–78, 97,
101–2, 109, 139, 141. 157,
174

Fossati, E. 146
Foxwell H.S. 71, 73, 78
France, 151
Friedman, M. 163

General equilibrium,
  and marginal utility theory, x,
  26
  confusion about the barter
  nature of Walras's, 2, 5, 10,
  39, 162
  epistemological status, ix, 51–
  2, 118, 130, 142–5, 158
  formal development, ix, xi,
  123
  internal coherence of, ix, xi,
  34, 86, 89, 110–49, 163
  interpretative content, ix, xii
  mechanism vs. process, ix, xii
  'realism' in, viii, xi, 34, 37,
  40, 82–3, 86, 89, 94, 118,
  130–1, 141–5
  static nature of Walras's, vii,
  ix, xi, 39–40, 74, 82, 89, 96–
  7, 110–12, 121, 138–9, 142
Geneva, 6, 12–13, 16, 41, 48
Gibson paradox, 77
Gide, C. xiii, 71–2, 78, 106
Goldfeld, S.M. 5
Gossen, H.H. 33
Goupillière, H. de la, 78
Gravitation, 35, 47, 81, 155, 172
Guggenheim, Th. 41, 76, 145

Hadley, A.T. 43
Hahn, F.H., vii, viii, xiii, 10,
  147–9, 169–70
Hall, S.G. 145–6
Hayek, F. 45, 54–5, 60, 68–9,
  74, 76–8, 169, 173, 175
Helfferich, K. 146
Hicks, J.R. xiii, 41–2, 45, 60,
  75, 120, 146, 150, 158–9,
  167, 169
Horton, S.D. 78
Howitt, P.W. 9, 36, 145

Hume, D. 15, 23, 27, 53

'Ideal types', ix, 46, 142–3
Index numbers, 106
Ingrao, B. ix, 145
Interest,
  loanable–funds theory of, 59,
  65–6, 77
  opportunity cost of holding
  money, xi, 79, 91, 93–5, 119,
  166
  rate of, xi, 52, 58, 94, 101–4,
  108, 124, 146, 174
  tâtonnement on the rate of, 94–
  8
  theory of, 56, 64, 124–5
  trailing–bankrate doctrine, 72,
  77
  two rates of, 64–6, 68–70, 72–
  5, 77, 108–9
Isnard, A.N. 4–5, 9, 41
Israel, G. ix, 145
Italy, 151, 168

Jaccoud, G. 106, 145
Jaffé, W., 3, 4, 11, 40–45, 106–
  8, 113, 121, 124, 130–31,
  144–8
James, E. 145
Jevons, W.S. 3, 11, 29, 41, 49,
  71, 106
Jolink, A. 106, 113, 124, 146–7
Juglar, C. 87

Kaldor, N. 78
Kemmerer, E.W. 43
Keynes, J.M. 48, 60, 74, 77,
  106, 146, 159, 167–8, 174
Kuenne, R.E. 107, 113, 145–7,
  172

Laidler, D. 43, 146, 173
Lange, O. 41, 113
Launhardt, W. 105
Laurent, H. 111, 135, 148
Lausanne, 1, 16, 152

Lausanne School, xii, 159, 168–9, 172
Lecoq, J. 145
Lendjel, E. 148
Lerner, A. 65
Levasseur, P.E. 43
Lexis, W. 78, 107
L'Huillier, J. 76, 145
Lieben, R. 171
Lindhal, E, 169
Locke, J. 43
Lucas, R.E. 77, 147, 148
Lundberg, E. 169

Maks, J.A.H. 78, 83, 145
Marget, A. 3, 15, 42–4, 55, 76, 146, 159, 168, 171, 174
Market,
    'continuous market', 30, 39–40, 91, 94, 96–9, 106, 111–22, 162, 167
    'once-and-for-all market', 30–36, 59, 86–7, 92, 94, 96–9, 113–22, 130, 172
    'periodical market', 30, 36–9, 46, 47–78, 91, 94, 96–9, 108, 113–22
Marshall, A. 21, 43, 45, 49, 64, 77, 105–6, 159, 167, 171
McKenzie, L.W. 121, 145
Ménard, C. 145
Menger, C. 11, 49, 78, 143, 162, 173
Menger, K. 173
Mercantilists, 10
Mill, J. 43
Mill, J.S. 43, 56, 76–7
Mises, L. von, 78, 146, 173, 175
Monetary policy, 81–2, 106
Monetary reform, 80–82, 100, 108
Monetary regimes, 81
Monetary theory,
    and expectations, viii, 167
    and forced saving, 71–5, 97
    and sequences, viii, 60, 86–7,
102, 120–24, 133, 144, 167, 169
    and theory of choice, xii, 150
    applied, 47–80, 82, 88, 99–100, 106, 131, 138
    circularity argument in, xii, 120, 146, 150, 159, 168
    Pareto's, 151–9, 171
    transmission mechanism, x, 48–50
    upheavals in Walras's, 10, 29, 45, 89–91, 101, 110–11
Money,
    allows synchronization between receipts and outlays, 94, 102, 112–22, 162, 165–7
    and banknotes, 52–4
    and marginal utility theory, x, 2, 11–15, 168, 173
    and perfect foresight, 117, 120, 162
    and theory of exchange, viii, 5–11, 83
    as a medium of exchange, ix, xiii, 1, 2, 4–11, 17, 40–42, 57, 83–4, 86, 120, 146. 154–5, 164
    as an add–on notion to general equilibrium, xi, 6–11, 79, 89, 91–2, 108, 141, 151, 163, 167, 170
    as a practical simplification and a theoretical complication, 6, 10, 64, 170
    as a social institution, vii, xii, 7, 152, 158, 162–3
    as a store of value, 119–20, 154–5
    as a unit of account (*see also* *numéraire*), 2–11, 41, 84, 120, 154–5
    as circulating capital, xi, 36–40, 64–5, 90–91, 94–9, 102, 113–30
    as savings, 29, 53, 95, 107, 114, 124, 134, 140, 172

–capital, 95–9
constant marginal utility of, 14, 42–3, 105, 151, 154
demand function for, 91, 93–9, 102, 106–7, 162, 171
depreciation of, 54–78
equation, 123–30
'essential' role of, viii, 10, 83, 169
exchange facilitating properties of, 1, 8
expected supply and demand for, 116–22
'false' (Pareto's), 153–8, 168, 171–3
fiat (paper), 43, 54, 58, 75, 87–9, 92, 101, 123, 152, 154–8, 162–3, 171
held out of technological necessity, 119
illusion, 21, 157, 174
in general equilibrium, vii, viii, xii, xiii, 1, 3, 6–11, 29, 40–42, 47, 74–5, 79–80, 89, 91, 94, 105–6, 108, 122–41, 160, 163, 168–70
in the utility function, viii, xi, 2, 8, 42, 74, 84, 89–99, 105–6, 110–22, 123–42, 146, 167–70
marginal utility of, 99–108, 154–5, 175
market for, 89–99, 101–5
neutrality of, 10, 23–4, 39, 45, 49, 68, 85, 105, 157, 169
Pareto and, 151–8
positive value of, viii, xi, 10, 83, 87, 92, 111, 154, 162, 168
precious metal as commodity–, 13–28, 47–50, 57–62, 66, 70, 77, 85, 92, 97–9, 154
price of, 17–22, 98–9, 100, 147, 166
qualities of, 14
'real' (Pareto's), 154–8, 168, 171–3, 175

rectangular hyperbola as demand curve (market equilibrium curve) for, 19–28, 43, 49, 57–9, 98, 108
service d'approvisionnement of, 13, 91, 94–5, 101–2, 119, 123–30, 137, 139, 147, 155, 168
supply of (monopolistic), 56–66, 71, 76, 82, 93, 104
transaction role of, viii, x, 2, 6–11, 93, 111, 119, 127, 140–41
value of, 12–28, 42, 56–9, 81, 98, 161, 165, 174
velocity of circulation of, 16, 20, 28, 39, 51, 77
without utility of its own (not a commodity), 92, 94
Montesano, A. 145–6
Montesquieu, C. de S. 4
Morgenstern, O. 173
Morishima, M. 40, 78, 145–6
Mornati, F. vii
Mouchot, C. 146
Murray, R.A. 168, 172, 175
Myrdal, G. 169

Negishi, T. 45, 145–6
Net income, rate of, 32, 37, 64–6
Newcomb, S. 43, 167
Newman, P. 45
Niehans, J. 105
Numéraire, ix, 1, 2–11, 17, 80, 83, 125, 129, 140, 147, 151, 161, 172, 174
and theory of exchange, x, 2, 29–42
as a commodity, 1–3, 13, 41
–capital, 95–9
change of, 4, 41
role in *tâtonnement*, 7, 35–6, 39, 41, 116–22

Ostroy, J.M., xiii, 9, 42, 145, 169–70

Pantaleoni, M. 168
Pareto, V. vii, ix, xii, 41, 78,
    108, 145–8, 150–59, 167–8,
    170–5
Patinkin, D. vii, xiii, 3, 21, 24–
    5, 42–4, 77–8, 106–7, 113,
    119, 129, 131, 135, 145–7,
    160, 169, 173–5
Period, 38, 54–75, 96–9, 102,
    165
Physiocrats, 4, 76
Pigou, A.C. 43, 159, 167, 169
Price determination vs. price
    formation, viii, xii, 32–4, 38
Price level, 21–5, 11, 10, 51, 50,
    61–2, 66, 73–4, 78, 88, 94,
    99, 104, 147
Probabilities, 165
Producers'cash holdings, 29, 114,
    117–22, 127–30, 134
Production
    theory of production, xi, 1, 29–
    40, 45, 89, 91, 110, 114–17
Proudhon, P.J. 52, 75, 77

Quantity theory of money
    ('proportionality theorem'), x,
    2, 43, 48, 80, 87, 94–9, 101,
    105–7, 129, 137–41, 148,
    156–8, 161, 165, 167, 173,
    175
    Walras's equation of exchange,
    12–28, 38–9, 47–87, 105
Quesnay, F. 37, 76

Rareté, 11, 42, 80, 85
Real balances, 59, 83, 166–70,
    174
Real-balance effect, xi, 21, 24–5,
    47, 104–5, 131, 136–8, 147,
    169–70
'Real types', ix, 46, 142–3
Rent, 67
Ricardo, D. 43, 56, 118
Robertson, D.H. 55, 60, 74, 106,
    146

Roscher, W. 43

Samuelson, P.A. 147, 150, 159,
    169
Say, J.–B. 43
Say, L. 78
Schlesinger, K., xii, 150, 159–
    68, 173–4
Schumpeter, J.A., xii, 1, 41, 43,
    79, 91, 107, 129, 145, 150–
    51, 159–62, 172–4
Selfsameness view, 32, 34, 99,
    130, 142–5, 148
Senior, N. 43
Sensini, G. 175
Smith, A. xiii, 9, 42–3, 53, 56,
    70, 106, 143, 172
Solow, R. 33
Spot economy, 120–21
Stability of a general equilibrium,
    viii, x, 2, 25–8, 47, 57, 74–5,
    85–6, 99, 112, 130–40, 164
Starr, J.M. 42, 169–70
Stockholm, 168
Substitution effect, 21, 44, 47,
    97, 148
Switzerland, 52, 76

Tâtonnement,
    as a bargaining process on
    actual market, ix, xi, 1, 32–3,
    91, 96, 99, 130, 138, 140,
    144, 147
    as a mathematical iterative
    solution (Gauss–Seidel), ix,
    34, 123, 132, 142–3, 149, 173
    as a mechanism, ix, xi, 30–36,
    40, 42, 45, 94, 96, 115–17,
    123–45, 147, 155–6, 171–2
    as a swindle, 33
    'at a given point in time'
    (timeless or instantaneous), 86,
    97, 112–22, 130–39, 141–5
    consecutive, 103, 136
    in historical time, 7, 34, 40,
    45, 94, 97, 121, 130, 132, 146

in theoretical/logical time, 7,
30–36, 40, 45, 82, 92, 94,
121–45
marchandage (Pareto), 155–6,
172–3
money vs 'real' markets, 86,
103, 131–2, 135, 148
on the money market, 130–9,
147
path-dependency of, xiii, 33,
155, 157
'realism of', 91, 94–6, 123,
132, 138, 156
role for money in, 7, 27–8, 30,
34–6, 39, 92, 94–9, 101–2,
141–3
static nature of, 30–6, 40, 86
sur bons, xi, 34, 45, 107, 112–
22, 131–2, 146
Taussig, W. 100
Theorem of equivalent
distributions, 7–10, 42
Thornton, W. 56
Tobin, J., xiii
Tooke, Th. 43
Trading-out-of-equilibrium ('false
trading' or 'disequilibrium
transactions'), ix, 30–35, 42,
45, 86, 107, 113–17, 131–2,
146, 155
Transaction technology, 83, 91,
119–20
Tsiang, S.C. 1

Uhr, C. 173

United Kingdom, 169
United States, 169
Utility, 2, 8, 10, 139, 148
marginal utility, x, 2, 10, 11–
15, 40, 42, 80, 83–5, 100
virtual, 11

Valade, B. 171
Van Daal, J. 113, 124, 146–7
Vienna, 168, 175

Wages, 67, 69
Wagner, V.F, 76
Wald, A. 147, 159, 173
Walker, D. 45, 77, 109, 131–2,
145–7
Walker, F.A. 41
Walras, A. 4, 9, 13–15, 41–2, 75
Walras, L. (*personalia*), 1, 40,
106, 108, 111, 135, 145, 148
Walras's law, 41
Wealth effect, 21, 24, 44
Weber, M. ix, 46
Weintraub, R. 173
Wicksell, K. 1, 41, 43, 50, 55,
58, 60, 64, 66, 71–8, 101–2,
108–9, 146, 159, 172–3, 175
Wicksteed, P.H. 108
Wieser, F. von, 173–4
Wilson, J. 76
Winiarsky, L. 111
Witteloostjuin, A. 78, 145
Wolkoff, M. 43

Zylberberg, A. 139, 148